T0290486

The Future of Feminism in Public Relations and Strategic Communication

The Future of Feminism in Public Relations and Strategic Communication

A Socio-Ecological Model of Influences

Linda Aldoory and Elizabeth L. Toth
University of Maryland College Park

ROWMAN & LITTLEFIELD
Lanham • Boulder • New York • London

Published by Rowman & Littlefield
An imprint of The Rowman & Littlefield Publishing Group, Inc.
4501 Forbes Boulevard, Suite 200, Lanham, Maryland 20706
www.rowman.com

86-90 Paul Street, London EC2A 4NE, United Kingdom

British Library Cataloguing in Publication Information Available

Library of Congress Cataloging-in-Publication Data

Names: Aldoory, Linda, author. | Toth, Elizabeth L., author.
Title: The future of feminism in public relations and strategic communication : a socio-ecological model of influences / Linda Aldoory and Elizabeth L Toth, University of Maryland College Park .
Description: Lanham : Rowman & Littlefield, 2021. | Includes bibliographical references and index. | Summary: "Aldoory and Toth present a socio-ecological model for understanding and building a feminist future public relations. This approach acknowledges previous gaps in scholarship and practice caused by ideological, societal, mediated, and organizational factors constructing norms and expectations for gender and race"—Provided by publisher.
Identifiers: LCCN 2021007283 (print) | LCCN 2021007284 (ebook) | ISBN 9781538128237 (cloth) | ISBN 9781538128244 (paperback) | ISBN 9781538128251 (epub)
Subjects: LCSH: Public relations. | Communication. | Feminism. | Social change.
Classification: LCC HM1221 .A488 2021 (print) | LCC HM1221 (ebook) | DDC 305.42—dc23
LC record available at https://lccn.loc.gov/2021007283
LC ebook record available at https://lccn.loc.gov/2021007284

Contents

Acknowledgments

"Feminism is the notion that we should each be free to develop our own talents and not be held back by manmade barriers."

—Ruth Bader Ginsburg

We have several people to thank for their belief in and support for this book. We are very appreciative of the encouragement of our friend and first editor, Elizabeth Swayze, past executive editor at Rowman & Littlefield Publishers, who brought our book proposal to publisher approval. We also thank Natalie Mandziuk, Rowman & Littlefield Publishers acquisitions editor, for her supportive efforts to achieve its publication.

We express our appreciation to the feminist scholars who contributed their expert observations: Kate Fitch, PhD, senior lecturer, Communication and Media Studies, Monash University, Australia; Denise Hill, PhD, associate professor, School of Communications, Elon University; Maria Angeles Moreno, PhD, professor, Group of Advanced Studies in Communication, TU Universidad Ray Juan Carlos; Katie R. Place, PhD, associate professor, Department of Strategic Communication, Quinnipiac University; Candace Parrish, PhD, director and assistant professor of Strategic Communication and Public Relations Online Master's Program, Sacred Heart University; Lana Rakow, PhD, professor emerita of communication, University of North Dakota; Bey-Ling Sha, PhD, dean, College of Communications at California State University, Fullerton; Martina Topic, PhD, senior lecturer in public relations, Leeds Business School, Leeds Becket University; and Jennifer Vardeman, PhD, associate professor and interim director, Jack J. Valenti School of Communication, University of Houston.

Finally, we thank our colleagues, friends, and feminist scholars who came before us and paved the way for this book to be acceptable to the public relations field.

Linda Aldoory and Elizabeth L. Toth

I

OVERVIEW OF THE BOOK

Model and Definitions

1

A Socio-Ecological Model for Public Relations and Strategic Communication

OUTLINE OF CHAPTER CONTENT

- Gaps in published research in public relations
- Goals of the book
- A socio-ecological model
  - o Models from media sociology
- Applying a socio-ecological perspective to public relations
  - o Descriptive goal: Organizing the body of knowledge
  - o Analytical goal: A feminist critique of public relations
  - o Dialogic goal: Co-constructed model and future research
- Conclusion: Summary and structure of the book

We have been studying and practicing public relations for a combined total of almost eighty years. Most of that time has been spent addressing gender issues in the workplace, fending off discriminatory practices, advocating for equity in leadership, and developing theory that advances feminist scholarship in the public relations discipline. With several remarkable coauthors, we published some of the original documented evidence of gender disparities over thirty years ago; through subsequent books, conference presentations, and journal articles, we have told the unfortunately oft-repeated story of the need for change in both the profession and scholarship. Today, we continue to see the need to create equity, but now we admit to what was our myopic view of difference and disparity; equity is not only for women—more importantly, people of color, LGBTQ populations, and other marginalized groups have been silenced by the field. On one hand, the body of knowledge addressing underrepresentation and marginalization is growing, with the help of dozens of researchers and students who have expanded the field's understanding of what and who is missing from the discourse in public relations. On the other hand, it is remarkable that we still have a significant dearth of literature and ongoing disparities.

GAPS IN PUBLISHED RESEARCH IN PUBLIC RELATIONS

When we looked back at the research on gender and feminism and started considering the future of public relations, we noticed three very critical breaches. First, our own past work over the years was almost always focused on the singular unit of analysis of the individual practitioner and on a dichotomous concept of gender. We most often focused on an individual woman and her story of discrimination and oppression in the profession of public relations. For example, our published work from a survey of members in the Public Relations Society of America illustrated the predominant Whiteness of the profession, and we relied on a White sample of practitioners in the focus groups and surveys. Aldoory and Toth (2004) examined how transformational leadership style was perceived as more effective in public relations than transactional leadership style and how leadership styles were gendered aspects of the profession. However, the data were based on individual opinions with little discussion of broader impacts, such as organizational influences and societal norms. We crafted a leadership principle that explained how women were perceived as better leaders due to socialized traits of empathy and collaboration, which are linked to transformational leadership. This theory generation was based on almost 90 percent White perspectives and 100 percent individual-level understanding. While on one hand the study was progressive because it was published at a time when so little was promoted about gender differences in leadership, it also perpetuated the singular White voice of gender scholarship of the time. In other research, we did address ideological and societal norms that acted as constraints for public relations professionals, but we left out key factors also playing a role in organizational decisions affecting the practitioners. One key factor rarely discussed was institutional and systemic racism. We looked around and noticed the same individual-level unit of analysis in other feminist efforts in public relations scholarship. While the scope of work addressing ideological and cultural influences on public relations has thankfully expanded, we could find no literature integrating ideology with the individual or integrating the organization with stories of discrimination.

Second, our earlier studies admittedly stuck to one type of woman. It was not until later in our academic careers that we noticed who was left invisible when we were explicating the experiences of practitioners from the 1980s, 1990s, and early 2000s. People who did not identify as female, White, or straight had limited voice in early gender scholarship. For example, in our 2002 article assessing perceptions of hiring, salaries, and promotion, our interpretations relied on opinions of the average participant, which was a forty-year-old, White, and married woman (Aldoory & Toth, 2002). Results showed that hiring was not perceived as a gender problem any longer, and salary discrepancies were based on several factors: skills differential, time in position, socialization, sexism, family commitments for women, and historical disparities. The few men left in the public relations profession led to favoritism and biased promotions. In discussing the findings of this article in the conclusion, we did not explicate the Whiteness of the voices that constructed our burgeoning theory or the other discriminatory factors at play, such as heteronormativity.

While, over the years, we have acknowledged the impact of race, class, and identity on studying and practicing public relations, we have never honed in on the lived experiences of "other" identities or the organizational and professional norms that act as oppressors. Other scholars have taken on the burden of illuminating the invisible practitioner, and we can turn to their work describing the lived experiences of practitioners of color and practitioners who identify as LGBTQ. For example, some recent research on LGBTQ has been done by Ciszek, who has examined activist publics and digital media (Ciszek, 2015, 2017a, 2017b, 2018). In one of her coauthored articles, Ciszek along with Pounders (2020) looked at how individual practitioners who identified as LGBTQ developed public relations messages targeting LGBTQ publics. Centering on the concept of "authentic communication," the authors suggested that practitioners who identify similarly to an underrepresented public may be perceived as more legitimate by that public. Following interviews with practitioners, the authors flagged key components of authentic communication, including social proficiency, consonance, and inclusivity. The findings were unique in that they were some of the first that focused on this special public and this identity as practitioner.

However, even with these advances in the public relations body of knowledge, we still find no one article that lays out the argument for a multilayered approach to understanding the causes and factors that facilitate sexism, racism, homophobia, and classism in public relations. Where are the influences from society, professionalism, and institutional routines? What along with individual-level factors contribute to inequity in public relations? Today's body of knowledge has not synthesized all the influences on the practice and scholarship of public relations.

The third breach we noticed while doing a historical review of gender research was that the U.S. body of literature is not as advanced as that of our international contemporaries and is missing key intersections with work from other countries to inform and develop feminism in public relations. Mainstream scholarly publications, such as *Public Relations Review* and *Journal of Public Relations Research*, publish international research, but U.S. research is still predominant. A recently published book on the history of women in public relations included the status of women in other countries, such as Turkey, Australia, and Malaysia (Theofilou, 2021). In this current book, to lessen the centrality of U.S. thought, we have engaged with essential and groundbreaking literature from across Europe (see, e.g., Tench et al., 2017); United Kingdom (Edwards, 2009, 2014, 2018a; Edwards & Hodges, 2011; L'Etang, 2005, 2014; L'Etang et al., 2015; Pieczka, 2002, 2018); Turkey (Demirhan & Cakir-Demirhan, 2015); Norway, Denmark, and The Netherlands (Ihlen et al., 2009); Australia (Fitch, 2020); and Spain (Xifra, 2017; Xifra & Collell, 2014). From these examples we highlight the European scholarship by Edwards to help inform this book. One of her case studies pointed to the use of public relations by marginalized young people in order to express voice, receive recognition, and engage with others as citizens. Other scholars from New Zealand and Australia have used sociological and critical lenses to interrogate the role of ideology in public relations (see as examples Daymon & Demetrious, 2016; Fitch, 2015; Fitch et al., 2016; Munshi & Priya, 2005). Munshi, McKie, and coauthors, for instance, have been critiquing public relations for over a decade, using a postcolonial lens for problematics such as appropriation and hierarchy. They have offered an approach to understanding theory from the point of view of resistance by peripheral publics (Broadfoot & Munshi, 2007, 2015; McKie & Munshi, 2009; Munshi & Priya, 2005). Throughout this book we cite authors not only from public relations but also from fields such as sociology and cultural studies, who offer theoretical tools to analyze public relations theory and practice.

Public relations scholarship needs to add proactive approaches to identifying root causes of disparities and appropriate solutions to the complex issues of gender and public relations. There have been examples of this, such as a recently published book, *PR Women with Influence* (Meng & Neil, 2020). Scholars from all over the world have helped advance U.S. knowledge about the various ways that power, social norms, and unwritten institutional expectations can guide meaning constructed about gender, race, and the practitioner's role in practice. This multinational body of work will be interwoven through each chapter in this book.

GOALS OF THE BOOK

After producing years of gender scholarship and discovering breaches in the current literature, we were motivated to produce this book in order to close the gaps and expand our understanding of feminism in public relations. The first goal of the book is to offer a comprehensive review of the literature in public relations that has addressed feminism, gender, race, LGBTQ practitioners, and related underrepresentations and marginalizations in the field. In particular, the book synthesizes scholarly territory some eighteen years after one comprehensive look at women completed by Toth and coauthors in 2001: *Women in Public Relations: How Gender Influences Practice* (L. A. Grunig et al., 2001). While *Women in Public Relations* was cutting-edge at the time, it did not speak to today's critical issues regarding racism, classism, and the heteronormative assumptions undergirding public relations. Thus, we also provide directions for future research and practice to address what is missing in current literature.

The second goal of the book is to analyze and critique the multiple factors that have constituted meaning about women, people of color, and LGBTQ practitioners and have influenced research and practice in public relations. There are ideological, societal, mediated, and organizational factors constructing norms and expectations for gender and race, for example, in public relations. These factors play out in the practice of public relations and in the research of the field. To illustrate the various factors, we borrowed "models of influence" from other disciplines and developed a model of our own, guided particularly by feminist criticism. We argue that a socio-ecological model of influence reflects how public relations is constituted as a body of meaning that is both practiced and studied. Through social, professional, and institutional norms and expectations, practitioners face oppression and marginalization and in fact reify hegemonic assumptions about identity—both personal and professional identity—that is contested.

The model presented here fulfills these goals. First, it is used as a framework to review the extant literature on gender, race, power, and feminism in public relations. We can categorize and summarize work by which level of influence it addresses. Thus, it is a prescriptive framework to help delineate and clarify existing research and its level of influence. Second, the model is an analytical tool. It explains why certain voices remain unheard and how disparities and discrimination continue.

Finally, the new model can be used as a spark for dialogue and change, which is the third goal of the book. We view this current project as a way to encourage professional and scholarly discourse that deepens an understanding of the problems of status, role, and legitimacy of public relations. The model here is new and has not been used before in the field, but it can be a helpful visual to discuss the field's history, current scholarship, and future work.

A SOCIO-ECOLOGICAL MODEL

The term *socio-ecological* describes a system of integrated units that are affected by their environment and that affect the environment. Typically, to get at the socio-ecological aspects of a phenomenon, authors use a visual model of the system in question to help explain how and why people adapt to certain situations. Visual models of socio-ecological systems illustrate who the social actors are, what institutions and ideologies play roles, and where influences are that facilitate or impede adaptation. They show the delimiting boundaries of the ecosystem and its level of complexity. Typically, if socio-ecological, the model is complex. At its minimum there will be more than one layer of influence, and thus there are overlaps. The layers tend not to be exclusive, which complicates explanations for these models even further.

The original conceptualizations for socio-ecological systems primarily emerged out of environmental science in order to explain human influence on the biosphere and ecological systems. Human choices have consequences on the natural environment, and the environment has influenced human decision-making (Petrosillo et al., 2015). In the field of public health, authors similarly developed socio-ecological explanations for systems to detect epidemiological spread of disease caused by economic, political, and social factors as well as biophysical ones.

Some refer to Bronfenbrenner (1979) as the first to label and define an ecological model of social influences. He was looking to explain the effects of the environment on children's development, but he also found that the individual in turn shaped their environment, hence his labeling the model as ecology. Using the term *socio-ecological* intentionally put the focus on a multilayered perspective of influences and on the interaction of the different layers of influence. *Socio-* defines the model as interactive and relational, as opposed to psychological or individual. *Ecological* describes the process by which influences move and interact with their environment, the individual, and each other.

The origins of the concept of a socio-ecological model can be traced back to a well-known systems approach, which posits that human behavior is a function of synergistic and reciprocal influences between an individual and the settings in which the person operates, the interaction among settings, the environments that indirectly affect the settings, and cultural ideologies (Lininger et al., 2019). Thus, multiple layers of influences interact to affect human and organizational behavior, and each layer can act both as facilitator and inhibitor to desired goals. For Bronfenbrenner (1979), there were four key layers: the microsystem (individual, family), mesosystem (relationships between multiple microsystems), exosystem (influencing systems that affect but do not contain an individual), and macrosystem (overarching sociocultural values and beliefs).

While the socio-ecological model has been used frequently in health-related fields and in environmental science, it is new to the field of public relations. To our knowledge, different pieces of the layers have been analyzed and used in studies, but there are no examples of using a full model with all its layers to assess influences in and on public relations. It has not been applied systematically to the body of knowledge or for areas of practice. Therefore, we must borrow literature and research from other fields to first conceptualize our own framework, construct it, describe its individual layers, and then explain the layers' contribution to norms and behaviors of public relations.

Hundreds of articles have applied socio-ecological models to world problems. In public health, for example, it has been used to address obstacles to treating chronic disease (Centers for Disease Control and Prevention, 2014; Salihu et al., 2015), to promote physical activity and healthy eating (Richard et al., 2011), and to identify global health concerns (Figueroa, 2017). In environmental science, models work to identify the factors affecting watershed management (Sanchez et al., 2014), and to predict patterns of sustainable development (Ursino, 2019). In communication research, we can find a socio-ecological model derived from media sociology, which is an area of study closer to public relations. Shoemaker and Reese (1996, 2014) developed their model to analyze and understand the layers of influence on media content. Their model is an exemplar for how to apply a socio-ecological model to a body of knowledge derived from communication scholarship.

Models from Media Sociology

Media sociology examines communication within the contexts of social forces, focusing on such elements as power, authority, identity, and institutional influence. Scholars in media sociology were some of the first to notice that areas of study in mass communication tended to stay decontextualized and separated. In other words, when individual journalists were studied, their perceptions and roles were not contextualized within the expectations of news routines or organizational constraints. News routines were studied separately from media ownership. And ownership did not include analysis of individual journalists. Each of these and the other areas of theory and practice influence each other and ultimately affect news. Media sociology argues that media and media workers are influenced by many social factors, including organizations, identity, autonomy, individualism, community, and power (Waisbord, 2014). Studies focus on power dynamics, socialization of journalists, and the functioning of media industries and occupations.

As Waisbord (2014) pointed out, these and other issues addressed by media sociology are constantly shifting. Ongoing transformations of media have aided in the "fragmenting" of communication/media studies and the difficulty of pinning down such important metrics as a singular definition for media and for mass communication. The analytical approaches and measures needed to study media became broad and fluid, creating a greater need for a socio-ecological perspective when considering influences on media content and audience behavior. As Waisbord (2014) put it, "'Media' are not simply what people consume when not working or sleeping; they are interwoven in social life, making 'mediation' integral to everyday life" (p. 6).

Media sociology thus offers guidance here as we analyze public relations factors that have influenced individual practitioners and research on practitioners. Like journalism, public relations similarly reflects constant transformations in definition, membership, and contributions to society. Public relations is also interwoven into everyday life, often in ways that organizations and publics do not notice. Power is at the core of decision-making in organizational contexts, and for both public relations and media, feminist researchers strive to uncover where power relations are and what and who they affect. Just as with media studies, postmodern and critical scholars in public relations have claimed that studies over the last century have been primarily concerned with psychological inquiries and have ignored important issues of historical context, inequalities, and political economy (Pooley, 2014). The significance of gender, class and race, identity, and subjectivity have been marginalized by this psychological domain. Media sociology corrects for this by introducing interrelationships between media factors and social and economic ones. We plan on doing that here in this book for the field of public relations.

Shoemaker and Reese (1996) created a model to bring together the different factors that influenced news in order to illustrate the forces that shape media content. They called their model the hierarchy of influences. The authors wrote in the newest edition of their book that the model shows the "multiple forces that simultaneously impinge on media and suggests how influence at one level may interact with that at another" (Shoemaker & Reese, 2014, p. 1). The value of the hierarchy of influences model is as an analytical tool. It helps scholars "establish a point of reference in locating their focus within the levels of analysis; offering an analytical strategy" (p. 242). By the same token, it reminds scholars to consider the different levels of influence and adapt a levels approach to their studies rather than focusing on singular or linear influence models (p. 241). The model helps identify key factors that are at work in shaping media content. Shoemaker and Reese (2014) explain that their model is meant to "simplify, highlight, suggest and organize" (p. 2), even though no model can capture all the complex interrelationships involved. However, they argued, models "can exert a powerful guiding effect in determining how questions are posed and defining the relationships singled out for investigation" (p. 2).

The hierarchy of influences model is based on a set of propositions derived from media sociologists Gans (1979) and Gitlin (1980). First, media content is influenced by media workers' socialization and attitudes. This proposition emphasizes the psychological, professional, and personal factors impinging on a person's work performance. Second, media content is influenced by media organizations. This premise holds that organizations have policies and norms that constrain and facilitate individual job roles. Third, media content is influenced by professional routines. Each professional practice has certain routines and habits that form a structure for work. Fourth, media content is influenced by other social institutions and forces. The major impact on content lies external to any one organization and includes the marketplace of discourse. Fifth, media content is a function of ideological positions and maintains the status quo. Content is hegemonic and succumbs to ideological status quo to support the interests of those in power in society.

With these propositions in mind, Shoemaker and Reese (1996) developed a visual model with five concentric circles. The largest and surrounding circle denotes the influence of social systems on all the other layers. The next layer of influence is social institutions. The next circle is organizations. The next layer indicates the influence of journalistic routines and professional practices, and the inner, smallest circle designates the individual journalists who are being affected by all the other factors found in the four outer circles. This type of model allows scholars to consider one topic from multiple angles and from intersecting perspectives. Shoemaker and Reese offered as an example the topic of professionalism. At an individual level, professionalism could be studied as a trait within an individual or as the extent to which a group of people join or identify with a professional association. At a routines level, professionalism can be associated with which routines are perceived as credible for the field and which ones are considered disrespectful. At the organizational level, professionalism could be the negotiated set of values structured by an organization, and one organization could be compared to another for their values toward professionalism. At the broadest level, professionalism becomes viewed as a construct devised by or refuted by a prevailing power structure. Professionalism as an ideology can become hegemonic, where certain ways of working become normalized as the better, more "professional" ways of acting. Shoemaker and Reese (2014) concluded, "The levels of the Hierarchical Model alert us to shifting meanings and implications in such important concepts [as professionalism] and help generate research questions appropriate to each level" (p. 10).

APPLYING A SOCIO-ECOLOGICAL
PERSPECTIVE TO PUBLIC RELATIONS

Media sociology is a useful paradigm for applying a socio-ecological perspective to the study of feminism in public relations. There are several similarities between public relations and journalism that make it possible to use a similar framework. For example, public relations is both a practice and a scholarly realm, and thus most of the scholarship addresses practitioners and their relationships with organizations and publics. Public relations also relies on professionalism and routines as part of its job expectations. It has a symbiotic relationship with journalism, as its outcomes are media messages and communication products, including news. Some studies have shown that journalists and public relations practitioners share the same news values (Shoemaker & Cohen, 2006; Sallot et al., 1998).

However, public relations also has distinct characteristics, organizational responsibilities, and scope. While the particular socio-ecological model used in mass communication is a helpful guide, it is not a perfect fit for public relations. We have reconceptualized a hierarchy of influences framework to best suit the needs of public relations research as it explains gender and practice. Our framework holds up the literature to criticism and offers a certain scaffolding for analysis.

Descriptive Goal: Organizing the Body of Knowledge

We began to build out the public relations socio-ecological model by first using it as a categorical scheme for the current topics of study in the field that commonly get addressed in research. Each of these topics was considered according to the levels of influence and then matched to the one that best fit the way it has been addressed in the field. For example, one fundamental area of gender research in the 1980s was roles taken on by practitioners and whether these roles were expected and assigned to women differently than to men. Roles theory developed, which explained how most practitioner work fell within two broad role categories: manager or technician (Broom, 1982; Broom & Dozier, 1986). Dozier (1988) subsequently studied these two roles and found that men tended to be managers and women tended to be technicians. For our exercise of level matching, roles theory and its large body of literature fell inside the individual practitioner layer. The work conducted was solely concerned with how individuals got paid in these roles, were perceived in these roles, and were satisfied with their role. Table 1.1 provides examples of different topics, such as roles, and how they match the layer of influence we believe they most address.

Conducting this exercise helped us consider and form the many layers of influence that seemed to be at play in public relations. We identified societal, media, organizational, individual, and professional "leverage points" where oppression, hegemony, discrimination, and marginalization are enacted and where change can happen. Once we did this, we then considered how the layers interact with each other and what layers might have greater implications on practitioners than others. The model that we adopted has five levels that reflect five broad areas of influence:

Table 1.1.   Issues Studied in Public Relations by Socio-Ecological Level

Socio-Ecological Level	Topics Studied in Public Relations
Ideological	Ideological norms create meanings about power, inclusion, equity, and identity. Dichotomous meanings constructed for gender limit voices. Lack of diversity maintains status quo. National policies reify discrimination and marginalization.
Mediated	Media and public relations are codependent and synergistic. Media reconstitute meanings of gender, race, sexuality. Political economy of media co-opt public relations goals. Public relations influences media content; thus control over influence is contested.
Organizational	Organizational culture, dominant coalition, and workplace initiatives affect how public relations is practiced in an organization. Glass ceiling and other barriers restrict women and people of color in their professional advancement.
Profession	Professional norms and rules define legitimacy for public relations and reify gendered and racial expectations. Governing bodies guide expectations such as around ethics. Professional associations reify sexism, racism, and other discriminatory practices.
Individual Practitioner	Salary and roles reveal disparities. Characteristics of individuals affect work, such as self-efficacy, gender, age, race, ethnicity, sexual orientation. Sexual harassment and microaggressions affect practitioners.

(1) ideological influences exhibited through social norms that are perpetuated by economic and political systems and manifested through communication; (2) mediated influences, which take into account the symbiotic relationship between media and public relations; (3) organizational influences from the characteristics and structures of organizations, their culture, policies, and practices; (4) professional influences that are guided by professional associations and govern ethics, rules, and routines for a profession; and (5) individual practitioner influences, where personal traits and factors affecting individual advancement are analyzed.

When we originally considered level interaction and implications, we positioned ideology as the largest concentric circle. Ideological pressures are often invisible and therefore most challenging to address specifically. Yet ideology affects all the other levels. In terms of the level with the least influence on other levels (i.e., the smallest circle), it was the individual practitioner level. While all the other levels affect almost all professional aspects of a person's job in public relations, the socio-ecological perspective argues that the individual does not have as much influence on the other levels. They are too powerful and purposely create limitations that prevent any one voice from enacting change.

For the three levels in between the most outer and inner layers, their positionality required some consideration and debate. When we began to collect literature and analyze influence level, we found evidence to suggest that the professional status defined the professional and that organizations had greater influence on both practitioners and professional identity. Thus, for the description of extant literature, Figure 1.1 was proposed as our initial visual that illustrates the five levels of influence and that were used to organize this book.

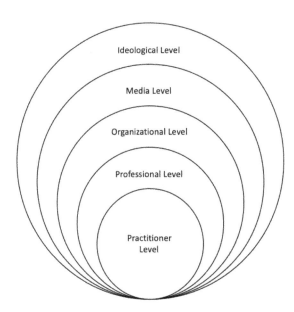

Figure 1.1.   Initially Proposed Socio-Ecological Model for Public Relations

Analytical Goal: A Feminist Critique of Public Relations

Once we laid out the levels of a socio-ecological model pertinent to all facets of public relations, we needed to go back and see how feminist theory would contribute to this book project and, hence, to the socio-ecological model we developed. At its core, this is a feminist endeavor. Both of us ascribe to a feminist identity and approach our scholarship and teaching from a feminist lens. Our goals were to consider what has been done in the field not only from a socio-ecological perspective but also from a feminist one. How can our book inform the future of feminist theory in public relations?

Feminist studies in public relations have traditionally focused on individual practitioners and historically emphasized the individual woman working in the profession. Today, feminism in public relations moves beyond just an individual analysis of how women experience discrimination or react to sexism. Ideology seeps into economic, organizational, and political systems and creates raced, gendered, heteronormative, and classist structures.

By adapting a socio-ecological model to analyze feminism in public relations, we can unpack the oppressive and hegemonic structures and "fit" in all the former research and future strains of research. Michell and coauthors did something similar for computer science (Michell et al., 2018). As they pointed out, "ecological approaches enable understandings of what supports existing social norms because masculinities are embodied and reproduced across the social ecology," and thus analysis and change must be at multiple levels (p. 326).

Michell et al.'s work is just one of several feminist pieces we can find that applied socio-ecological perspectives to examine gender inequity. Sociologists Thornton Dill and Zambrana (2009) argued for a multidomain approach to analyzing power and generating knowledge. They believed that four domains existed for analysis: structural, disciplinary, hegemonic, and interpersonal. Risman (2004, 2009) was a sociologist who took Bronfenbrenner's original socio-ecological model and used it to focus on gender and how gender is a structure. In her earlier work, Risman (2004) developed three levels to analyze gender's influence: individual, interactional, and institutional. Risman showed how women are both constrained by and resist the constraints of gendered structures. Later, Risman and Davis (2013) used this three-level framework to assess how gender is a social structure that shows how we hold different expectations for each sex and the mechanisms by which gender is embedded into social institutions. In organizational studies, an example comes from Bond and Pyle (1998), who analyzed workplace diversity. Their findings offered four lessons: (1) the influential role of organizational history and tradition in shaping current diversity dynamics; (2) the importance of understanding how participants' experiences of events may differ; (3) the power of informal organizational processes; and (4) the connections between individual, organizational, and broader cultural values. In computer science, Michell and colleagues used four levels to discuss influences on current norms and expectations in computer science education that have kept women out of the field (Michell et al., 2018). Underrepresentation of women in computer science reflects the underrepresentation of women at the highest levels of government and business in Australia. The authors argued that while they pinpointed certain influences at four levels, there are not clear distinctions between the levels: "Rather it is a way by which we can analyze the need for, implement, and monitor multi-level interventions" (p. 327). The levels operate continually and reciprocally in daily life (West & Fenstermaker, 1995, p. 24).

Based on interviews with Finnish journalists, Ruoho and Torkkola (2018) developed a typology to interrogate gender in journalism. They claimed that journalism is a gendered institution, and thus all practices and practitioners within the profession have a relationship to gender just as they do to journalism: "An individual journalist does her or his gender in everyday routines by using certain gestures, manners and language, all of which form a person socially and culturally as a woman or man" (p. 70). Their socio-ecological approach analyzed three layers: the individual, the profession, and the organization. They found nine dimensions within those three layers that explained the relationship between gender and journalism: (1) organizational symbols, (2) professional ideals, (3) gender expectations, (4) media management, (5) professional practices, (6) social conventions, (7) organizational specialization, (8) daily routines, and (9) individual reflexivity (p. 72). These aspects are quite similar to areas of study in public relations. These other bodies of knowledge were helpful roadmaps for us as we began to examine gender in public relations from intersectional levels of influence.

Dialogic Goal: Co-Constructed Model and Future Research

This book is a feminist approach to understanding socio-ecological impacts on public relations. We used our model to begin the dialogue about feminism and how we can make change to research and practice in public relations. We invited other feminist scholars and practitioners from different countries to talk to us about our newly created model. These nine women had also done research on gender, race, and intersectionality in public relations. Together, we discussed feminism in the field, the model, and certain impacts it has at different levels. The dialogue is represented in this book in chapter 11. As an outcome of the dialogue, we changed some of the aspects of the visual, we added content to chapters, and we enhanced the suggested areas for future research. Notably, the levels of influence were moved around to better reflect the co-constructed meaning provided by the group of dialogue participants. The final model to be used for future research is provided in chapter 12.

CONCLUSION: SUMMARY AND STRUCTURE OF THE BOOK

This book is a collection of chapters framed by a socio-ecological model that explains public relations and that can be used to retool research and practice for the future. Chapters are divided into sections. Section 1 is an overview of the book's perspective and thus defines socio-ecological perspective, critical approach, and feminism. There are enumerable definitions for *feminism* and *feminist thought*, and we lay out the way we use these terms so that readers understand our lenses by which we structure our assumptions and propositions. Section 2 and each subsequent section takes a different level of the socio-ecological model and lays out historical and current literature that can be used to characterize that level. Some of the chapters include a case study to use as an example of how that level focuses in on different challenges. Section 2 addresses the ideological level, social norms, and media influences. Section 3 focuses on the institutional level, where organizations make decisions that affect public relations. Section 4 gets at the professional level, such as discourse created by professional associations. Section 5 drills down to the individual level, the practitioner and how their identity is constituted by the larger levels. Finally, section 6 moves beyond any one level and pulls the different aspects together to look at the future of a feminist socio-ecological model in public relations. We engage in a dialogue to model the type of discursive meaning construction that we believe constitutes the future of feminist theory in public relations. We bring in both experienced and new scholars to talk with us about this book's main concepts. We recorded our conversations and used transcriptions of the dialogue to share feminist perspectives on some of the arguments made in this book. We use the literature found and the dialogue to end the book with a chapter that synthesizes themes found, recommended changes to our model, and areas for future research.

2

The Backstory

Conceptualization and History
of Public Relations and Feminism

In this book, we intend to share a comprehensive review of feminist and gender research in public relations and to argue for a socio-ecological model that critiques the ideological, societal, mediated, political, and organizational factors in public relations. These goals are built on the core constructs of public relations and feminism, two very general terms that are difficult to measure and define. Critics have not agreed with "mainstream" definitions, and there is little consensus on parameters that mark what is included and what is excluded from such general concepts as feminism and public relations.

First, *public relations* includes a wide array of definitional perspectives, which guide different streams of research and theory. For example, rhetorical and dialogic definitions of public relations have developed questions about discursive meaning making, while a definition stemming from a management paradigm of public relations creates the need for empirical research in organizational settings. There are also definitions stemming from critical and postmodern perspectives that dismantle the traditional, organizational view of public relations. In the profession, the term *public relations* is used to define both legitimate employment and unethical forms of work, while in many cases, work takes on many forms, such as public information and advocacy. Strategic communication, an outgrowth of public relations, has developed its own set of presuppositions, and there is a growing number of alternative definitions that are outside these parameters.

Second, the extant literature on definitions of *feminism*, *feminist*, and *feminist research* have filled volumes. There are multiple feminisms and diverse ways that feminists define their scholarship. We have found, however, that in most cases there are two common elements in any definition of feminism: gender and power. Some twenty-first-century definitions include race, class, and other social constructions that cause oppression, though gender is still the crux of any feminist definition. Similarly, power has been expanded and modified, yet forms of power continue to base definitions of feminism.

Given the vast array of definitions and background on these terms, we could not possibly offer a comprehensive survey here, so we instead selected the definitions that are most helpful to us in our feminist public relations work and that are most prevalent in public relations. We recognize that the definitions we are using stem from our Western worldview of what feminist public relations is. Nevertheless, it is critical for readers to know where our worldview is when we use the key terms that form the basis of our new model and the arguments we make about it.

PUBLIC RELATIONS

Unfortunately, we cannot begin our definitional section on public relations with a unified understanding of what public relations is. While we might agree that a mainstream paradigm has dominated the discourse and defined how public relations has been studied over the last half century, parallel efforts have existed and have used very different definitions. The mainstream paradigm situates public relations within an organizational context and views public relations as the management of communication between that organization and its publics (J. E. Grunig & Hunt, 1984).

Most textbook accounts of public relations use this definition and historically discuss four phases of time that have led to this definition and four models for public relations practice. The four phases are press agentry/publicity, public information, two-way but asymmetrical communication, and symmetrical communication (J. E. Grunig, 1992). In general, however, most public relations used one-way, intentional communication to persuade targeted publics. Nineteenth- and early twentieth-century synonyms for public relations included *publicity, promotion,* and *propaganda* (Myers, 2017). Whether the messages were truthful or did not matter; press agents and publicists used public relations tools, such as the press release, to achieve "free publicity." Myers (2017) pointed out that early publicists were mainly from France and Germany, where they used the popular press as a vehicle for advocacy as well as some early research methods to support their claims.

In almost every undergraduate public relations textbook, the turning point for U.S. public relations is the mid-twentieth century, when Edward L. Bernays first used strategic and theory-based efforts to persuade publics (Cutlip & Center, 1958). Bernays was a nephew of Freud and implemented the new ideas around psychology to persuade audiences (Myers, 2017). He also published several autobiographies and claimed himself to be a pioneer of modern public relations. Indeed, most of public relations history touts other "fathers" of public relations, neglecting to even hint at any influence on the field's advancement by grassroots organizations, women, or people of color. Every college student of twentieth-century public relations memorized Bernays's name and the efforts that painted him as the father of professional, strategic public relations. While there are limited historical accounts that provide different narratives about the origin of today's public relations, we are aware of several insightful biographical accounts of the contributions of women and people of color. One such example is Dr. Inez Kaiser, who was the first known African American woman who owned an international public relations firm (Parrish & Gassam, 2020).

The popular definition of public relations that continues to prevail in scholarly discourse is that public relations is a strategic management function within an organizational setting (J. E. Grunig, 2006). This definition arose in the 1980s, along with the "two-way symmetrical movement," at a time that has been termed "the Romantic Age of public relations research and theory building" (Heath et al., 2019, p. 2). There are other definitions that focus on specializations, such as crisis communication, or focus on audience, such as activist public relations. Other definitions viewed public relations as two-way communication (L. A. Grunig et al., 2002), negotiation and conflict resolution (Plowman, 2008), accommodation (Reber & Cameron, 2003); dialogue (Sommerfeldt & Yang, 2018; Taylor & Kent, 2014), and engagement (Johnson, 2018) to build and maintain effective relationships with key constituent groups.

We believe that twenty-first-century definitions for public relations continue to base principles and practices within a strategic and purposive model within an organizational setting—be it government, interest group, or agency setting. While we are not in agreement with the notion that this is the primary or principal concept of today's public relations, we must acknowledge that this is the commonly acceptable definition that is taught.

There have been new paradigms for the field that reflect greater complexity and depth to public relations and what it entails today. Rhetorical definitions of public relations have focused on meaning making and how discourse constitutes the work and the worker in public relations. While most of the research in the rhetoric tradition still resides within an organizational context, it highlights the "wrangle in the marketplace" and the complexities behind communication, which is the basis of public relations work. Critical and postmodern perspectives unpack what has been invisible and missing in public relations definitions. Publications in the critical tradition are not based on empirical studies but instead assess power relations, hegemony, and what has become normalized in public relations.

Toth (2009) organized definitions and perspectives about public relations into three broad categories that have guided its body of knowledge: methodologies for research, topics for study, and approaches to understanding the role of gender and race. These three categories are not the only ones, but they still prevail today and capture many of the theories and principles studied in the field. Each of the perspectives—functional structuralist, rhetorical, and critical and postmodern—are detailed below. In addition, we discuss strategic communication to illustrate a more recent perspective that stemmed from the discipline.

Functional Structuralist Definitions

The research literature that has dominated twentieth-century public relations has been based in the functional structuralist perspective (Botan & Taylor, 2004), which produced the excellence theory and organization-public relationship theory, two metatheoretical premises that use systems theory to delineate normative expectations for the practice. Functional structuralism stems from system theory and assumes that a phenomenon can be defined and understood by knowing how it is structured and how it functions in a society. In this perspective, public relations is viewed as a strategic management function housed within an organizational context. Most textbooks and mainstream scholars rely on the function of public relations within an organization in order to define the practice and the field of study (Coombs, 2001; J. E. Grunig & Hunt, 1984). For example, Ehling (1992) argued that public relations management must make its primary mission that of attaining and/or maintaining accord between "its organization and other organizations or social groupings" (p. 618). Another example comes much later, from Lattimore et al. (2012): "Public relations is a leadership and management function that helps achieve organizational objectives, define philosophy, and facilitate organizational change. Public relations practitioners communicate with all relevant internal and external publics to develop positive relationships and to create consistency between organizational goals and societal expectations. Public relations practitioners develop, execute and evaluate organizational programs that promise the exchange of influence and understanding among an organization's constituent parts and publics" (p. 4).

The development of the excellence theory was one of the first metatheories to emerge from the functional structuralist definition of public relations. The excellence theory, sparked in 1992 by the publication of J. E. Grunig et al.'s first book, led to subsequent theoretical streams that have guided much of the research published in the late twentieth century and early 2000s in public relations (see, for examples, Hon & J. E. Grunig, 1999; Huang, 2001; Huang & Zhang, 2013; Hung, 2005; Ki & Hon, 2007). The theory was based on a synthesis of the research done on excellent practice and outcomes from public relations. Data were then modeled into a normative guide for organizational success.

The definition of public relations by the Public Relations Society of America comes from the functionalist tradition. It states that public relations is "a strategic communication process that builds mutually beneficial relationships between organizations and their publics" (Public Relations Society of America [PRSA], 2020). A relationship is viewed in this context as a tactic that benefits the organizational host. The Public Relations Society of America stated, "At its core, public relations is about *influencing*, engaging and building a relationship with key stakeholders across numerous platforms *in order to shape* and frame the *public perception of an organization*" (italics added, PRSA, 2020, np). The core concepts in the definition make it clear that the organization is the entity that remains in control of decision-making. The process of communication is one-way, unless two-way is implemented as feedback in order to influence the target.

The Public Relations Society of America defines public relations by what its functions are within an organization. It included the following duties:

- anticipating, analyzing, and interpreting public opinion, attitudes, and issues that might affect, for good or ill, the operations and plans of the organization
- counseling management at all levels in the organization with regard to policy decisions, courses of action, and communication, considering their public ramifications and the organization's social or citizenship responsibilities
- researching, conducting, and evaluating, on a continuing basis, programs of action and communication to achieve the informed public understanding necessary to the success of an organization's aims—these may include marketing; financial; fundraising; employee, community, or government relations; and other programs
- planning and implementing the organization's efforts to influence or change public policy—setting objectives, planning, budgeting, recruiting and training staff, developing facilities

The stream of research that focused on a relational goal for public relations came into view as the primary function for public relations, albeit still with an eye toward organizational benefit (see, for examples, Ki et al., 2015; Ledingham & Bruning, 2000; Ledingham, 2003). Most authors attribute the genesis of the organization-public relationship perspective to Ferguson (1984), who, in a conference paper, challenged public relations scholars to study the relationship that measures whether public relations meets its goals. Bruning and Ledingham (1999) argued that by re-defining public relations as a process of relationship building, the discipline gains a distinct identity from its close cousins of advertising and marketing.

Issues management, an area of work in the management paradigm, is defined as a theoretic tool applicable across all of public relations. Issues management involves the detection of a problem, the attachment of significance, and organizing activities to influence the issue. Organizing activities can include research, response develop-ment, and communication strategies. Botan and Taylor (2004) associated issues management with applied communication because it addresses the current and most important issues that need to be the target of organizational communication strategies.

Less well-known definitions within a structural functionalist perspective have sim-ilarly attempted to distinguish public relations as a strategic and ethical function and move it away from a unidirectional perspective of influence. For example, Kim and Ni (2010) defined public relations "as a problem-solving process in which problems arise out of consequences resulting either from the organization's behaviors or from the stakeholders' behaviors. . . . Public relations as communication management thus engages in communicative efforts to seeking, selecting, and sharing problem-relevant information from the problem-casing entities (e.g., organization) and for problem-solving opportunities (e.g., resource or power holders)" (p. 48).

Rhetorical Definitions

A second group of definitions stems from the rhetorical tradition for the field that defines public relations through a discursive lens, thus emphasizing symbolic communicative behavior. The rhetorical tradition in public relations dates as far back as the functionalist one described above and has often run afoul of some of the strategic principles for functionalism. The most prevailing debate has been with the outputs and goals of public relations. Rhetorical definitions of public relations focus on its discursive process and the role it plays as a mediator of dialogue and meaning making, whereas functionalist definitions require material outputs and measures of organizational success that affect the bottom line.

Most public relations students in the United States associate the rhetorical tradi-tion with Heath, who has coauthored with dozens of scholars to codify rhetorical principles that compose public relations (Heath et al., 2009; Toth & Heath, 1992). Rhetorical public relations is prolific and varied outside of the United States, with European scholars in particular as frequent authors of the work. The rhetorical definitions step away from a focus on products and strategy and turn attention toward the discursive tools and messaging used to create meaning (Heath, 2006, 2009). A "rhetorical rationale of public relations," according to Heath et al. (2013), premises goals of democracy that can be fulfilled by public relations, which provides information for people to make informed decisions (p. 272). However, in most cases, rhetorical public relations still prioritizes an organizational context. Heath (2001), for example, defined public relations as "the management function that rhetorically adapts organizations to people's interests and people's interests to organizations by co-creating meaning and co-managing cultures to achieve mutually beneficial relationships" (p. 36). Thus, the unit of analysis tends to be organizational discourse and organizational meaning making.

Prime examples of studies based on a rhetorical definition of public relations can be found in the two edited volumes of *Rhetorical and Critical Approaches to Public Relations* (Heath et al., 2009; Toth & Heath, 1992). For example, Stokes and Holloway (2009) analyzed a documentary about Walmart to show its struggle with defining its corporate identity in the face of activist opposition. Meisenbach and Feldner (2009) pursued the question of how organizations can reduce obstacles to enacting a "truly dialogic model of public relations" (p. 254) and answer the question through a case study of Walt Disney Company and its Save Disney campaign. A dialogic model or theory for public relations was developed by Kent and Taylor (1998) for organizations to find ways to better engage with their stakeholders. Theirs is an extension of the rhetorical perspective for public relations, and it primarily applies to the Internet and the use of websites. Dialogic theory was used in an examination of public relations in China, where the occupation suffers from a negative reputation. Authors recommended implementing dialogic theory, along with other principles, to enhance the professionalism of public relations in China (Chen et al., 2020).

An example of a rhetorical approach to defining public relations outside the organizational setting was led by Bourne (2019), a British scholar who defined public relations as discursive boundary work. To understand public relations, Bourne compares it to adjacent professional fields such as advertising and marketing and claims that its boundaries have been defined by struggles over market control, elite status, and reputation. Bourne approaches public relations uniquely yet still within a rhetorical paradigm. She contended that public relations is "an ongoing professional project struggling over jurisdictions in order to survive" (p. 2) and that rhetorical analysis of its texts and products will define its success over the other professions. Thus, to identify what is public relations and what its value is, Bourne created and applied a discourse analysis framework. There are three areas of discourse to be included in the framework. First is expansionary discourses, which expand authority and expertise into other domains. Second is protectionist discourses, which are defenses against encroachment. The third area is fragmentation or hybridization discourses. In this category you find innovation, entrepreneurship, and subspecialties emerging. Bourne's framework is a significant way to find meaning in public relations products and the organizations that produce them.

Critical and Postmodern Definitions

Critical public relations has grown significantly over the last three decades, moving from "the margins" of scholarship to having dedicated journals and books about it (Weaver, 2016). Critical definitions of public relations focus less on what public relations is and more on what public relations is not or should not be. A critical perspective of the field and its scholarship raises questions about who public relations serves and how public relations reifies power relations. The work of the critical scholar is to unpack sites of power and note what is absent or not said in communication (McKie & Munshi, 2009). Critical public relations has been named a transformative emancipatory project, as it "seeks to identify and expose systems and causes of domination" (Weaver, 2016, p. 43). Critical inquiry of a scholarly field originated out of Marxism and the critique of political economy (Weaver, 2016). Scholars today situate public relations in the larger context of capitalism, democracy, and citizenship and analyze public relations work, content, and meaning according to its values and ethics (Munshi-Kurian et al., 2019). Munshi-Kurian et al. (2019) explained, "In correcting mainstream public relations' myopic focus on corporate and organizational interests, the emerging field of critical public relations has provided a much broader vision for public relations scholars and practitioners" (np). Basar (2019), a Turkish scholar in Vietnam, argued that a critical approach to public relations will improve the profession's "negative public image" as it would call into question the "intentionality, genuineness, sincerity, wider context, power dynamics and social and political implications of public relations practices" (p. 1).

Critical scholars define public relations as symbolic communicative processes used by entities of power to pursue and sustain their own goals (Toth, 2009). Daymon and Demetrious (2013), for example, defined public relations as "communicative activity used by organizations to intervene socially in and between competing discourses in order to facilitate a favorable position within a globalized context" (p. 3). Their definition highlights the political role of public relations in seeking to influence the meaning-making process purposefully. The authors clearly reflect a critical paradigm in defining public relations by claiming that the public relations industry "exerts significant influence and power in society through the production of meaning, the commoditization of discourse and the creation of consent" (p. 3).

Critical and rhetorical approaches are related to each other in that both focus on meaning and typically analyze texts as the unit of analysis and disdain positivist methods for research. Munshi-Kurian et al. (2019), for example, used a critical lens to analyze the #MeToo movement and its social media messages. The authors expounded on the campaign's successful use of feminism but also explained how the hashtag fell short of achieving significant structural change.

Postmodernism in public relations arose out of the critical paradigm and in attempts to problematize the accepted opinion that public relations is an objective and rational mediator between an organization and its publics. Public relations in this vein can be defined as a "source of moral power" that plays an important role in creating discourses that construct society (Holtzhausen, 2015, p. 771). The materials and information created and moderated by public relations practitioners can be viewed as symbolic capital that is necessary for retaining economic and social wealth by those in power (Holtzhausen, 2002). Thus, postmodernism defines public relations as sustaining ideology via the use of media for purposes of organizational power and control.

While there is a growing number of critical scholars in public relations, two key figures that helped to originally develop the acceptance of critical definitions for public relations are Lee Edwards and Jacquie L'Etang. Edwards (2018b) examines the field through a sociocultural lens. She believes that public relations has a significant influence on societies and culture in both good and bad ways. Edwards views public relations as "both an imposition of hegemony and a resistance to domination" (in Hou, 2019). L'Etang critiqued the notion that public relations is the appropriate function to claim responsibility for organizational ethics. She illustrated how public relations discourse about itself has constructed the "myth" of "ethical guardian" and "conscience of the organization." She used the growth of corporate social responsibility as a subfield of public relations as an example of how public relations has taken on the mantle of ethics keeper. Further, the idea of public relations as the "conscience" of the organization fits the definition of public relations creating ethical and two-way relationships with its publics (L'Etang, 2003).

Strategic Communication

Strategic communication is a deliberative, holistic, and convergent communication domain, and it is considered a part of, as well as separate from, the scholarly boundaries of public relations. It evolved out of public relations and still shares many of the same principles and goals of public relations. It is a much newer form of communication management, with its journal *International Journal of Strategic Communication* created in 2007. In the inaugural issue of its journal, strategic communication was defined as deliberate communication practice on behalf of organizations, causes, and social movements (Hallahan et al., 2007, p. 3). Plowman and Wilson (2018) defined strategic communication as the management of communications between an organization and its key stakeholders on a long-term basis to meet measurable objectives in a realistic timeframe (p. 127). This definition is remarkably similar to the original definition for public relations given by Grunig and Hunt in the 1980s: the management of communication between an organization and its publics (Grunig & Hunt, 1984). Strategic communication thus falls within a definition of public relations as an organizational function and heavily relies on a social scientific paradigm for methodology and theory (Lock et al., 2020). Strategic communication scholars examine public relations, marketing, human resources, and management. Strategic communication merged "scholars from public relations, corporate communication, organizational and internal communication, public diplomacy, political communication, advertising, marketing, health and intercultural communication" (Future Directions of Strategic Communication, 2017, np). Strategic communication prioritizes persuasion. As stated by Hallahan et al. (2007), "Lest there be any misunderstanding, persuasion is the essence of strategic communication" (p. 24). Public relations claims the use of persuasion as a tool among many depending on goals and publics. Added to the working definition of strategic communication was the context of the public sphere. As Holtzhausen and Zerfass (2015) explained, "the ultimate aim of strategic communication is to maintain a healthy reputation for the communication entity in the public sphere" (p. 5).

While scholars emphasize the integrated, multidisciplinary perspective used in strategic communication and carve it out as a separate scholarly domain, its position as a body of knowledge is typically related to public relations, and thus we include strategic communication in this book. While we personally do not identify as strategic communication scholars, we have examined its body of literature for how it addresses marginalized identities, gender, and race as well as whether its scholars have used a feminist approach to understanding its premises. Initially, feminist scholars were welcomed into the subset of strategic communication scholarship that began to flourish at the turn of the twenty-first century. Referenced in an early call for scholarship on strategic communication, Hallahan et al. (2007) posited that strategic communication should allow for those interested in gender studies to have a place in the dialogue. He suggested the study of, for example, "how language privileges male leadership and strategic decision-making processes; how women use language strategically to reach their goals, and how gendered lives affect organizational strategies" (p. 13).

To uncover the landscape of strategic communication scholarship, a content analysis was conducted of the *International Journal of Strategic Communication* (Werder et al., 2018). Findings showed that 77 percent of articles were empirical studies, and of those over 50 percent included quantitative methodology. Only half the articles took on interdisciplinary approaches. The most studied topics included management and leadership consulting, crisis communication, social media, and corporate social responsibility. Only one study had ethics as the central topic, and none focused on gender, women, race, or LGBTQ issues as the central topic.

In addition, postmodernism was applied to strategic management scholarship thanks to the work of Holtzhausen (2015; Holtzhausen & Voto, 2002), who helped encourage critical thinking about the organizational role and power. The vision for strategic communication acknowledged a continuous participation in the shaping of messages between actors, such as organizations and their constituent groups, to reach "an array of fragmented and continuously fragmenting audiences who have power in the shaping of meanings" (Smith, 2013, p. 78). Gender study was welcomed in a postmodern acknowledgment of the tensions in meaning making that dispute the goal of one overall organizational strategy.

FEMINISM

Feminism has been defined and redefined for decades, and while most authors might agree that it is the analysis and praxis of gender and power, they would not agree on any specific definition beyond this simplistic conceptual base. In our own work several years ago, we defined feminism as comprising three core concepts—that of gender and power but also diversity (Aldoory, 2005). More recently, Fitch (2015) regarded feminism as a social movement that seeks to end discrimination on the basis of gender. Fitch (2015) believed the feminist movement emerged out of capitalism and modernity (p. 54). This definition is less about its body of knowledge and scholarly endeavors and more about feminism's end goal. Whether praxis or research, feminism has as its goal social justice.

Definitions of feminism tend to vary by nation and culture. For example, in the United States, feminism has historically been defined by liberal ideals of equal rights, labeled as liberal feminism. The Equal Rights Amendment movement in the 1980s is an illustration of the predominant liberal feminist perspective. In contrast, feminism is more often approached from radical and socialist perspectives in Europe and the United Kingdom. Radical feminism is defined by its intent to topple systems of patriarchy and redefine society itself for women's power. Socialist feminism centers its arguments regarding oppression around class and women's lack of economic power. Socialist feminists are interested in "building inclusive movements organized by and for working class, indigenous, and rural women" (Brenner, 2014, p. 20).

Some authors today argue that women of the millennial generation condemn feminism and its potential to contribute to their lives. Crossley (2017) conducted research on college campuses and found that young women disavow traditional definitions of feminism. Her research participants regard older feminists as bureaucratic and conventional. On one hand, this battle between the old and the updated feminism is not new and has been made by feminist scholars for decades. For example, Creedon and Cramer (2007) wrote that feminism and "equal rights" were dismissed as "passé" by many women entering mass communication professions in the 2000s (p. 276). Ten years ago, McRobbie (2009) wrote of postfeminism as a time marked by "a new kind of anti-feminist sentiment which is different from simply being a question of backlash against the seeming gains made by feminist activities and campaigns in an earlier period" (p. 1). She described the third-wave feminists of the 1990s and their lack of focus on sexual power in contemporary feminist media and cultural studies. By the 2000s, feminism had become fragmented even in its basic goal of addressing women's oppression. While this might sound like an innovative turn for what feminism meant, fifteen years earlier, van Zoonen (1994) similarly argued that a reluctance to associate with feminism had occurred among young women: "feminism was a battle of their mothers or older sisters and their own struggles are of a different kind" (p. 3). Van Zoonen explained that young women did not wish to be associated with an outdated and rigid lifestyle. Furthermore, the introduction of Black feminism, womanism, poststructuralism, and critical feminism "undermined such like structuralist analyses of women's oppression in pointing out their ethnocentric proclivity, their untempered belief in rationality and progress and their 'Enlightenment' conception of a universal, unified human subject" (p. 3).

Still, among scholarly circles, feminism is a perspective that is relevant for young women and for changing the social hierarchy that exists in societies between men and women. Contemporary authors do acknowledge the usefulness of feminism in theoretical terms. As Swirsky and Angelone (2016) stated, "While there are many different factions of feminism that differ in their specific goals, generally speaking the feminist movement works to end the social dominance of women and supports gender equality in social, political, and economic arenas" (p. 445).

Many authors accept a "wave" framework to delineate and categorize historical moments in the development of feminism and its corresponding theories. Second-wave feminism encompasses the 1960s through the 1980s, and the goal was gender equality, mostly for White women and mostly in the workplace. In communication and public relations scholarship of that time, these second-wave intentions were reflected, and thus literature focused on equality for women, who in the practice at the time were predominantly White. Third-wave feminism, 1990s through the 2000s, rejected the grand narrative of equality for all, which was invisibly benefitting only White women, and instead took a postmodern, individualized approach. The third wave included rights for men, focused often on the household, and promoted diverse feminisms. Furthermore, feminist theory presented intersectionality and the demand for analysis of other areas of oppression: race, age, social class, and disability.

Today's feminists, however, debate whether a "wave" approach is useful and whether a unified set of theoretical propositions could exist. Younger feminists reject the "wave" perspective and cite the fragmentation of feminism today (Crossley, 2017). Baumgardner (2011) believes the wave approach is a useful guide to feminist history as a road map and not so much as a specific and detailed treatise. The approximate time periods allow for discourse to emerge about how the movement advanced and how it stymied (Phillips & Cree, 2014). There are others that view 2008 as the beginning of a fourth wave (Phillips & Cree, 2014). These scholars cite social media as the catalyst for today's feminist movement, opening up significant spaces for the rebirth of debates and resistance. Fourth-wave feminists are not cognizant of the online universe as distinct from who they are; it is just a part of life. The fluidity of online media and identity similarly create a fourth-wave feminism that is fluid and nonbinary. "Transgenderism, male feminists, sex work, and complex relationships with the media" characterize fourth-wave feminism (Baumgardner, 2011, p. 245).

Swirsky and Angelone (2016) list three principles important to today's feminism. First, there is a need to recognize and disseminate the historical exploitation, devaluing, and oppression of women. Second, while a goal is to improve women's social standing, it works toward equality for all genders and groups. Third, scholars should maintain active criticism of traditional intellectual pursuits and gender ideologies. In public relations, this third point is commonly represented through critical and rhetorical analysis of mainstream discourse that reinforces structures of power and social relations. The centrality of discursive meaning emphasizes the role of stories in articulating ideological-level assumptions and norms. Public relations feminists strive to illuminate the constraining meanings of symbols, norms, and values—all of which are difficult to measure and "see"—to make visible the impact of ideology on organizations and individuals. Universal narratives often take hold of professions and bodies of scholarship, which we argue defines the profession of public relations. These narratives are used to keep women "in their symbolic and literal places by denigrating and discounting those who do not stay there" (Rakow & Wackwitz, 2004, p. 103)—even when most practitioners are female.

Feminist Research

Feminist critique as a scholarly method can break the structures created by normative and reifying narratives of a discipline and a profession. A critique brings to the foreground questions of voice, power, and agency, all of which are essential concepts to understanding levels of influence on public relations. A recent example of feminist critique is Vardeman and Sebesta's (2020) analysis of the 2017 Women's March on Washington and the campaign messages that exposed both consensus and dissensus for purposes of political change. An estimated five million people around the world marched for women's rights on January 21, 2017. Vardeman and Sebesta used this moment as a chance to analyze social media and organizationally produced messages that defined the march and its goals. Their study focused on specific language used in the messages produced by WomensMarch.com, found in social media posts, and quoted by organizers interviewed in news articles. Using thematic analysis, the authors searched for representations of intersectionality, dissensus-based communication, and organizational decision-making. Their findings led Vardeman and Sebesta to conclude that while the women's march succeeded in publicly promoting the need for intersectionality, "its messaging consistently relied on a single-axis approach—that of gender—to gather followers and unify support" (p. 23).

The critical feminist research found in public relations is one methodological approach that is used to enact feminist ideals. A great deal of controversy exists among feminists, though, about what defines appropriate and valuable feminist methodology. Many feminists, for example, see no place for statistics and positivism in research, while others have argued that only through empirical evidence can feminists influence policy. Reinharz's (1992, 1993) work was helpful for defining feminist research and what should be excluded. She characterized feminist research by themes rather than by methodology. After a comprehensive review of all sociological feminist research published at the time, she found the following themes cut across the range of research, regardless of method used:

1. With few exceptions, feminist is a perspective, not a research method.
2. Feminists use a multiplicity of research methods.
3. Feminist research involves an ongoing criticism of nonfeminist scholarship.
4. Feminist research is guided by feminist theory.
5. Feminist research may be transdisciplinary.
6. Feminist research aims to create social change.

7. Feminist research strives to represent human diversity.
8. Feminist research frequently includes discussion of the researcher as a person.
9. Feminist research frequently attempts to develop special relations with the people studied.
10. Feminist research frequently defines a special relation with the reader. (1993, p. 72)

Reinharz noted that every research project did not have to incorporate all these themes to be defined as feminist. She believed these were descriptive rather than normative. While some of these themes are central premises for feminist research, such as criticism of nonfeminist scholarship, others are choices made based on methodology, such as having special relations with the people studied. Reinharz's perspective seemed more inclusive of methodology than others because it remains open to the possibility of quantitative methodology and positivist epistemology, two very prominent traditions in public relations scholarship.

While our own research may have varied over the decades with how much it could be defined as feminist, we identify as feminists and consider Reinharz's themes general markers for scholarship that can be defined as feminist. In writing this book, we considered these themes for our own analyses of the scholarship in public relations that we included in this book.

Feminist Communication Theory

Feminism and feminist theory began to be formalized and published in communication in the 1970s and took on its own body of knowledge as scholarly outlets such as *Women's Studies in Communication* and *Feminist Media Studies* were formed (Byerly, 2018). The original authors of feminist communication theory melded their feminist ideology and focus on women with principles of communication and media studies. Feminist communication theory served to debate and study how gender discursively constituted society and how those in power used discourse for their own gain.

A number of scholars mapped out specific principles that feminist communication theory employs. In 2004, Rakow and Wackwitz argued that difference, voice, and representation were main points of analysis for speech and mediated communication that formed the units of analysis in feminist communication theory. Their main goal for feminist communication theory was the transformation of social structures such as media to be more egalitarian. Valdivia (1995) explained that feminist communication theory explains how gender constructs individuals and their world through media, representations, and discourse. Her criteria for valid theory included being intersectional, taking account of race, ethnicity, class, and other identities in analyzing and explaining communication. More recently, Byerly (2018) set up three tenets for feminist communication theory. First, gendered social transformation typically begins with language and the speech acts that bring it into public discourse. "Thus, communication is the initial and central component of women's liberation" (Byerly,

2018, p. 28). Second, there is a dearth of feminist theories explaining women and communication that has prevented feminist communication from advancing. Third, better theory building will create more rigorous and productive feminist communication scholarship. In other words, Byerly called on scholars to strive for theory building that is intentional, specific to a field and a phenomenon, and addresses the challenges women face in communication.

INTERSECTIONALITY

We debated where to put a section defining intersectionality, since it can be used as an ideological lens and studied as an individual identity. Thus, we decided to include it in various levels given its multiple contributions to understanding marginality and discrimination in public relations. Here we define the term, and then later we describe essays that encourage its analysis for practitioner studies. We believe intersectionality should be a mandate in order to consider the multiplicative effects of identities and oppressions. We have written before about intersectionality and its imperative to examining public relations, its professionals, and its products for purposes of a more realistic lens. Intersectionality does not prioritize any one social factor but instead examines the impact of the intertwining of factors. In other words, a Black woman has a different experience at work because of her intersecting identities, visible markers, and experiences as a Black woman. Thus, her experiences are different from those of women who are White and different from those of Black males. While we describe the historical research on gender, it inevitably will focus on White experiences, as public relations research and practice has and continues to be predominantly White. In public relations, LGBTQ, disability, and age are neglected intersected identities. As feminist scholars who strive to uncover hidden power relations, we will work to address these and other contested and constrained intersections as we discuss the scholarship and practice of public relations.

Intersectionality was first developed in women's studies and ethnic studies. It originated with researchers of color who sought to have their voices and lives acknowledged in theory and scholarship. Intersectional analysis means the examination of social identities, including race, gender, class, and sexual orientation, in a connected and multiplicative manner. While each social category is typically perceived separately and has its own oppressive contexts, no one person occupies only one of these identities. At one point in time the authors of this book are White female heterosexuals, and thus our lived experience lies somewhere at the intersection of these and other personal identities. The interconnected identities reflect and define our environment, which in turn defines us. Multiple consciousness is how most of us experience the world, in different ways and on different occasions, because of who we are. "The hope is that if we pay attention to the multiplicity of social life, perhaps our institutions and arrangements will better address the problems that plague us" (Delgado & Stefancic, 2001, p. 57).

One of the first to use intersectionality as a theoretical lens was Crenshaw (1989), who applied it to the understanding of Black women and their experiences in the justice system not just as women or just as Black. From her original work, Crenshaw (1991) devised a set of principles to develop intersectionality theory:

1. Individuals and groups understand themselves and others based on power differentials between groups, and these power differentials rest within social constructions of multiple identities.
2. Identities include race, ethnicity, class, sex, gender, age, sexual orientation, nationality, religion, geographic location, and dis/ability, among others, and they coexist, are always present, and are multiplicative rather than additive.
3. A single identity may become salient at any one time.
4. Different identities may be privileged or marginalized depending on context, and thus a group may achieve more power in one context but be marginalized in another, thus producing a "matrix of domination" (summarized in Vardeman & Sebesta, 2020, p. 10).

There are ways to use intersectionality at all socio-ecological levels. As Thornton Dill and Zambrana (2009) explained, it can be used at the individual level to reveal the way the intermeshing of ideological systems has created opportunities and constraints on the expression and performance of individual identity. For example, it can analyze how a person who may feel subordinated under one form of identity, such as gender, may feel no need to view herself as a possible oppressor or beneficiary within another form, such as race (Wildman & Davis, 1996). Also, language used by practitioners, and in discourse and materials produced by practitioners, can be a unit of intersectional analysis. At the societal/ideological level, it can reveal the ways systems of power are implicated in the development, organization, and maintenance of inequalities and social injustice. Intersectionality also helps to promote social justice at an ideological level. It produces an alternative knowledge, one that addresses social issues and is used to solve problems of inequality.

CONCLUSION: GUIDEPOSTS
FOR OUR FEMINISM GUIDING THIS BOOK

We take a hybrid approach to defining public relations, and based on our own experiences and knowledge about the practice and its scholarship, we view public relations as a domain of work that maintains power, constructs identity, and emphasizes strategic discourse focused on creating meaning for organizations and publics. We intentionally employ the term *emphasizes* because we do not exclude other efforts beyond those that are strategic, though the practice is focused on intentional strategic communication for organizations. The goal of creating meaning reflects the rhetorical and critical views for public relations, where outcomes are not measured by a deliverable or organizational gain only but by discursive meaning production. We do not exclude relationship building in our definition because this has been a frequent goal of public relations as a practice and an educational endeavor. However, we attest that public relations does not lie solely in an organizational domain, and relationships are not always the goal.

We believe in the criterion of reflexivity and promote it among our students and in our paper. Thus, for transparency and analysis purposes, we describe below some of our reflexive thoughts about our own feminism and how we came to be feminists. Each of us came to feminism at different times and from different philosophies. Each is described below in order to provide readers context for how we produce meaning about feminism and public relations and why we are writing this book.

Elizabeth is a White American second-wave feminist. She faced overt gender discrimination in the 1970s when she sought to enter a doctoral program that until then had been almost exclusively male and in the 1980s as a new assistant professor. As a teacher, her feminist awakening happened when she saw the makeup of her public relations undergraduate classes go from 50 percent female and 50 percent male to 80 percent female in the 1980s. She had examined gender issues in public relations from a liberal feminist perspective, but she includes all feminism in her current work to advance understanding of the masculine norms that pervade public relations practice.

Linda is a White American Arab third-wave feminist who began her feminist awakening in her doctoral courses in the mid-1990s. Having been taught by radical feminist professors at Syracuse University, Linda took on the radical belief that the masculinist systems guiding society must be dismantled in order for any oppressed groups such as women and Black Americans to have a voice. Linda saw value in postmodernist claims that no singular meaning existed for feminism, nor was there a singular theory best for dismantling the oppressive patriarchal regime that guided public relations. As a professor, though, she teaches and studies multiple theories and approaches to public relations, allowing students to consider their own ontological and paradigmatic views as they decide to enter academia.

The two authors speak here from their positions as White cis-gendered hetero-sexual women who recognize their narrow perspective and limited ability to write about marginalization, racism, and homophobia in the field. No writer is "uncontaminated" of their identities and experiences when telling their story (Rakow & Wackwitz, 2004, p. 103). Thus, we are aware that our identities cloud our interpretations in ways that we cannot always know due to privileges we have. There will be readers who criticize our myopic views that may present even when we do not realize it. "Woman" is not an inherent and universal identity that allows us to tell one story that affects all public relations the same. Thus, we welcome criticisms and hope this book opens up the discourse in order to expand the knowledge in public relations and break down some of the filters that we do not recognize in ourselves and our research. As White feminist authors, we do not believe we have the right to give up trying to engage these difficult issues, and we hope this book will be helpful to others in understanding how to consider and study influences on public relations from a feminist framework.

II

IDEOLOGICAL LEVEL

Social Norms, Hegemony, and Media

3

Ideological Level

The Overarching Power
of Hegemony and Social Norms

Ideology can be defined as the belief systems governing and constraining a society. Ideology stems from the rules, often invisible and unspoken, that guide expectations, beliefs, and behaviors of people within a society. For example, religion, politics, economics, education, and family conjure up different images and expectations because of the ideology that created these systems for society.

The most outer layer of the socio-ecological model addresses ideology and its construction of norms, ideals, and expectations. Ideology shows up as the expectations for how people "should" behave in social settings. These social norms create constraints and judgments on how people live their lives, and they also create meanings for gender, sexuality, race, ethnicity, class, age, and other social determinants that can affect professional values and organizational structures.

These norms and expectations enact control, oppression, and invisibility of certain thoughts, beliefs, people, and entire communities. Yet ideology and its manifestations are the hardest of all impacts to measure and are the most debated. We believe that ideology constructs meaning for professions, organizations, professionals, and researchers, yet there are critics who believe that if you cannot observe and empirically measure cause and effect from ideology, it has no influence or control over manifestations of a society.

Power is what defines the ideological level that hovers over and influences all other levels. Power has been defined as both a force that some groups use to oppress others and "an intangible entity that operates throughout a society and is organized in particular domains" (Collins, 2000, p. 275). This chapter explores some of the main ideological power schemes that create tensions in and for public relations. We are not arguing that the ones we selected are the only ideological premises governing society or, specifically, public relations. They are just some of the more major oppression frameworks that we have seen addressed in public relations research and examined for the field. Importantly, we also wish to acknowledge that we merely scrape the surface of the bodies of literature and perspectives found about each of the below ideological constructs.

HEGEMONY

Hegemony is a key construct to understand how ideological premises seep into an industry, an organization, and an individual, controlling beliefs, practices, and decision-making. As mentioned previously, ideological influence is not empirically visible for us to observe or count. It is manifested through social norms, assumptions about who holds power, about gender, race, and what is valued. It is the process of hegemony that typically allows these assumptions and norms to take hold and guide behavior.

Hegemony as we think of it today was developed by Gramsci (1971) to explain how the dominant classes in a society construct a view of reality that is the accepted, commonsense way of living by all other classes. This was an alternative option to military rule and direct threats of force by imperial power. Instead, hegemony was exercised via economic, political, cultural, and civic spheres (Gramsci, 1971). Roper (2005) stated, "Hegemony can be defined as domination without physical coercion through the widespread acceptance of particular ideologies and consent to the practices associated with those ideologies" (p. 70). Gramsci described the manufacturing of consent as the primary hegemonic process that leads to moral and philosophical leadership by the dominant class and its way of thinking.

Four concepts that comprise hegemony were conceived by Howson and Smith (2008). First, subalternity is the status of social groups who lack political autonomy and voice in the political process. Examples over time have included slaves, peasants, and women. Subalternity in civil society creates disunity and conflicts, and the subaltern will never gain political voice until their power rises to such a level that they can become a "state" within the system. Second, *common sense* is the term for beliefs and traditions that become the norm for subaltern groups. Common sense defines and describes the everyday life and status quo for subaltern groups that create conformism. Publics and professions accept mainstream norms without realizing that there may have been different realities that were worthy. Third, Howson and Smith include power, "one of the most difficult concepts to explain because it is precisely power that must be reconfigured through a war of position to produce hegemony" (p. 5). Here, power is conceived of as asymmetrical operations that lead to domination and resistance. Finally, their concept of the ethico-political is the representations of a dialectical method that foregrounds everyday praxis. A "concreteness" that is organic, this produces moral and intellectual leadership expressed as civil society (Howson & Smith, 2008, p. 9).

Hegemonic Evidence in Public Relations

There is a dearth of public relations literature on hegemony and how it constrains the field. Only a few articles were found that tackled hegemony and its construction of modern public relations (Coombs & Holladay, 2012; Xifra & Heath, 2015). Roper (2005) might have been the first author to examine public relations theory from the perspective of hegemony. A scholar from New Zealand, Roper critiqued symmetrical communication as a form of hegemony. She examined cases of organizational excellence in public relations, arguing that while concessions and small changes were made, the organizations maintained existing hegemony. Another important article was authored by Gregory and Halff (2013), who analyzed global public relations and mainstream theories as hegemonic devices that offered simplicity and certainty for public relations in the United Kingdom and Singapore. They claimed that the excellence theory is an example of a hegemonic theoretical domain that has proved difficult to challenge (p. 418). As a metatheoretical all-inclusive approach, it "lends itself to normative proselytizing" (p. 419).

This type of convergent model, where complex and diverse practices are simplified and codified into easily understood categories, is created to make the public relations profession easier and expedient. However, as authors pointed out, the convergent theoretical models become irrelevant for professionals and scholars who do not recognize their own local, complex daily roles in them (Gregory & Halff, 2013, p. 418). Furthermore, these types of models become hegemonic in that scholars and professionals might not realize that they have bought in to the simplistic assumptions that were developed in one culture, that of the United States, and adapted for use within other cultures, in the context of global public relations. Gregory and Halff (2013) pointed out that the excellence theory was used by several other scholars to apply its generic principles to other cultural contexts. However, these scholarly applications "reinforce hegemony at least as much as they challenge it, by accepting the 'Excellence Matrix' and its 'Western' context of pluralism as reference points, thereby rendering other forms of public relations as different or peripheral" (p. 420).

CAPITALISM, MARXISM, AND CLASSISM

Class refers to the categories of economic and material wealth in a society and is based on ideological premises defining economic privilege, material and capital access, and political influence. Educational attainment and professional advancement are influenced by class as well as by the economic system of a society. The emphasis here is on the systems level of economics that governs professions, organizations, status, salary norms, educational expectations, and other factors defining a field. We argue that public relations as a profession and a body of knowledge is an economically privileged one and based on capitalist assumptions, even as it operates on a global level. For example, many campaigns today rely on social media and websites as the primary channel for messages when large groups of potential target publics are low-income and not able to access media. Public relations research is most frequently analyzing how public relations practices benefit an organization's bottom-line economic goals. Another example is feminist criticism about salary disparities and the emphasis on financial equality between genders. Thus, a prevailing theme of most research is how public relations is linked to economic success, though the hegemonic assumptions about capitalism and classism undergirding the scholarship are not articulated or discussed in the scholarly discourse.

A political approach for understanding the classist assumptions undergirding public relations can be derived from Marxism. Marx formed much of the modern thought about productive labor and how it is a means by which we make meaning of a particular society. Marx believed that labor productivity was the way humans expressed individuality, self-realization, and fulfillment (Weaver, 2016, p. 44).

Capitalism, however, was a limiting system on that creativity. According to Marxism, capitalism severed the connection between people and products that is necessary for society's value. The goal of capitalism is profit and productivity. However, "capitalism enslaves humanity and prevents the realization of its species potential" (Weaver, 2016, p. 45). Caldera (2020) similarly wrote, "Capitalism succeeds based on its dehumanization of women and people of color. . . . It forces us to neglect our personal and communal well-being for the sake of thriving industries and robust economies" (p. 711). This neglect, based on "White male domination," is "the engine that drives sexism, racism, and classism." Thus, in industries such as public relations, we have salary disparity, glass ceilings, microaggressions, and work-life conflict that devalues women and people of color. Worse, we have an almost 90 percent White field that continues its racist and classist operations even when most of its workers are women. We discuss these professional issues in subsequent chapters of this book.

Political Economies of Public Relations

While class emerged in some critiques of the field, it has not been analyzed and interrogated fully enough as a central challenge for the field (Lawniczak, 2009). There are several reasons for this neglect in research, and Lawniczak highlighted these explanations. He argued that unfair practices in the profession are glossed over in the body of knowledge and that a managerial context has acted as cover for what is actually the economic context. For example, ethics research examines how communication and tactics can be employed by individual practitioners rather than critiquing systemic economic drives that govern organizational ethics. This lack of attention is concerning given the "role of public relations in promoting the economic theories and the neo-liberal ideology that encouraged deregulation, discouraged oversight, and created an environment conducive to greed-focussed managerial practices" (Lawniczak, 2009, p. 346).

Indeed, a Marxist lens should be applied to public relations in order for us to examine the political economies that structure the practice and the body of knowledge. As Weaver (2016) put it, "Marx would have undoubtedly regarded the public relations industry's ubiquitous use of the news media to propagate the ideological interests of business and capitalism, and public relations practitioners who sell their labour to work as propagandists for capitalism, with contempt" (p. 45). One study that exemplifies the marketing of identity by public relations is an analysis of "Pride collections" or limited-edition, often rainbow-patterned products created for Pride month and marketed as part of social responsibility campaigns by corporations. These products receive criticism for co-opting LGBTQ symbols for commercial purposes. Champlin and Li (2020) investigated how heterosexual and LGBTQ participants perceived these types of products. They found that heterosexual participants favored these types of branding more than LGBTQ participants. The findings illustrate an awareness of economic co-optation by the marginalized group being co-opted in ways that the dominant group does not see. There is power in public relations, according to Marx, as those with economic capital are able to dominate public debate and decision-making. Yet this power is rarely acknowledged in theory and research. Weaver (2016) said, "Public relations has always been implicated in capitalism's exploitation of the working classes" (p. 46).

There are arguments to be made that a postcapitalist view reflects today's public relations, perhaps better than other professional industries. Thompson (2020) laid out the characteristics of tipping points that changed capitalism. First, value is created through intellect at work, and scientific or expert knowledge becomes the source for wealth. Second, knowledge capital, or the value gained by having information, corrodes the value placed on output or a product and price. Third, a new economy has been created via digital, Internet sectors, where scarcity is no longer a threat and market discipline and managerial hierarchy has disintegrated. This by no means suggests a diminished work intensity or quantity. In fact, critics have argued that the postcapitalist workplace has created an increased amount of work and cognitive load due to a twenty-four-hour, fluid work space and skills needed to utilize software and other online management systems. Also, some research has found less job identity and workplace engagement in the postcapitalist society. In former labor societies, sources of happiness and meaning resulted from work, even for low-paid care workers and other laborers. Nevertheless, as Thompson (2020) pointed out, "professional workers can and do enjoy the positive features of their circumstances, whilst kicking back against threats to their autonomy, work-life balance or pensions" (p. 303).

This view of postcapitalism also has its problems. The main limitation is that it leaves out two-thirds of the global population who still labor for pennies and produce outputs that are now less valued in the postcapitalist view. The Fourth Industrial Revolution creating postcapitalism and driven by technology has generated a significant digital, economic divide that is more real than ever, and those without the knowledge and skills to advance in the digital world are left behind (Hughes & Southern, 2019). Public relations is not immune to this divide. As a profession, the ideological premises of postcapitalism influence who can join professional associations, who can facilitate online communication, and who has the digital knowledge and resources to succeed.

The feminization of the public relations field has interacted with the appropriated middle- to upper-class professional norms to create what can be termed a "pink-collar" service industry. This term defines the middle management professional workers from typically metropolitan environments who are entrepreneurial in spirit and younger in age. The label *pink collar* normalizes gender essentialism while reinforcing class differentiation of the profession. Zhang (2018) argued that the pink-collar workers in China were technologically empowered entrepreneurs caught between the interactive, fluid communication independence they gained on the Internet and the traditional cultural values of motherhood and femininity.

CRITICAL RACE THEORY AND RACISM

Public relations scholarship has not yet paid sufficient attention to the "raced" nature of the field (Munshi & Edwards, 2011). Whiteness is unexamined and adopted as the norm not only in public relations but also in U.S. society, institutions, and professions. Whiteness is invisible and thus read "human" for most White people (Dyer, 1997). This culturally embedded invisibility has been an essential part of the power of Whiteness and its control over cultural and discursive representations. Research, as Dyer (1997) indicated, "repeatedly shows that in Western representation whites are overwhelmingly and disproportionately predominant, have the central and elaborated roles, and above all are placed as the norm, the ordinary, the standard" (p. 11). As a result, White people do not see themselves as raced because they see the varied nature of their other identities discursively constituted for them across all cultural representations. In other words, "whites are not of a certain race, they're just the human race" (p. 11). Yet race and racism affects all humans in society. Race refers to the social categories constructed based on physical appearance, particularly skin color (Center for the Study of Social Policy, 2019). The classification system is not determined by biology, although it is used in that way, but instead created for social and political reasons.

While, indeed, postmodern multiculturalism has become a contested and prevailing discourse in its own right, it has not dismantled the hegemonic racialized assumptions within industries such as public relations. Although diverse voices advocate for alternative theory and inclusive practice, multiculturalism has simultaneously functioned "as a side-show for White people who look on with delight at all the differences that surround them" (Dyer, 1997, p. 12).

According to Rothenberg (2005), White people have the entitled position of creating their own world—in this case, professional and institutional norms of public relations—and a system of professional and organizational values that reinforces the power and privilege of White people. White privilege is a core theme addressed in this book, as it has been an ideological framework for constituting the meaning of public relations practice and research. Dalton (1995), one of the most well-known cultural critics, argued that the most significant consequence of race obliviousness by Whites is their failure to recognize the privileges that society confers on them just because of their White skin: "White skin privilege is a birthright, a set of advantages one receives simply by being born with features that society values especially highly" (p. 110). "It is often easier to deplore racism and its effects than to take responsibility for the privileges some of us receive as a result of it. By choosing to look at White privilege, we gain an understanding of who benefits from racism and how they do so. Once we understand how White privilege operates, we can begin to take steps to dismantle it on both a personal and institutional level" (Rothenberg, 2005, p. 1).

Some illustrative work comes from international authors who study race as a social category that affects the ways people are perceived and positioned in society (Munshi & Edwards, 2011). These authors define race as "a process of structured events over time" that demonstrate a system whereby groups and individuals are racialized" (p. 350). They argued that if race is a process rather than a moment or a distinct variable, then it cannot be analyzed merely at an individual unit of analysis. The focus of analysis must include social context as well as organizational practice and historical events. As Munshi and Edwards (2011) explained, "Despite its virtual invisibility in the scholarly literature, race is firmly embedded in the context and practice of PR" (p. 349).

Moreover, it is imperative that race analysis include the interrogation of Whiteness as a system that privileges elite groups. It is not just the argument that the power of Whiteness is invisible to scholarly discourse; it is the argument that the invisibility facilitates the normalcy of Whiteness and the power formed for the White practitioner. In other words, studying practitioners of color or articulating discrimination from the point of view of a person of color is a limited slice of the larger construct of public relations today. Studying Whiteness and its lead on power and influence in the field offers a more complete picture of public relations and what needs to be addressed in order to bring equity to the field. Furthermore, explicit and implicit discursive norms often place the burden of protest on people of color to justify their positionality (S. Robinson, 2018). By focusing on White privilege and power at the ideological level, it shifts the burden on to us as White researchers and to larger systems of oppression. White people in this country are accustomed to advocating for themselves, to advance their own causes, within a system run by people who look like them (S. Robinson, 2018).

Another rationale for studying Whiteness is that it reduces the tendency for "race" to be inherently defined as "Black." There is a paradigm in U.S. race discourse that prioritizes a Black-White binary. This binary operates in everyday culture, through media, and in organizational practices, for example to increase "diversity" among staff. Discourse that reflects this binary dictates that racial minority groups who are not Black are less valuable to efforts in diversification. According to Delgado and Stefancic (2001), "The risk is that nonblack minority groups, not fitting into the dominant society's idea of race in America, become marginalized, invisible, foreign, unAmerican" (p. 70). This results in other minority groups being forced to "join" a majority group, either to assimilate with White as the authority in society or to appeal to the same oppressive rhetoric of Black populations. Furthermore, a binary paradigm simplifies the two groups that are the focus of the binary model. Blacks are essentialized into a unified, stereotypical group rather than perceived as varied, nuanced individuals with differing backgrounds and characteristics. Binary thinking can "conceal the checkerboard of racial progress and retrenchment and hide the way dominant society often casts minority groups against one another to the detriment of both" (Delgado & Stefancic, 2001, p. 71).

Within the black-white binary, white has historically been associated with goodness and purity. Bridal dresses, Snow White, the white hat of the "good guy" in popular film—all are juxtaposed to the black dress of the witch, the black hat, and use of terms such as *blacklisted* and *blackballed* (Delgado & Stefancic, 2001, p. 76). Racial goodness and badness has become so ingrained into our culture that even the "natural" color of Band-Aids reflects healing the White-skinned person over other, darker-skinned people, and pantyhose colors typically use the descriptor "natural" or "neutral" for lighter, cream-colored hose. These examples help illustrate the level of White privilege that U.S. society offers people who identify with the White racial group. White privilege manifests through all contexts of everyday life, and yet it is often a controversial topic to bring up in the workplace and other social and economic settings. As Delgado and Stefancic (2001) argued, the U.S. system of race does not just consist of "outright racism—the oppression of people on grounds of who they are." It consists of White privilege, "a system by which whites help one another."

Critical race theory (CRT) emerged in the mid-1970s out of legal studies to examine how law and policy reproduce and reify White privilege and power. The founding of the CRT perspective and, ultimately, movement has been attributed to Derrick Bell, who was a professor of law at New York University (Delgado & Stefancic, 2001). Scholarship using CRT as a perspective "works toward eliminating racial oppression as part of the broader goal of ending all forms of oppression" (Logan, 2011, p. 448). CRT "questions the very foundations of the liberal order, including equality theory, legal reasoning, Enlightenment rationalism, and neutral principles of constitutional law" (Delgado & Stefancic, 2001, p. 3).

One of the main premises of CRT is that race is a social category and not a genetic or biological variable. Historical evidence of this can be found in the shifts in political economic benefits of different minority groups based on race. Delgado and Stefancic (2001) give examples of when the Japanese were in disfavor and cultivated as the enemy of the United States, and then Mexican agricultural workers had a time when they were demonized, showing that "popular images and stereotypes of various minority groups shift over time" (p. 8). A second premise is that racism is endemic to American society; it contributes to all contemporary manifestations of social norms, such as media, laws, organizational policies, and research. Third, the United States embodies a system of "White-over-color ascendancy" that serves important purposes (Delgado & Stefancic, 2001, p. 7). It makes racism difficult to identify and address. It offers benefits to all Whites in such a way that few work at eradicating the deeper, systemic racism that abides. It also allows for the notions of "color-blind" selections for purposes of equality to be perceived as resolutions to manifest racist practices. The liberalist approach to race guides U.S. policy and law that mandates equality that ignores racial difference. This avoids having to dig into systemic racism that continues to privilege White authority (Delgado & Stefancic, 2001).

Since its origin, CRT has been helpful in several scholarly fields, such as education, political science, and sociology, to expose what is silent or invisible in mainstream discourse and social relationships. A main tool to use with CRT is to construct counternarratives to fill in the invisible. Scholars not only identify where there are gaps in other voices but also fill gaps with stories that counter stereotypes, myths, and preconceptions. As Delgado and Stefancic (2001) put it, "Many victims of racial discrimination suffer in silence, or blame themselves for their predicament. Stories can give them voice and reveal that others have similar experiences." Importantly, this storytelling has an ideological impact. It can disintegrate social norms and redirect assumptions about race at an ideological level: "If race is not real or objective, but constructed, racism and prejudice should be capable of deconstruction; the pernicious beliefs and categories, are, after all, our own" (p. 43).

Decentering Whiteness in Public Relations

We argue that a core cause of the racial disparity among the practitioner population is systemic racism. Systemic racism is at the ideological level of analysis and thus
it is wide-ranging in type of impact and typically invisible as a cause of individual
behavior. Historical moments illustrating the racist origins of the field serve as re-
minders of how little has changed today. At the turn of the twentieth century, when
public relations was forming as a profession and White men such as Ivy Lee and
later Edward Bernays were defined as "founders," African Americans were not legally
allowed to be hired for public relations management positions in White-owned
businesses. Even though the legal access did change over time, the racist and racialized norms defining value and success in public relations continued and were reified
through educational programs with textbooks affirming the White male heroes who
formed the field. As Logan (2011) argued, these circumstances laid the foundation
for what she called the White leader prototype to emerge.

Logan (2011) offered an innovative, theoretical premise for how systemic racism facilitates racial disparities in public relations. The White leader prototype is "a
historically constituted, ideological discursive formation that organizes professional
roles along racialized lines in ways that privilege people who are considered a part
of the White racial category" (p. 443). An unspoken norm that emerges out of the
belief in the prototype is that leaders in public relations are White and should be
White. This in turn makes White leadership appear normal, "natural," thus not
based on any racism and, ultimately, accepted and self-sustaining.

Using a CRT analysis, Logan found that although affirmative action created
structural access for African Americans in organizations, it did not alter everyday
practices that reinforced racist hierarchies in public relations. This argument can be
found in the fact that while there is still gender discrimination in public relations,
White women are hired more and excel to management positions faster than women
of color. For Logan, this means, "although issues of race, gender, and class intertwine,
race may emerge as the most salient factor in determining professional outcomes,
especially in the context of leadership in public relations" (2011, p. 451).

The White leader prototype serves several ideological functions in public relations.
First, it limits the meaning that gets constituted about and from public relations.
Leadership becomes assumed as White, and other racially diverse and inclusive
meanings are not normalized. It "fixes the representation of leadership firmly in
the realm of Whiteness" (Logan, 2011, p. 453). Second, it becomes normalized to
devalue non-White professionals. Specific beliefs and practices become internalized
within professionals themselves so that they are not aware of their racist lens when
hiring or selecting decision-making teams. The White leader prototype thereby becomes hegemonic in its sustained and yet unconscious influence.

Scholars and critics have published treatises arguing for greater attention to race,
multiculturalism, diversity, and the racism plaguing the field (Aldoory, 2001b;
Banks, 1995; Kern-Foxworth, 1989; Munshi & Edwards, 2011; Pompper, 2005a;
Sha, 2006; Vardeman-Winter, 2011). There have been attempts at improving di-

versity in research by some who have purposefully sampled non-White participants (Aldoory, 2001a; Sha, 2006; Sison, 2009). There have also been studies that highlight the voices of underrepresented minority professionals, revealing their perceived powerlessness and their attempts at fitting in to an almost all-White profession. Kern-Foxworth's (1989) assessment of public relations practitioners might have been the first published attempt to provide empirical data on the roles of practitioners of color. She found that, at that time, "the profile of the typical minority public relations practitioner would be a Black female, age 38, who has worked for nine years in public relations and has attained a middle level position earning $38,337 annually" (p. 45). She was one of the first to document salary and roles disparity for Black practitioners. In the twenty-first century, Edwards (2010) interviewed practitioners in the United Kingdom and United States and found that most were uncomfortable talking about the impact that race has had on them. These studies will be discussed in more detail later when we expound on the individual practitioner level of influence. At an ideological level, however, CRT was introduced to public relations scholarship by Pompper (2005a) to offer a broader set of tools to dismantle racism and the power that Whiteness has provided the mainstream body of knowledge. As Vardeman-Winter (2011) pointed out, Whiteness "manifests in public relations research as the disembodiment of race" in all aspects of methodology, theory building, and research protocols for the body of knowledge (p. 413). Vardeman-Winter (2011) argued that antiracism and decolonization should be used as lenses to "reclaim the nuances of lived experiences and personal identities" in theory and research. Grimes (2002), for example, examined corporate communication literature and revealed where White privilege was masked and perpetuated. Findings illuminated how Whiteness continues to be a symbol of freedom, power, and access.

Other studies like Grimes's are encouraged, where the social, historical, and cultural domains that lead to racist research are interrogated. Logan (2011) offered practical ways public relations can dismantle the White leader prototype and make efforts from an individual and institutional level to combat the ideological impact of racism. First, public relations scholars should encourage discussions of Whiteness and the White leader prototype to improve understanding of how White people are also raced as well as privileged. Scholars need to center and contribute to ideological discourse that will eventually hone in on organizational practices and professional roles that are racist (Vardeman-Winter, 2011).

Second, leaders should confront their own complicit participation in racist assumptions and use their power to help point out racism in the goals of public relations. Leaders should be aware of not only their racial privilege but also their complicities in colonization and how it has constructed public relations professional culture, authority, and norms for their organizations (Vardeman-Winter, 2011).

Third, further research should be conducted on the White leader prototype and other racialized norms that reinforce racist practices in public relations. This research needs to begin with the conceptualization of public relations as a sociocultural force and not just as an organizational activity (Munshi & Edwards, 2011). Hence, constructing a model that includes an ideological level of influence helps turn the focus toward sociocultural forces, such as racism, when studying public relations.

FEMINISM AND SEXISM

Feminist theory has centered on gender as a social construct. Sawyer and Thoroughgood (2020) wrote, "Gender is one of the most fundamental attributes by which individuals categorize and perceive others and by which they categorize and perceive themselves" (p. 60). As Rakow and Wackwitz explained, "Gender (and race) are meaning systems arising from the cultural activity of creating similarities and differences rather than as biological or metaphysical givens that culture modifies" (p. 13). The ways that people dress, speak, act, and relate to others are indicators of the social construct of gender (Sawyer & Thoroughgood, 2020, p. 60). Public relations scholarship, including our own, has used the term *gender* to really mean the biological traits given by birth that have been defined as male or female. We have written this way in most of our articles, mostly because it was the acceptable term used to construct the meanings between men and women in public relations. In this book, we attempt to remedy this error in writing and purposely reserve the term *gender* for when we are discussing the social construction and gender expression of meanings for womanhood, femininity, masculinity, or manhood. As a meaning system, rather than a biologically distinctive set of traits, gender then can be interpreted as fluid and dynamic rather than fixed and thus problematic and, in fact, misinterpreted. Rakow and Wackwitz (2004) argued that there is a dominant belief about a natural basis for dividing gender into the biological sex of female and male. This is used to justify different economic, social, and political treatment of people.

It is at an ideological level that gender can be analyzed as a political, social, and economic marker for oppression, which affects how organizations are structured and how professions are defined as well as the personal well-being of individuals (Poleshuck et al., 2017). According to Poleshuck et al. (2017), "There is much at the societal level that contributes not only to women's depression, but also their experiences of powerlessness and systems mistrust" (p. 1001).

Gender is made "normal" in the interplay of social, cultural, and institutional practices. Social norms shape the meanings given to gender identity. Social norms are also the basis of communicative practice that uses gender to achieve relationships, both personal and professional. Feminist communication scholars have argued for a reconceptualization of theory and analysis that reveals the fluid nature of gender rather than focus only on women or only on men.

In their book, Creedon and Cramer (2007) did not observe much of this desirable revisioning of gender in mass communication literature. They claimed that a growing number of studies in the 2000s used "sex" as a demographic variable and that "gender appears to have lost its explanatory power. . . . The hope that gender would challenge discriminatory practices had all but evaporated" by the early 2000s

(p. 276). In their summary, the authors argued that an example of this was women in public relations, who at the time comprised two-thirds of the profession but still were paid less and promoted less often than men. Toth and Cline (2007) wrote, "Women in public relations face barriers that existed in 1989, which serve to subordinate their roles and their potential contributions to the profession" (p. 277).

The rationale for why women were continually constrained even when they were in the majority is twofold. First, it is at the ideological level that oppression and discrimination have their roots. If gendered expectations are being guided at an ideological level, then change at the individual level will not eliminate oppression. Authors thus have been arguing for feminist values—a revisionist feminist ideology—to be promoted and then infused into public relations professional norms, organizational decisions, and ultimately individuals' lives (Creedon & Cramer, 2007). The second reason is that gender is still seen as a binary sex distinction that can be marked by difference for women versus men. While women were welcomed into the public relations workplace, they still battled the sexist frames that governed how they should act, how they should dress, and how much they should be able to achieve. The same sexist expectations also limited men. Men are constrained by professional norms and by expectations of work-life integration, though in different ways than women.

HETERONORMATIVITY AND HOMOPHOBIA

A related ideological schema that intersects with sexism and co-constructs gender identity and expression is heteronormativity. The term *heteronormativity* was introduced in the early 1990s (Warner, 1991). Heteronormativity is the ideological assumption that heterosexual relationships are the expectation and assumption for society. Herz and Johansson (2015) defined heteronormativity as a body of lifestyle norms as well as how people tend to reproduce distinct and complementary genders. These authors stated that "the concept works as a critique not only of gender divisions and hierarchies but also of more specific ways of organizing family, sexuality, and lifestyle" (p. 1011).

Herz and Johansson (2015) argued that heteronormativity has its roots in second-wave feminism. The critique of patriarchy and gender structures assumed an interrogation of sexuality and a promotion of a better way of life through lesbianism (Butler, 1990). Wittig (1997) claimed that the oppression of women can be eradicated only through the destruction of heterosexuality as a social system, "which produces the doctrine of the polar differences between the sexes" (Herz & Johansson, 2015, p. 1010). Heteronormativity marginalizes and erases all other sex/gender systems and is inextricably linked to gender discrimination on all levels. This is exhibited in public relations scholarship by the maintained invisibility of any labeling of the sexual orientation identity of participants in research or practitioners in organizational settings. In this book, we use the acronym LGBTQ to describe communities and practitioners whose sexual orientation is not heterosexual only; it stands for lesbian, gay, bisexual, transgender, and queer. GLAAD (2016) stated that the Q at the end can also mean *questioning*. This acronym has been designated as the preferred one to use by the Human Rights Campaign (2020) and GLAAD (2016).

Heteronormative Public Relations

In public relations literature, there has been limited discourse addressing the ideological underpinnings of heteronormativity that motivate organizational and individual behavior (Ciszek, 2018). On an individual and organizational level, however, there are a few books and articles, by Ciszek (2015, 2017a, 2020) as well as a couple others, that survey the experiences and advocacy of publics and practitioners and that critique LGBTQ discrimination (Tindall & Waters, 2012, 2013). One notable exception is the critique by Ciszek (2018), who expanded the arguments to a broader call for "queering public relations." She saw the need to decenter existing structures of the field that legitimize heterosexuality and its identity, knowledge sources, and politics. Instead of discussing heteronormativity as an ideological state, Ciszek turns to an activist stance by suggesting use of the term *queer* to depict "a political and intellectual endeavor that is . . . dependent on . . . critiquing normative values and assumptions" (p. 135). Queer theory is thus a response or reaction to the heteronormative ideology that governs dominant institutions and social relationships.

Application of queer theory to organizations and individuals is discussed in different chapters. Here, it is important to know that queer theory is inextricably linked to the ideology that it attempts to dismantle. Some have claimed that it focuses on identity politics (Ciszek, 2018). Halperin (2003) linked it to feminism and gender studies, arguing that queer theory "re-opened the question of the relations between sexuality and gender" (p. 341) and "harmonized very nicely with the contemporary critique of feminist and gay/lesbian identity politics" (p. 340). Ultimately, queer theory opens possibilities to theory development and to dismantling the ideological constraints of heteronormativity and sexism. According to Halperin (2003), queer theory moves away from narrowly conceived notions of gender and lesbian and gay identity. It has supported non-normative expressions of gender and sexuality. It has also allowed for both theoretical and political resistance to normalized discourse (p. 341).

CONCLUSION: AT THE INTERSECTION OF "ISMS"

Ideological assumptions determine authority, voice and representation, and who does not get to speak. We wish to find a multiplicative, paradigmatic approach to addressing conflicts at all levels, where broad understandings of society frame the multiple interconnected identities of organizations, professions, and people. Different subgroups are defined by society's values and beliefs and by who holds power. One such approach is intersectionality, which might help minimize essentializing subgroups according to race, gender, or class.

Intersectionality offers a systematic approach to understanding human life and behavior that is rooted in the experiences and struggles of marginalized people. For example, many critical race scholars look at not only poverty but also how poverty and race intersect in complex ways so that the predicament of very poor minority families differs in degree from that of their White counterparts. As Gatta (2009) put it, "Not everyone has an equal chance to be in poverty. Race and gender, and, more aptly, the intersections of these identities, influence one's life changes" (p. 103). Delgado and Stefancic (2001) showed that White poverty usually lasts for only one or two generations, whereas poverty for families of color sustains over generations. Similarly, middle-class status for Blacks is less secure than for Whites, "yet a general theory of race and economics remains elusive" (Delgado & Stefancic, 2001, p. 111). Critical scholars have debated the question of how class intersects with race and gender, while some authors suggest that since race and/or gender are dominant factors in the subjugation of people, class is not as relevant a point for facilitating professional or scholarly discourse. Delgado and Stefancic (2001) claimed that critical race theory, for example, has not developed a comprehensive understanding of class and its impact on racialization and racism. Few scholars, they argued, have shown that Black poverty is different from other poverty or that denial of loans is both a class and a race issue (p. 108).

There are ways to use intersectionality at all the socio-ecological levels. At this broad ideological level, it reveals the ways systems of power are implicated in the development, organization, and maintenance of inequalities and social injustice. Intersectionality helps to promote social justice, which is also a theme and goal of feminist research. It produces an alternative knowledge, one that addresses social issues and is used to solve problems of inequality.

4

Media Level

Symbiotic yet Contested Terrain

OUTLINE OF CHAPTER CONTENT

- Media sociology
- The digital mediascape
  o Social media and public relations
- Political economy of media
- Framing theory
- Information subsidies
- Conclusion: Contested yet symbiotic terrain

We single out media as a strong, high-level influence on social life, politics, and public relations. It constitutes and is constituted by ideology and thus like the other levels can be a tool for change or for reifying the oppressive and discriminatory values that are constructed via traditional, mainstream ideologies. Media also holds power as its own level because of its highly contested and symbiotic relationship with public relations. The complicated, yet mutually beneficial, relationship stems from historical evolutions in both industries, where training used to be limited to journalism for both, but then formal education as well as specialized practice developed so that public relations and media became distinct training grounds and advanced professions, which yet still relied on each other for reaching goals. Moreover, people who work in one industry may have worked or been trained in the other industry, allowing for insider knowledge of the routines and practices that result in the outputs. Ultimately, conflict emerges from the negative perceptions evading both industries of the other while simultaneously depending on the other for success—media needing public relations for subsidies and access to information and public relations needing media to promote intended campaign, organizational, or advocacy goals. Ideological, political, and social structures pit the two professions against each other while also creating dependent need between them.

Ideologically, while media is used by public relations professionals to succeed in their goals, it is also a reinforcer and creator of damaging social norms that inhibit the public relations profession and its professionals. Specifically, media reinforce and create sexist, racist, and classist norms in public discourse. There are three paradigmatic approaches helpful to analysis of media influence on social, political, and, hence, professional life. First, the field of media sociology assists us with theoretical frameworks and guidelines to analyze media industries, text, and audiences. Media sociology questions "stratification, order, collective identity, sociability, institutions, domination/control, and human agency" (Waisbord, 2014). Second, political economy of communication and media examines the economic and material systems that guide media decisions. In particular, a *feminist* political economy theory of media explains how media ownership, systems, and policies regulate media content in ways that are political and oppressive to marginalized groups, such as women and people of color. Third, we include framing theory here as a paradigmatic approach to understanding media influence on public relations and power. While framing theory is used as a theoretical lens, Scheufele (1999; Scheufele & Tewksbury, 2007) argued it acts more as a paradigm, for it helps explain ideological assumptions and hegemony of media workers who construct meaning through their stories.

MEDIA SOCIOLOGY

Media sociology is defined as the analytical linking of "media industries, texts, and audiences to questions about stratification, order, collective identity, sociability, institutions, domination/control, and human agency" (Waisbord, 2015, p. 15). This linking is a model for our interests in building a socio-ecological model to understand influences on marginalization and underrepresentation in public relations. Media sociology in the United States has its roots in the Chicago school of sociology and the Frankfurt school of cultural studies and then grew as a subdiscipline of sociology and mass communication in the 1970s (Revers & Brienza, 2018). It originally focused on how print and broadcast news was socially constructed and influenced by many structural and ideological factors. Media sociologists were less concerned about the effects of media on audiences and more about what effects different factors had on media content. McQuail (1972) edited a volume of collected articles that addressed the sociology of mass communications. In his introduction, he wrote that "knowledge of the empirically measured 'effects' of the media, as they are usually conceived, does not contribute a great deal to the understanding of the part played by mass media in modern society" (p. 10).

One primary area of original study examined the values of journalism, such as prominence, impact, and conflict, and their influence on content. Several ethnographies of news rooms attempted to demystify journalistic professionalism. Traditional values were called into question along with the idealized objectivity stance of journalism. Some of the more famous sociologists who helped uncover the strategic and socialized rituals of newsrooms included Tuchman (1978), Gans (1979), and Altheide (1976).

In addition to examining rituals and routines at a practitioner level and in a newsroom, sociologists analyzed the influence of ownership, interlocking boards of directors, and organizational structures. Research revealed constraints put on editors and reporters by ownership and boards of directors. It also uncovered the myth of the "scoop" and the reality of outlets following such outlets as *The New York Times* for what was newsworthy (Altheide, 1976; Gans, 1979; Tuchman, 1978). All these structural and often invisible constraints affected individual editors and reporters and the content they produced.

THE DIGITAL MEDIASCAPE

One guiding premise of media sociology is that the structures and formats of media influence it as much as the functions and professionals do. As far back as 1972, when McQuail first introduced a volume of media sociology research, he predicted that mass media will survive only as long as its currently recognizable institutional form and technology would. Mass media, he argued, "take their predominant character from other features of modern society—from its level of technology and economic development, its particular class and status structure, its centralized and bureaucratic forms of organization, its ways of handling work and leisure, its predominantly democratic political forms" (p. 12). It was as if he was able to predict the significant impact that digital evolution would have on media and its content.

Media sociology now works to uncover the economic, political, and social factors influencing online and other digital formats as well as bricks-and-mortar media institutions and their content. For example, Deuze and his colleagues studied how new journalism companies challenged former ways of operating while also reinforcing traditional understandings of journalism, holding on to old routines such as the use of sources (Wagemans et al., 2016). One reason for this is that the "virtual" and boundless newsroom accelerated the pressures on writers to produce newsworthy material (Ramaker et al., 2015).

However, analyzing media has become far more complicated, given the twenty-first-century blurring of distinct channels and messages. As Revers and Brienza (2018) suggested, "formerly valid distinctions between news and entertainment, old and new media and associated institutions, and media consumers and producers have been blurring" (p. 353). The Internet, social media, and user-generated content have created a synergy of platforms, which has confused not only who is reporter and who is audience but also what is news and what is entertainment (Pavlik, 2001; Reese & Shoemaker, 2016). Developments in technology have removed distinctions, and authors have argued that a "mediatization" of constructed meanings and "convergence" of channels has occurred (Deuze, 2011; Revers & Brienza, 2018; Zerfass et al., 2016). Importantly, this has caused media to be seen as constructing social life even more than in previous decades. Its influence on attitudes and norms governing gender, race, and class is more insidious and effective. Deuze (2011) described our current world as "a comprehensively mediated public space where media underpin and overarch the experiences and expressions of everyday life" (p. 137). He concluded that this pervasive and fluid context of media in our lives causes us to see the impacts of it as invisible and hegemonic.

Deuze (2006) argued that while digital technology is a diverse and new form of communication, it is also within the same cultural threads that people have used to share stories and information for generations. Deuze defined the principal components of an "emerging global digital culture" as values and standards ascribed by groups of users. These values and standards are embedded in everyday life to such an extent that they become wholly undetectable by users. According to Deuze, three core values of a digital culture shape expected social arrangements and meanings. First, we—the audience and user—are expected to be active agents in the process of meaning making. In other words, we must become participants. The level of participatory production within the U.S. media system has increased rapidly. Today, "everyone is a journalist" (Deuze, 2006, p. 67). Jenkins (2004) called this shift toward a more inclusive production process "cultural convergence," fostering "a new participatory folk culture by giving average people the tools to archive, annotate, appropriate and recirculate content. Shrewd companies tap this culture to foster consumer loyalty and generate low-cost content" (p. 93). Participation as a core value is reflected in the "DIY" trend that can symbolize people's wish to be autonomous and heard and participate as meaning makers while seeking an audience for their meaning.

Second, while we often hold on to former understandings of social relationships, we value a process of remediation to modify and revise ways of understanding reality within the new media environment. Remediation in this context suggests that old forms and ways of understanding society still manifest themselves albeit veiled in very different and new formats. For example, individual users can post their creative ways of applying makeup, for the goal of "public interest," and yet applying makeup and tutorials are standard message fare dating back through U.S. history. Social media and the Internet illustrate a "hyperindividualization"—the extreme fragmentation of contemporary society into private public spheres (Deuze, 2006, p. 69)—yet with "mainstream" symbols, images, and other notions that reinforce traditional assumptions about women, men, family, public relations, and so on.

Third, we assemble our own particular versions of reality from media as if we were bricoleurs. Bricolage is the creation of objects with bits and pieces of different materials. The bricoleur is a common metaphor to describe the media user who finds information online through searching and clicking through different sites. Media writers and journalists search and combine sources and hyperlinks to create new meaning.

Social Media and Public Relations

Social media have come into sharp focus for public relations, with research on its use, impact, and meaning growing exponentially. Social media are fast, cheap, interactive channels for reaching targeted audiences. They are conversational Internet and mobile platforms that allow for asynchronic as well as synchronic conversations and user-generated material. They are also viewed as important to the field because of their afforded opportunities to nourish relationships with publics (Valentini, 2015). The development of social media has given greater legitimacy to public relations as a communication profession, since public relations is typically the central office for handling the digital platforms in an organization. This is in countries where media are democratic and accessible; many countries do not have the same access to social media for public relations and for users.

The research in public relations about social media primarily explores potential benefits to organizations and practitioners (Valentini, 2015). Studies often seek out ways that public relations practitioners gain from using it. This growing body of knowledge illustrates norms and expectations produced by a capitalist society that has constrained most of public relations to be about gains to bottom line and reputation. Davies and Hobbs (2020), for example, explored the growing trend of public relations agencies using social media influencers as part of intentional campaigns. The researchers interviewed practitioners in Sydney, Australia, to explore their perceived value of social media influencers to public relations goals. Another study showed that European and Latin American public relations professionals did not take advantage of social media influencers yet did distribute massive amounts of social media content themselves (Navarro et al., 2020). The authors used a media gatekeeping approach in the study, suggesting that, like other journalistic gatekeepers, social media influencers are important for public relations goals. White and Boatwright (2020) used an ethics approach to analyze the use of Facebook by public relations practitioners. They argued that using Facebook to communicate with target publics may be ethically questionable and therefore not as beneficial to intended goals. These studies and numerous others frame their assumptions on a gains-loss model, where their goal is to assess the benefits that public relations can gain from social media. Kent and Li (2020), for instance, wrote about developing theory in this area in order to understand the benefits of social media and how to use it in public relations.

Social media platforms, though, have been viewed as a potential tool to change the power dynamics of society, particularly for marginalized groups in democratic societies. Social media are sites of public commentary and offer opportunities for bridging communities and engaging in social action. Social media has been praised for its democratizing influence in society and for allowing participation by those who before had no voice in a plural society. The content shared can increase learning and information sharing and extend public services such as voting and telemedicine and has substantially changed interpersonal communication and relationships. Overall, van Dijck (2013) argued that, for users, social media are likely "to emphasize human connectedness when [the users are] explaining a platform's value in their lives" (p. 12). However, this argument is weak when it runs up against the ideological constraints on social media due to ownership, access, and discrimination. An analysis by scholars in Turkey showed how Twitter content embeds and reifies patriarchal discourse on women that limits its ability to push democratic ideals (Demirhan & Cakir-Demirhan, 2015). Social media is based on an ideal of access for all groups, yet several marginalized voices still need to be heard (S. Robinson, 2018). S. Robinson's argument reflects a problematic within public relations: "White majority paradigm whose systemic policies and insular professional and social networks tend to benefit majorities and reinforce marginalization" (p. 34).

POLITICAL ECONOMY OF MEDIA

Political economy is the analysis of the socioeconomic factors that influence media structures and industries. Political economy is its own distinct body of knowledge but has its original ties to media sociology. In the United States, McChesney's (1999) work on the political economy of media led the first wave of scholarship to critique the corporatization of media and the influence of industry and ownership on content.

Political economists have used the particular paradigm of Marxism to examine the economic problematics of U.S. and other Western media organizations (Parkin,

1979). Within a capitalist system, the media hold economic power and can create the rules and laws while determining how resources are allocated (Byerly, 2018). Moreover, the unified concentration of ownership, where most of the media industry is owned by five global conglomerates, puts the power in very few hands. This has serious implications for democratic and pluralistic values. The few companies control the production of social meanings and produce "hegemonic visions of the world" (Montiel, 2012, p. 311).

The digital revolution has allowed for an even greater dominance of capitalist norms and assumptions to guide media structures and content. As McChesney (2014) put it, "the internet has become a, if not *the*, dominant force in modern capitalism" (p. 92, italics in original). Much of the ownership and wealth of the Internet is monopolized, argued McChesney, and thus limits opportunities for true public debate and democracy. While on one hand, digital media allows for varied and vast voices to be heard, on the other, all the channels for those voices are owned by the same company or a few companies; "as such, they pose a direct threat not only to smaller enterprises but to democratic governance" (McChesney, 2014, p. 96). The result of this has been a related threat to journalism values and the notion of an informed, participating citizenry. McChesney argued that the Internet gives the illusion of a multivocal democratic global citizenry, but in actuality, economics, advertisers, and a few conglomerate owners have created hegemonic values that most digital users accept and enact. McChesney (2014) quipped, "By giving the illusion of an information rainforest with every Google search, it has made people oblivious to the actual information desert we increasingly inhabit" (p. 97).

Political economists have also examined American and European capitalist media systems through a feminist lens. Feminist criticism of political economy has focused on the gender neutrality of its analysis. Authors have shown how women have been devalued due to their lack of economic power and are subject to exploitation for purposes of material gain. Riordan (2002) used a political economy lens to critique gender relations found in U.S. media structures, employment practices, and media content. Montiel (2012) studied the relationship between women and communication industries in Mexico. She argued that with men controlling the property, economies, and cultural industry that is media, women in Mexico have had limited rights to their own liberty and participation in the public arena. Byerly's work has highlighted the influence of White privilege and masculinity on the economic control of media and its content. She used critical analysis to expose the control that White men have in print and broadcast media (Byerly, 2006, 2011, 2013). Byerly and Ross (2006) described the "patriarchal capitalism that values male forms of organization and knowledge" and that constrained women who were employed at these media organizations. Byerly (2011) combined critical political economy with intersectionality to show how media ownership and its products are based on "processes that have affected women's ability to own media and to advance into decision making ranks within news organizations" (p. 27).

FRAMING THEORY

One robust theoretical area that stemmed from media sociology is framing theory, considered "one of the most influential, enduring sociological contributions to mass communication research" (Revers & Brienza, 2018, p. 355). Framing theory was initially developed by Goffman (1974) and explained how mass media influenced public opinion by defining boundaries of what information is and what information is not. Entman (1993) further clarified that framing "is to select some aspects of a perceived reality and make them more salient in a communicating text, in such a way as to promote a particular problem definition, causal interpretation, moral evaluation, and/or treatment recommendation for the item described" (p. 52).

Framing research typically analyzes the particular media frames and messages via content analysis but can also focus on the producers of the frames, the media workers. There is another, smaller branch of research that focuses on effects of media frames. Media frames are interpretive schema that activate certain ideas or meanings based on predictable and normative concepts that are known by individuals in a particular society. Thus, complex issues and events are organized and simplified into understandable interpretive shortcuts. This is problematic when it comes to interpretations of gender, race, sexuality, and other modes of difference because simplified and interpretive shortcuts rely on mainstream understandings and constrain diverse thought. The frames selected limit views presented and enable hegemonic opinions (Nicolini & Hansen, 2018). As Entman (1993) argued, frames "highlight some features of reality while omitting others" (p. 53). By the same token, then, framing also makes certain attitudes and viewpoints more salient. This filtering and emphasizing of meaning is hegemonic, so we do not notice the process (Carragee & Roefs, 2004; Kuypers, 2010).

Public relations is integral to framing theory because public relations practitioners can be the framers or can supply journalists with the information for them to frame content. Hallahan (1999) might have been the first to take a rigorous analysis of framing theory and apply it to public relations. He devised seven topics for framing that comprise public relations work: situations, attributes, choices, actions, issues, responsibility, and news. As Hallahan argued, framing involves processes of inclusion and exclusion as well as emphasis, and public relations professionals, as communicators for organizations, have the important role of deciding these characteristics. As Hallahan concluded, "Public relations professionals fundamentally operate as *frame strategists*, who strive to determine how situations, attributes, choices, actions, issues, and responsibility should be posed to achieve favorable outcomes for clients" (p. 224).

Feminist media researchers have examined the framing process as a reification of power. Hardin and Whiteside (2010) claimed that journalists engage in "gender-related myths in their reporting of events and issues" and "reinforce commonsense assumptions that privilege men in the social hierarchy" (p. 312). In studies of media framing of women's movements and feminists, common frames observed include demonization, personalization, trivialization, goals of feminist movement, victimization, agency in which feminists are presented as strong and capable, and site of struggle that emphasizes location (Lind & Salo, 2000). While many of these frames are negative, the same researchers found that feminists were more positively framed over time and more likely to be presented as independent and powerful in recent decades.

Public relations is the professional mediator and often creator of messages, resources, and, ultimately, frames for mediated content. Public relations professionals help decide what is to be paid attention to and what is not and how so. For some scholars, framing theory helps explain a significant role of public relations in media work (Lee & Lin, 2017). Sallot and Johnson (2006) found that journalists with more years of experience valued public relations more and perceived greater benefit from information and source access. In their analysis of media frames in coverage of the Women's March on Washington, Nicolini and Hansen (2018) explained that public relations influences what aspects of messages to emphasize in order to frame their organization's unique perspective on the event in question. When media select the frames generated by public relations, they ultimately shape public opinion and construct meaning for their audiences. In particular, through its supply of information subsidies, public relations contributes to the framing of media content.

INFORMATION SUBSIDIES

In the hierarchy of influences model, Shoemaker and Reese (2014) listed public relations as a relevant influencer on journalism. They situated public relations within the routine level. According to the authors, "The rise of public relations has played a major role in routinizing and making more systematic the link between the press and other institutions" (p. 187). In this argument, the need for journalists to continually fill the news void created a need for public relations. Public relations helped fill this void by providing information subsidies.

Information subsidies are tools that help journalists get out their product faster and with better content and relevant perspectives. Gandy (1980, 1982) was one of the first to explore the value of information subsidies from public relations. Subsidies can comprise knowledge, materials, or human capital. They might include press releases, spokespersons, or access to data and archives. Also included are op-eds, news conferences, and social media templates. In some cases, subsidies could be fully written drafts of stories by public relations representatives for use by media personnel who have limited time to fully expound a story in time for a feature deadline.

The content of information subsidies is regarded as official communication from the source, which in most cases is an organization, government, or other type of institution (Park et al., 2016). Numerous studies in public relations have explored the effects and types of information subsidies (see, for examples, Choi, 2012; Kleininjenhuis et al., 2013; Lee & Basnyat, 2013). In most cases, findings show that information subsidies affect media content and hold value for media workers. For example, Sherwood et al. (2017) found that news of an Australian football club was solely limited to the high-quality information subsidies delivered by the club to sports journalists but that the subsidies met the journalists' news requirements and needs. Another study analyzed information subsidies provided by governments in the United States, China, and Singapore. The authors found different frames for content covered by the media in the three different countries based on human rights policies and other influential factors in each (Lee & Lin, 2017). One public relations study focused on Black newspapers in the United States and the utility of information supplied by public relations practitioners regarding cancer (Lumpkins et al., 2010). Black newspapers are influential and trusted news sources for Black communities in the United States. The authors claimed that almost 88 percent of individuals who regularly read Black newspapers do not regularly read mainstream newspapers. Thus, they argued that public relations efforts to address Black communities with health information would be served if subsidies were to target Black media outlets.

Public relations' subsidies have been shown to influence up to 80 percent of news content (Sallot & Johnson, 2006). Very little has been done, however, in public relations to critique the role of information subsidies on maintaining status quo ideological norms and assumptions. Some research on war, military, and crisis communication have shown the constraining power of information subsidies. For example, Sweetser and Brown (2008) examined information subsidies provided by the U.S. military to media during the 2006 Israel-Lebanon conflict. Findings showed that media coverage was more neutral to positive about military assistance given to Americans leaving Lebanon. Coverage of U.S. government sources portrayed a positive view of the United States. This study and a few others have revealed the powerful role of information subsidies. As media rely on information subsidies, public relations can narrow perspectives covered. The resulting content limits viewpoints and diverse representations of the topic being covered.

CONCLUSION: CONTESTED YET SYMBIOTIC TERRAIN

The digital platforms for media have changed the ecological system affecting journalists and have shifted meanings for such concepts as routines and news values. In 2016, Reese and Shoemaker (2016) revisited their hierarchy of influences model and incorporated digital media research into it. The model was nimble enough to accommodate new realignments of media and the journalist. As the authors stated, "Emerging spaces in the network public sphere may not fit as easily into the once familiar professional, organizational, and institutional containers, but the new media configurations supporting these spaces must still be understood with reference to a larger framework of power" (p. 390).

The relationship between public relations and media is symbiotic in nature and yet very contested. It has been the topic of research for almost a century, with researchers in journalism and public relations claiming the greater influence on the other industry or a better way to work together. The relationship is symbiotic because both professions benefit from each other and thrive off of what the other one can provide it in reputation and material gain. It is synergistic in that their outputs produce a combined effect that is greater than the sum of their separate outcomes. Thus, the relationship is based on a political economy where capital gain and reputation are at the forefront.

In the new digital culture, this relationship has become even more contested. The expectations that come with the values of participation, remediation, and bricoleur directly affect public relations as a profession. According to the American Press Institute, to stay afloat, media companies had to reimagine storytelling to vie for user attention (2015). The role of public relations as a subsidy of information is threatened by the user-generated content and the turn toward audience as both creator of content and rater of it. Public relations therefore must change its way of working and its content as a direct effect of how media has changed. It can play a role in unearthing the invisible values that a digital culture has generated, but to do so, it needs to forgo many of the traditional ways of work. The public relations practitioner must know both the media sources and the media users in order to play her role in subsidizing digital information. They are in a uniquely advantageous position to be an interpreter of meaning as well as potentially creator of meaning. This is a powerful position but one that is often not recognized or harnessed.

On the other hand, the public relations practitioner can do the work of the bricoleur for both journalist and audience. The practitioner of public relations can take on the responsibility of curating the artifacts and activities of a digital culture. They can track users within a certain media source; they can monitor the enrollment and disengagement of social networks; and they can analyze posts and news as members, participants, or observers. The practitioner considers suitability of information, accessibility, relevance to their goal, ease of understanding, and other factors. She can repurpose and refashion other sources in order to construct a story. However, while freedom and creativity are a part of this process, the public relations bricoleur is also constrained by pragmatic barriers such as timeliness, online access to information, and skill and competence in the digital landscape.

Another impact of the digital media environment is a breaking down of professional stereotypes. The norm of neutrality by media representatives is often contrasted with a perceived norm of bias or spin by public relations professionals. However, within a digital culture, boundaries between who is audience and who is source have disintegrated, thus blurring the accountability for bias and the expectation of neutrality.

This intertwining and contested relationship is the reason why we carved out a level of influence for media. The influence of media is greater than just on any one public relations practitioner. While most of the research focuses on an individual re-lationship level or on professional-level norms, findings from this body of knowledge reveal a much greater impact. Media influence expectations about public relations goals, perceptions about its relationship with media, and constraints on its profes-sional routines and understandings of audience. Thus, a layer of influence in our socio-ecological model must be devoted to this contested terrain.

III

ORGANIZATIONAL LEVEL

Issues and Theories

5

Organizational Level

Their Role in Maintaining the Status Quo

OUTLINE OF CHAPTER CONTENT

- A feminist view of the organizational level
- The online environment's unfair advantages
- Work-life policies and practices
- The glass ceiling
- Organizational mentorship
- Case example: NBC sidelined female public relations professionals
- Conclusion: Two steps forward, one step back

From a neoliberal perspective,[1] we believe that public relations is influenced by organizations even when the public relations itself may not be practiced within organizational settings. For example, activist public relations may have an organization as its target, independent consultants may have organizations as clients, and social media influencers may have organizations as sponsors. Thus, the importance of an organizational level of influence cannot be overstated.

While there are several types of organizations, such as governmental, nonprofit, and corporate, the public relations unit tends to be the same, except in agencies or firms (Smuddie, 2015, p. 32). Agencies differ from nonagency organizations because their missions are distinct. Agencies seek clients who pay them to conduct public relations work. To "get" clients and "keep" them, agencies must be willing to adapt their structures. Nonagencies have "in-house" public relations personnel who function to achieve their organization's goals. In-house public relations work is considered more fixed because the organization's mission remains stable. Each type of organization reflects differences in preferences for what employees, stakeholders, and publics do; how they are treated; and whether they can advance in their careers. In this chapter, we provide a brief introduction describing how public relations is found in organizational structures and outline the issues we found to be particularly relevant when analyzing organizational influence on public relations. The issues include the online environment, policies that limit women's advancement, employee/workplace initiatives, the glass ceiling, and mentorship. But first, we explain our feminist view of including an organizational level of analysis in our model.

A FEMINIST VIEW OF THE ORGANIZATIONAL LEVEL

We take a decidedly feminist stance in depicting the institutional level of our socioecological model, but we see the imprint of neoliberal research that has identified how public relations is mostly gendered and raced in organizational contexts. The nature of organizational reality is such that masculine values predominate, causing barriers for women who work in public relations functions. In chapter 6, we lay out the paradigmatic theories that mainly play out in an organizational context and how they have focused on gender in public relations while ignoring the racist and classist assumptions of the discipline.

Public relations is done in organizational contexts. Organizational decision makers create organizational structures to achieve goals through deliberate role assignments that control individual behaviors. Structures embed organizational values in orientation programs, ongoing socialization, and messaging. Structures are found in practices, policies, and norms, both formal and informal, that dictate individual rights and responsibilities. Because organizational actors perceive value in structures to expedite organizational behavior, structures are not easily changed. When organizational policies and norms normalize preferences for employees because of gender, race, ethnicity, class, or sexual orientation, issues of disparity and oppression result.

In a study of top public relations executives, it was discovered that 72 percent of organizations did not have diversity and inclusion goals tied to compensation and reward of the executive. Only 40 percent of these executives had completely integrated a comprehensive diversity and inclusion plan. The most effective practices in recruiting and retaining diverse public relations staff were led by leadership support for proactive strategies (Jiang et al., 2016).

Structures and policies become spaces in which power relationships are negotiated. For example, Werder and Holtzhausen (2011) explored how public relations practitioner role enactment, decision-making behavior, and leadership style relate to and influence organizational structure. From an online survey of 885 practitioners who were members of the Public Relations Society of America, the authors found that male practitioners were more likely than female practitioners to work in virtual organizations. They speculated that senior male communication managers were more likely to be working in virtual structures because they are more trusted to work independently. Structure in their study became a means of privilege for male practitioners' flexibility not available to the female practitioners despite their similarity in role assignments.

The problems of public relations have been minimized as either "just a woman's issue" or as no issue at all (Aldoory et al., 2008). Similarly, race is ascribed only to people of color. Organizations are entrenched in efforts to achieve goals of survival, and thus reflecting on their power systems and structures that discriminate and marginalize would prevent efficient paths to strategic goals. By minimizing concerns about their racist, sexist systems, organizations maintain the status quo, which has generally worked for them. Dubrowski at el. (2019) reported that male participants in their study said they didn't think there were systematic barriers to women's rise to leadership positions. Their female participants disagreed, "frequently citing challenges such as work-life fit" (np). Some participants said they had no desire to climb higher in the ranks because of the "costs" of workplace inflexibilities. The research on microaggressions and sexual harassment provide evidence that racism and sexism are negatively affecting practitioners and their work. In a follow-up quantitative study, McCorkindale and Rickert (2020) reported that 16 percent of women in their sample had seen gender bias "always" or "often" in their organizations compared to 4 percent of the men; 36 percent of the women in the sample said they had "sometimes" seen gender bias compared to 12 percent of the men.

THE ONLINE ENVIRONMENT'S UNFAIR ADVANTAGES

The online environment of the public relations practitioner is now a 24/7 social and professional world (Gilkerson et al., 2018, p. 1). This has caused three issues: work-life as antiquated myth to cope with, exploitation of emotional labor, and false narratives that deepen inequities. Gilkerson et al.'s (2018) qualitative study of agency public relations practitioners found that "the rise of social media led to issues of employee burnout, challenges related to keeping pace with quickly evolving technology and of need to maintain a personal brand conveying cutting edge expertise" (p. 1). Gilkerson et al. (2018) participants thought that the concept of "work-life balance had become an antiquated idea or an unachievable 'myth'" (p. 13). These agency practitioners had developed pragmatic strategies for their employer and client expectations. They'd developed internal team strategies, processes, and protocols for responding to emergency situations that occurred outside of business hours. They developed shared responsibility systems and team scheduling and used automated media monitoring and management services to work against the rapid response needs or policies for when to alert senior staff (pp. 15–16). Their participants reinforced the unique challenges of social media for junior employees and work-life challenges faced by parents, especially mothers.

Gilkerson et al. (2018) described structural challenges of the online environment defeating practitioners' expectations of life as well as work. Bridgen (2011) identified the drain of emotional labor work of social engagement reaffirming existing gender roles. Emotional labor referred to using one's personal feelings and emotions, a "learning to please" character of new media work. Bridgen (2011) theorized that although practitioners gained pleasure through online conversations and connections being carried out on behalf of employers, their personal interests shared online were "part of the employer's product and subsequently responsible for some aspects of organizational success" (p. 63). Bridgen reasoned that social platform interactions acerbate the use of emotion in public relations because "communication technologies have been used to facilitate remote forms of interaction with customers that seeks to emulate the feeling relationship of the direct encounter" (Bridgen, 2011, p. 65).

To illustrate her position, Bridgen (2011) recruited five public relations practitioners in the United Kingdom—three men and two women—to examine the extent to which they used their own emotions and feelings in social media work. Her participants reported that online conversations took emotional commitments beyond the boundaries of journalist-practitioner relationships. "They brought more of their personal life into their work and took it home due to the portable nature of online work and the 24-hour nature of online communications" (p. 73). These practitioners accepted their "self" as a commodity for the client and didn't have any ethical or moral contrition in doing so (p. 65).

Keating (2016) examined dominant organizational discourses that "purport to value 'flexibility' and 'diversity' to limit awareness of systematic sexism" (p. 22). She pointed to the "new labor" associated with social media and the resulting organizational narratives' narrowing of resistance to gender inequality. She gave the example of practitioners who held the view that "gender inequality is not an issue or misrecognized their long work hours and limited career advancement as individual choices" (p. 23). Adjusting to the online environment, practitioners seemingly faced reallocation of budgets, personnel, and skills training to adjust, unaware of how the narratives of "new media" reinforced gender inequality. In her essay, she points to Australian local councils where public relations workers report anxiety about increased social media work because such work has a low internal profile, is undertaken in ad-hoc ways, and attracts few resources. As young women predominate low-profile public relations roles, these new practices and divisions deepen inequalities, in contrast to organizational discourses around "family friendly hours and flexible conditions" (Keating, 2016).

WORK-LIFE POLICIES AND PRACTICES

Work-life integration addresses efforts by workers, both male and female, to juggle various personal, home, and work responsibilities (Aldoory et al., 2008). Jiang and Shen (2018; Shen & Jiang, 2013) have done research on work-life conflict, focusing on the experiences of employees in integrating their job responsibilities and activities outside their work, such as family, leisure time, and community service. They identified three types of work-life conflict: behavior-based, time-based, and strain-based. Behavior-based means contradictory expectations between public and private domain or bringing home inappropriate behavior: "managerial roles often characterized as independence, aggressiveness, objectivity, impersonality, logic, power, ambition, and authority when one's spouse and children would expect home behaviors that were communal, nurturing, intuitive, sensitive, dependent, warm, accommodating" (p. 261). Time-based refers to situations demanding time away from nonwork activities (p. 260). Strain-based issues are circumstances when employees are "psychologically pre-occupied with work" and fail to meet nonwork commitments (p. 261).

Organizations typically attempt to increase job satisfaction and retention through the development of family-friendly or work-life integration policies and initiatives. For example, policies might include maternity leave, financed day care, and flexible telecommuting. However, today, there are still organizations that limit female advancement due to lack of policies for leave, childcare, and elder care. While it is far more normal to have these types of policies, organizations present inconsistencies with their policies and often judge parenting and family obligations even with policies in place. Feminist scholars have argued for decades that consistent, equitable work-life integration policies are beneficial for women. Hayden (2010) claimed that "they are central . . . in the ongoing battle against sexism and the struggle to create a more just and humane society" (p. 119). Yet critics have shown how the policies in many cases are discriminatory (Hayden, 2010). A study by Dubrowski et al. (2019) based on focus groups of senior and midlevel public relations practitioners from agencies, corporations, and nonprofits provided several themes related to organizational barriers to female practitioners who sought to achieve leadership roles in public relations: (a) "inconsistencies among managers in the same organization around flexibility, while some allowed employees to work from home, some managers in the same department did not"; (b) "missing out on social/family activities because of after-hour work demands"; and (c) "shamed if they took advantage of flexibility-offers" (np). Women without children felt "they deserved the same leave for their own personal endeavors as those who took parental leave" (np).

The Mind the Gap: Women's Leadership in Public Relations survey assessed work-life integration perceptions and organizational practices related to it (McCorkindale & Rickert, 2020). Based on a convenience sample of 865 practitioners, their data reinforced the notion that women experience more stress and conflict over work-life balancing than men. Women cited a desire for equality when it came to leaves of absence yet acknowledged that utilizing benefits often carried a stigma. Only 56 percent of respondents' organizations offered paternity leave, though 92 percent offered maternity leave. Nearly half of respondents said a leave would "hurt my career" (McCorkindale & Rickert, 2020). The authors concluded, "Both men and women agree that flex work arrangements are important benefits, but in practice, they're not uniformly applied across genders. Often, there are workplace culture barriers (the policy or options exist, but we don't do that here) or managers inconsistently approve the arrangements" (McCorkindale & Rickert, 2020, np).

One study was found that highlighted the additional stress on Black practitioners during the COVID-19 pandemic (Barnes, 2020). Fifty-two percent of the Black professionals in the study reported that they felt more pressure to perform at a higher level than their White counterparts. More than 75 percent reported experiencing on-the-job stress that reduced their productivity. Fifty-four percent felt their employers were not offering enough support or decreasing support in the wake of COVID-19. Finally, 77 percent were women who expressed difficulties with balancing work and family responsibilities, including homeschooling and childcare.

Workplace initiatives are beneficial to the work-life integration, health, and job satisfaction of employees. While these organization-sponsored initiatives often emerge out of policy, they can also be created by volunteer employee groups or as special projects of executives and other employees. There are four typical categories for workplace initiatives, according to Thiefels (2017), and if done well, they can all improve office culture, mental health, and perceived job satisfaction of employees. The categories are health and wellness initiatives, "kindness" programs (such as recognitions and awards and setting characters or pillars that everyone follows), volunteer and social service activities, and work-life integration options (such as flexible Fridays).

For women and people of color, workplace initiatives could make the difference in their ability to feel empowered at work, seek professional advancement, and succeed in professional goals. However, research has shown that if not done well, organization-led programs, particularly those related to health and wellness, for example, can lead to greater feelings of exclusion, resentment, and perceived discrimination. For example, if only one way of doing health is promoted or if employee voices are not included in the decisions about which health actions to incorporate, employees feel neglected, burdened, and resentful (Zoller, 2004).

In public relations research, workplace initiatives have not been the focus of feminist studies or work-life integration projects. One study was found that considered how transformational leadership, procedural justice policies, and family-supportive workplaces affected employer-employee relationships. Jiang (2012) measured how managers helped mitigate work-life conflict with a transformational leadership style defined as the dimensions of charisma, inspirational motivation, intellectual consideration, and individual consideration. She defined procedural justice as how employees perceived the fairness of the procedures through which outcomes were decided. Family-supportive workplace initiatives included (1) policies on job flexibilities, (2) childcare services, and (3) personal leave. Jiang's model tested how these organizational-level concepts affected time-based and strain-based work-life conflicts and employer-employee relationships. She collected surveys from 396 full-time employee participants from forty-four organizations over a five-month period. Jiang's analysis supported the hypothesis that transformational leadership, fair formal procedures used to make work-life decisions, and a family-supportive workplace affected the quality of employee-organizational relationships, defined as higher levels of satisfaction, trust, commitment, and control mutuality or power sharing (p. 243). Her study concluded that senior management should pay more attention to employees' work-life experiences and the critical role of supervisors in organizational efforts to enhance employees' organizational lives. Jiang's work provides models for organizational structure to alleviate stress related to the inability to integrate work and personal life.

THE GLASS CEILING

The glass ceiling aptly defines a structural barrier beyond which women and marginalized groups of practitioners have difficulty advancing. Beginning with "Under the Glass Ceiling: An Analysis of Gender Issues in American Public Relations" (Wright et al., 1991), studies have documented how female practitioners and people of color cluster in lower technical roles while White and male practitioners dominate upper-level managerial roles. This glass ceiling effect in organizations is seen worldwide. According to the *European Communication Monitor*, the glass ceiling continues to be evident in both Europe and Latin America (Moreno, 2018).

The glass ceiling effect showed up in the Dubrowski et al. (2019) focus groups as three reasons why White men were more likely to be in public relations leadership roles. First, senior-level male practitioners said that there was sexism in the C-suite and that unless it was addressed at the macro (organizational) level, "gender inequity in public relations will persist" (np). Second, female participants said that male leaders were more comfortable choosing from their network's other male leaders for leadership positions. Third, women were left out of the "boys' club," excluded from opportunities to make client pitches and to join social outings, which created a barrier to leadership opportunities. The exclusion of Black practitioners was evident as well (Ford & Brown, 2015).

In 2017, two optimistic reports cited an increase of White women in senior agency positions, from 20 percent to 30 percent (Lukitsch, 2016). Increasingly,

White women can be found on executive or leadership teams (Shah, 2017). Less optimistic is the finding that women and people of color achieving leadership positions will receive unequal pay.

While White women have arrived in some top management positions, Black women have not been as lucky, and even those who are in leadership roles find that their roles reduced status and power (Place & Vardeman-Winter, 2018, p. 166). Organizations diminish the informal power and respect when women step into leadership roles. Place and Vardeman-Winter (2018) pointed to the unequal gender assumptions about role enactment and positioning based on gendered social and institutional practices. Factors included the value of the role's work, lack of access to individuals in power, and lack of mentoring opportunities. The authors referenced how organizations lessened the value of the leadership role by using gendered stereotypical perceptions of gender roles (caring); women defaulting in their work to be more socially acceptable in nurturing, participative, or supportive leadership roles; and women feeling compelled to adopt more stereotypically masculine leadership roles, "resulting in women occupying organizational positions of less power and status" (p. 167).

The Plank Center's 2019 report found continuing gaps between male and female leaders' perceptions of their leadership performance. Men ranked themselves significantly higher than women in all six dimensions of leadership performance. The male senior managers reported higher scores than the women managers on self-insights, ethical orientation, participation in strategic decision-making, team leadership capabilities, relationship-building skills, and communication knowledge management (Meng et al., 2019, np). These dimensions reflect organizational culture and its systems that impede value and advancement by women and people of color in the communications field (np). The 2019 report found that the top male leaders rated their cultures significantly more positively than did the women. The men believed more than the female leaders that their CEOs valued and understood public relations. Most notably, the women rated significantly lower than the men the organizational culture elements in which they worked. "Women were significantly less trusting of relying on their organizations to keep promises, taking opinions of employees like them into account when making decisions, and treating employees like them fairly" (Meng et al., 2019, np). The research team posited that leadership performance and organizational culture strongly influence each other (Meng et al., 2019). The lack of trust in the organization is of concern if women need to hit expected performance indicators of leadership.

Barriers such as stereotypical expectations, lack of mentorship, and exclusionary organizational practices are only exacerbated for women from marginalized identities. Tindall (2013), for example, described a lavender ceiling—the name for the barriers to promotion for women in sexual minority groups. Ford and Brown (2015) conducted a survey with 199 respondents who derived from Black diaspora groups; they self-identified as African American, biracial White/Black, Black British, Black/African Brazilian, Hispanic/Black/Native American, Black Puerto Rican, Caribbean, Latina, mixed multicultural, and Nubian. The sample was 71 percent female. The study authors claimed that progress had been made by U.S. practitioners from the Black diaspora. About 50 percent of the participants were at the managerial level. However, none of the participants had reached the executive level of vice presidents or chief communications officers, and 22 percent reported owning their own firms, thereby opting out of the traditional process of advancement within an organization. Ford and Brown (2015) stated, "Several expressed concerns about being able to reach executive positions particularly because of a perceived glass ceiling" (p. 8). One participant commented that her greatest fear was "hitting the ceiling (in my career)" (p. 10).

The glass ceiling was created originally as a metaphorical device to highlight the professional limitations of White, cis-gendered women. While we may assume that the feminization of public relations has diminished the glass ceiling effect for White women, we need to be vigilant in our exposure of its continued existence for women of color and other marginalized groups who deserve equitable access to professional advancements.

ORGANIZATIONAL MENTORSHIP

An organizational initiative considered vital to employee advancement is formal mentoring programs. Mentoring programs have been called an important contributor to workplace success because they provide insider one-on-one guidance from senior advisers. However, in the public relations literature, formal mentoring programs have had mixed results. Tam et al. (1995) examined the outcomes of superior-subordinate gender mentorships in surveys of two professional public relations associations. The authors found that female supervisors offered more active and intense mentoring relationships but yielded fewer career advancement opportunities than those who had male superior mentors. "Practitioners with male mentors, regardless of gender, tended to have more access to management advancement and have more opportunities to enact the manager role" (p. 268). One conclusion offered was that the male superiors were in more powerful positions to provide advancement opportunities (p. 269).

Pompper and Adams (2006) argued that mentoring is a gendered and raced organizational activity. Based on forty interviews with Florida-based public relations practitioners, the authors found that factors of compatibility and structural features explained successful mentoring. The gendered structures of the mentor-protégé relationships included female practitioners seeking male mentors because they were of better help in climbing the management ranks. The female practitioners spoke of both the positive emotional connections they had with mentors and the conflicts with male mentors who held them back. But, most significantly, female participants reported choosing male mentors. One reasoned that she felt that women elsewhere in her organization failed to support one another. They were "tougher on female employees to the extent that it was detrimental" (p. 313).

The male participants chose male mentors who could help them with career-related support. They preferred male mentors because they could identify with them: "Someone who I identify as a role model and whose thought patterns and general behavior probably will influence mine" (p. 314). The men had clear attitudes toward working with female mentors, joking that men at the firm were at a disadvantage. One expressed that taking an instruction from a woman didn't bother him, but, on the other hand, some male participants selected female protégés because they were perceived to be less threatening. Results from this study reflected how organizations' mentoring initiatives perpetuated gendered social roles (p. 314).

While not studied in public relations per se, similar outcomes can be expected for people of color and LGBTQ practitioners. A desire for not only support from a mentor but also an innate understanding of racism and homophobia guide mentor selections. According to Ford and Brown (2015), U.S. practitioners from the Black diaspora desire public relations sustainability and career growth. Their participants were looking for help with networking and professional development. Only 50 percent reported having mentors, and 19 percent had formal sponsors who offered guidance and critical feedback and connected them with important players and assignments (p. 10).

A Public Relations Society of America Foundation study that included focus groups and surveys with United States–based Black and Latino practitioners gained greater insight into their professional and personal experiences with mentorship (Applebaum et al., 2015). The survey included 108 practitioners with the following demographics: 42.6 percent Hispanic/Latino, 60.4 percent Black/African American, 80.6 percent female, largest single age group in the twenty-three to twenty-six range (50.9 percent). Applebaum et al. (2015) found that fewer than half of their Black and Latinx practitioners reported having a mentor, with all the men and the African Americans more likely to have a mentor. Six in ten felt "family feelings" with other young professionals with the same ethical or racial backgrounds, with this feeling more prevalent among the women than men and more so among Latinx than African Americans. Official mentoring, according to Applebaum et al. (2015), was rare in participants' first jobs, with one in ten reporting that they were part of formal mentoring programs. Those who went to work in agencies were more likely to report that they had a senior colleague to respond to their needs, but only one in five of these senior colleagues were themselves African American or Latinx. One in five surveyed felt that mentoring was best if a senior executive in the department or an immediate supervisor was African American or Latinx. Still important was an immediate supervisor who was not African American or Latinx or a peer who was African American or Latinx (pp. 28–30).

Dubrowski et al. (2019) found mixed perceptions from focus groups about organizational mentorship initiatives. Participants found that formal mentorship programs were not as effective as informal programs. They found the formal programs to be forced "if the chemistry isn't right" (np) and that mentorships didn't stick "over the long haul." However, "while informal mentorships seemed to work best, all organizational structures didn't lend themselves as well to that" (np). Participants thought that coaching or training programs to learn how to be a good mentor or sponsor would be beneficial (np). In the Dubrowski et al. findings, both male and female practitioners found that a sponsor or career advocate was beneficial for "supporting career mobility and serving as a sounding board for guidance" (np). "You need an advocate. So, whether it's a mentor or your boss, you have to have an advocate. And I think that's what we hear a lot now in general, and also in the discussions of why there are more men at the top. Well because they've had advocates, they've had people pushing them up" (Dubrowski et al., 2019, np). McCorkindale and Rickert (2020) listed several areas important for mentorship: "Women need to be mentored and educated on how to lean-in, how not to be offended by direct, sometimes aggressive business conversation, how to be less emotional during critical, difficult business decisions, more analytical, less gossipy, less reactive, and more deeply centered during turbulent times. Use humor more often and be confident."

In prior research, female public relations practitioners have been less than supportive of other female practitioners, with some preferring to work for male supervisors. Documented in public relations research are individual-level accusations of "queen bees" (Wrigley, 2002; Pompper, 2016). A queen bee situation is a "symptom of institutional patriarchy wherein women advance their careers by sabotaging the careers and work of other women" (Pompper, 2016, p. 71). We argue for an organizational-level view of the power structures of organizational "in groups" that hold power and create beliefs about their "right" or privilege to admit like group members. Pompper (2016) described male advantage and privilege in public relations in this way: "Men validate their privilege despite being a minority in the feminized field of public relations and women use defense mechanisms to accept a disadvantaged status" (p. 71). What female public relations practitioners perceive to be sabotage is more likely women who succeeded in getting ahead but are still too limited by masculine structures to be of help to other women.

Dubrowski et al. (2019) found a positive cultural shift in female public relations professionals' perceptions of female colleagues: "Executive participants reported the environment had changed from when they came up, a time when there was more apprehension about helping other women rise because of the scarcity of opportunities for women leaders. Now there's more openness" (np). On the other hand, female public relations practitioners still have unrealistic expectations of their "sisters'" ability to help, for example, of having women leaders resenting having to "pick up the slack" for working mothers (Pompper, 2012; Dubrowski et al., 2019) and expectations that women seeking to advance must work as hard as their female predecessors.

In Pompper's (2012) interviews of forty-two female practitioners working in different types of organizations and across the United States, finding expressions of positive experiences in building and maintaining working relationships, her participants were still experiencing inhospitable workplaces created by women "that prevented management track women from achieving their full potential" (p. 94). That between these 2012 and 2019 qualitative studies of women's public relations workplace experiences, the competitive issues remain suggests that the boundedness of organizational structures remains. As Pompper concludes, "Women are still working in environments that limit relational opportunities because of the 'zero-sum,' 'limited pie,' and patriarchal organizations in which women work" (p. 99).

CASE EXAMPLE: NBC SIDELINED FEMALE PUBLIC RELATIONS PROFESSIONALS

A feminist analysis of the careers of two White female information managers in the early days of NBC's public relations efforts illustrate how organizational beliefs and structures showed explicit and implicit bias toward the work of the women. The analysis shows that the organization reduced the women's perceived expertise to acceptable feminine roles (Martin, 2019). Anita Barnard and Kathryn Cole, information department managers, oversaw the incoming network audience's mail and telephone calls, "exerting significant influence on public relations, program standards, advertising and sales" (p. 89).

In the 1940s and 1950s, the NBC Department of Information, a forerunner of the research function of public relations practice, supplied monthly audience statistics including all of the audience communications that NBC received. The department's monthly reports to departments of publicity, continuity acceptance, and sales provided detailed analysis of positive and critical letters and telephone calls regarding programming. Barnard, succeeded by Cole in the Information Office, led nine staffers (p. 88) to respond to each letter and phone call, evaluate and categorize them, and issue reports to top decision makers. Their reports, preserved in an archive of NBC papers, required judgment calls on what to emphasize or leave out, helping to gauge public opinion, offset possible regulatory efforts, and justify new content policies (Martin, 2019, p. 94).

NBC would have had few female managers at the time. Those such as Barnard and Cole were located in acceptable "female and/or service-coded areas, such as Public Affairs, Women's Programming, Continuity Acceptance and audience relations" (Martin, 2019, p. 92). In these departments, women were little acknowledged by the organization. In fact, the responses to audience letters written by women were signed by male executives, reflecting the gendered norm that a male signature would be more authoritative (Martin, 2019).

An NBC profile of Barnard, when she became the Information Office manager, described her "as the lady who sits surrounded by cackling typewriters and screaming telephones [in room 3021], calmly soothing that insatiable bird, curiosity" (Let's Get Acquainted, 1941). The author further described Barnard as "a mother confessor to an average of 38,000 souls a month." Both descriptions fit within the acceptable gender roles of sympathetic mother and head of a religious order (Martin, 2019, p. 97) as opposed to a highly knowledgeable influential supervisor of nine employees.

These two women had roles that influenced corporate decision-making. However, their decisions were influenced to enact organizational beliefs. Martin found that

Cole created complaint categories reflected in audience feedback. In a March 1957 report, a "racial" complaint category appeared, representing criticism of racist jokes and portrayals. Cole headlined her report without mentioning the new racial complaints category but instead noted criticism of crime and Western-style programs and audience appreciation for a Noah's Ark special. Cole made choices "biasing in favor of culturally conservative audience members" (Martin, 2019, p. 94), helping to "perpetuate racial and gendered disparities in networking programming . . . whether she embraced these priorities or simply told her bosses what she thought they wanted to hear" (p. 94). Both examples underscore how organizational norms and expectations create the gendered roles that employees carry out and reinforce the organization's beliefs and values.

CONCLUSION: TWO STEPS FORWARD, ONE STEP BACK

This chapter examined the research on organizations and public relations and illustrated how organizations create structures, policies, and role expectations that define gender, race, and class norms and hinder advancement for women. We took a feminist stance with this examination in order to identify the institutional sexism that women in public relations encounter through organizational structures, policies, norms, and practices. Issues of workplace inflexibility affect women's opportunities for advancement.

The research, however, shows that there have been significant advances for women, particularly White women, in the field. The glass ceiling has shattered a bit, mentoring has been beneficial, and organizations have taken strides to support work-life integration. However, the greatest beneficiaries of these programs are White women in Western countries. A masculine work culture results in women competing against women even though a culture shift may be happening because of more women achieving top management positions. When women in public relations move through the glass ceiling, they perceive their leadership to be less effective and lack trust in their organizational cultures. The online environment has led to mistrust, emotional exploitation, and false narratives. Women's coping with workplace stress may be mitigated theoretically through transformational leadership, procedural justice, and family-friendly workplaces. Organizational mentoring programs received mixed reviews because organizational cultures continue to favor masculine approaches.

NOTE

1. We define neoliberal as an ideology reflecting a capitalist system that features economic enterprises to achieve maximum profits.

6

Organizational Level

Facilitating Inequity and Marginalization

OUTLINE OF CHAPTER CONTENT

- Systems theory
- Excellence theory
- Strategic communication
- Feminist approaches
  - o Organizational structures are discursively gendered and raced
  - o Socialization: Cultural barriers to upper-level influence
  - o Structuralist perspective
  - o Structuration theory
- Conclusion: Feminism decenters status quo organization

This chapter addresses public relations theories of the organizational level, which helps reinforce inequity found in the field. We also examine here feminist perspectives that can assist in interrogating the organizational level. The theories derive from various traditions, such as functionalism. Citing Burrell and Morgan (1979), Trujillo and Toth (1987) introduced functionalism to public relations research, defining it as "approaches emphasizing how instrumental aspects of organizational life can be designed to run and regulate the organization" (p. 201). Botan and Taylor (2004) described the functional perspective as focused on "the use of public relations as an instrument to accomplish specific organizational goals" (p. 651). The functionalist theories described here—systems theory and excellence theory—are the two most well-known theories in the public relations field. They focus on how organizations can achieve goals most efficiently and effectively, and they perceive gender as a variable to either hinder or facilitate those goals. Race, class, and sexual orientation have not come into play and remain invisible in the mainstream discourse. Strategic communication took a different approach, a postmodern one, to address marginalization.

There have been feminist approaches to examining the influence of organizations on public relations. These approaches explain organizational structures not through functions but through discourses, cultural socialization, and structuration. We detail each of these theories and approaches below.

SYSTEMS THEORY

We start with systems theory, a worldview that has contributed paradigmatic understanding of how public relations functions in organizations (Cutlip et al., 1985; J. E. Grunig & Hunt, 1984). L. A. Grunig et al. (1992), in their introduction to the Excellence Study's literature review, expected systems theory to have particular promise for understanding how public relations is or could be managed strategically (pp. 73–74). Systems theory promised public relations scholars and practitioners a lens for thinking of organizations' communication processes as made up of "interrelated parts, adapting and adjusting to changes in the political, economic, and social environments in which they operate" (Lattimore et al., 2012, p. 52). Kennedy and Sommerfeldt (2015) described systems theory as a worldview wherein an organization is "dependent on strategic relationships with its environment" (p. 34).

Defined as how organizations design their internal departments contingent on the environment (J. E. Grunig et al., 1992, p. 73), systems theory outlined three concepts central to how public relations is understood: the environment, boundary spanning, and the dominant coalition. The environment external to an organization contained potential opportunities and constraints, such as outside forces and special interest groups. The internal environment of an organization included opportunities and constraints related to employee satisfaction and productivity. Environmental uncertainty or instability caused organizations to monitor and bring information about threats and opportunities into organizational decision-making through a process of inputs, throughputs, and outputs. The more uncertain an organization's environment was, the more likely that it would practice two-way communication through its public relations function (J. E. Grunig, 1984).

Public relations practitioners monitored an organization's environment as boundary spanners who moved in and out of an organization's boundaries with information about public perceptions and issues that could affect the organization's goals. Practitioners shaped information coming into an organization (input), shared it with decision makers (throughput), and sent out messaging on their organization's behalf. Boundary spanning was influenced by whether organizations had an open systems management or whether organizations closed off bringing in information, choosing instead to send out one-way communication. The dominant coalition represented an organization's influencers, who chose whether to operate in closed or open ways and chose which elements of an organization's environment to address (L. A. Grunig et al., 2002). The dominant coalition's power to choose which elements of the environment to prioritize explained why organizations failed. The dominant coalition's choices represented mixed motives of what benefited those in power and sufficed with respect to organizational viability (Robbins, 1990).

Systems theory continues to influence scholarly thinking about public relations' role in organizations. Systems theory has informed analyses of external consulting functions and roles (Rottger & Preusse, 2013), internal nonprofit conflict management and decision-making (Gallicano, 2013), intangible resource management (social capital) (Dodd, 2016), advanced information technology (Jiang et al., 2017), and conflict ecology (Hobbs, 2020).

Critiques of systems theory challenge its functional perspective from rhetorical, critical, and functionalist perspectives. Heath (2009) thought that systems theory was useful for understanding and improving the processes of public relations but "failed to explain the role of ethics, language, and meaning in efforts to foster or correct imbalance or achieve balance" (p. 21) between organizations and their publics. Critical theorists Kennedy and Sommerfeldt were skeptical of organizations' aims to build relationships because of their need to ensure organizational stability (2015, p. 34). In rethinking their foundational support for systems theory in their search for excellent public relations practice, J. E. Grunig and L. A. Grunig concluded that systems theory's goal of organizational survival was extremely weak (2000, p. 306). Only Creedon (1993) critiqued systems theory for its overly rational promise, particularly with regard to gender and the use of power by the dominant coalition.

Creedon (1993) challenged systems theory's uncritical explanations for how organizations relate to their environments. She foresaw the influence of instituted values or norms on organizational decision-making, such as organizational assumptions about gender, race, class, and sexuality, which she named the "infrasystem." She used the concept of the infrasystem to contest the public relations systems' rational assumptions of "equal opportunity, equity, and symmetrical communication . . . without regard for preserving the system of privilege" (p. 160).

Creedon illustrated how infrastructure's masculine values explained the case of how the National Collegiate Athletic Association, as a male-driven dominant super-system valuing competitive exclusionary elite athletes, was able to push out through economic incentives a female system, the Association of Intercollegiate Athletics for Women, which believed under Title IX of the Higher Education Amendments Act of 1972 in a women's sport ideology of "the greatest good for the greatest number" (p. 162). By 1990, the National Collegiate Athletic Association controlled both men's and women's collegiate athletics, "gutting women from leadership roles in women's sport" (p. 162). In her conclusion, Creedon argued for the concept of dis-symmetry as a "goal to value various symmetries, rather than to achieve homeostasis by minimizing differences" (p. 164) as a better way for the field of public relations to value diversity. However, no work followed her early breakthrough article on the infrasystem concept.

Two additional mentions of systems theory relate to issues of inequities and include work by Rakow and Nastasia (2009) and Witmer (2006). Rakow and Nastasia (2018) urged recognizing "taken for granted gender systems," which they argued were masculine (p. 252). Witmer (2006) contested systems theory because of its missing role for human interaction and inadequate conceptualizations of culture as lived experience, although she failed to address gender head-on (p. 364). She argued that systems theory does not adequately address organizational culture, defined as patterns, routines, habits, rites, and rituals, in which public relations practice is situated. We return to their work in the structuration section of this chapter.

From a functional perspective, only Rakow and Nastasia (2009) have critiqued public relations' complicit role in organizations because of its influence in choosing from the countless information messages received and interpreted for the benefit of an organization's goals. In their argument, it is this choice of what to receive and transmit that is gendered, in the sense that the public relations practitioner will use his or her skills that will be developed and reinforced through the organizational masculine values/dictates as well as their own values. Systems theory has also continued to significantly influence the individual-level work on roles (see chapter 9 on roles research) but has had little formal following work to measure the impact of organizational structure on gender discrimination.

EXCELLENCE THEORY

The dominant organizational theory paradigm of the field of public relations is a group of theories that came from the Excellence Project, a landmark research study sponsored by the International Association of Business Communicators to identify best practices for the public relations field. The Excellence Project reflected a comprehensive review of the literature in public relations and related disciplines, such as communication, management, feminist studies, organizational sociology, psychology, political science, and culture, published in 1992 (L. A. Grunig et al., 2002,

p. 5). Included in the literature review was a comprehensive chapter summarizing the research on women in public relations (Hon et al., 1992), including reference to Creedon's (1993) contention that a masculine value system in organizations must be transformed (p. 429).

The Excellence Project's output of theories represents a grand theory of why public relations is of value to organizations. Its framework came from four perspectives: systems theory, strategic constituencies, competing values, and goal attainment (Management-by-Objectives). Based on surveys of 327 organizations in four countries, the excellence theory resulted in a fourteen-item theoretical profile of "critical success factors and best practices" (L. A. Grunig et al., 2002, p. 6). These success factors were organized according to four levels of an organization: the program level, the department level, the organizational level, and the societal level, referring to contributions of organizations to the welfare of society (J. E. Grunig, 2008, p. 98).

Excellence theory generated several public relations theories, as summarized in L. A. Grunig et al. (2002). These theories focused on individual knowledge and skills required and how to get them, best practices of strategic management roles, integration of communication functions, participatory/authoritarian cultural influence, and the relationship of the public relations function to the dominant coalition. However, excellence theory has been mostly identified with one theory—two-way symmetrical communication as the ideal model of public relations practice—defined as "balancing the interests of the organization with the interests of publics on which the organization has consequences and that have consequences on the organization" (L. A. Grunig et al., 2002, p. 11). Botan and Hazelton, in *Public Relations Theory II*, refer not to the Excellence Study but to the "Symmetrical/Excellence Theory" (2006, p. 8).

One of the fourteen factors of excellence referenced gender as part of the departmental-level ideals. Reflecting liberal feminism, at the department level, a measure of excellence would be equal opportunity for men and women in public relations. This factor reflected a quantitative survey containing twenty-two items about the treatment and opportunities for women (L. A. Grunig et al., 2002, p. 63). Survey results confirmed that the excellent treatment of women was a characteristic of excellent organizations. The subdimensions of treatment of women were nondiscrimination policies, providing a supportive work environment, and mentoring and advancement programs (p. 63). The quantitative and qualitative data of the Excellence Study found positive relationships among support for women, participative culture, symmetrical communication, and employee satisfaction (L. A. Grunig et al., 2002, p. 527).

The Excellence Study authors sought to discover how excellent organizations empowered women and "minorities." They reported suggestions from qualitative interviews that did move beyond the simplistic suggestions that women would have to have talent, personality, work harder, and be at the right place at the right time, or that women needed to emulate the male mode and downplay their femininity—the "blaming the victim" position (L. A. Grunig et al., 2002, p. 528). There were several suggestions to empower women and practitioners of color, though the suggestions reflected liberal feminist ideals:

- Use total quality management programs to create a culture to influence diversity goals.
- Promote from within with proactive advancement programs.
- Get to the mindset of the people who hire with the caveat that as more women become top managers, sexism will gradually disappear.
- Become more conscious of the need to work with women and minorities to overcome barriers to advancement, such as providing diversity training programs.
- Hire a diversity recruiter or a diversity manager.
- Create women's groups to "make a little noise" (L. A. Grunig et al., 2002, p. 231).
- Move to another job to enhance skills and opportunities.

The Excellence Project achieved its goal of providing a benchmark for the public relations field on how to practice effective public relations. Its finding that successful public relations means equal opportunities for men and women and people of color found no traction in feminist studies of public relations. There has been no excellence critique of the barriers to equality; the organizational level of analysis; or the promising connections among gender, race, organic structure, participative culture, and symmetrical communication.

STRATEGIC COMMUNICATION

Gender and class appeared in strategic communication discourse when postmodernism began to frame some of its prevailing research. Holtzhausen (2016) referenced the traditional understanding of the public sphere to include only the "wealthy, aristocratic, and well-connected." She continued, "Women, peasants, and trades people were typically excluded from the public sphere because they were viewed as second class citizens who did not have the necessary competency, education and background to make decisions for themselves or others. This was also true for a number of ethnic and race groups" (p. 28).

Holtzhausen (2016) added gender to her depiction of new technologies, allowing voices "previously silenced" to be heard and to remain vigilant against the dangers of the private sphere. She referenced the "feminist critique of the private sphere to which many issues of gender discrimination were relegated" (p. 28). While the balance of Holtzhausen's article on datafication's threat or opportunity for strategic communication in the public sphere was not concerned with gender, her choice of example encouraged us that gender critiques at the earliest stages of the strategic communication project were welcomed.

Theorizing about feminism and the public sphere was included in the call by Overton-de Klerk and Verwey (2013) for strategic communication to "shift in power and control from management to individual stakeholders, allowing them to make decisions based on the value systems they are able to support" (p. 372). Overton-de Klerk and Verwey argued that dissent will encourage multiple voices to be heard, of "particular relevance where conflicts are the result of class, economic, racial or gender differences" (p. 372).

Besides these few notable exceptions, we cannot find an exposition of marginalization and discrimination in the extant strategic communication literature. No recognition of racism and heteronormativity, for example, keeps strategic communication within a cloak of tolerance and lip service rather than within a model of equity. It retains traditional power structures and eliminates the ability for nonmainstream voices to be part of the strategic communication paradigm. One area in the strategic communication literature where this invisibility is particularly potent is crisis communication. The crisis communication research is limited to how to maintain profits, reputation, and client loyalty in the face of human error or natural disasters. Crisis communication theories have become fixated on how to minimize damage to reputation and stock prices, thus exhibiting inherent classism. Reputation repair looks at the deficits or gaps in plans, processes, or expertise during a crisis. A "what can go wrong" mentality subsequently normalizes a "fix-it" perspective. Feminist critiques thus become deficits if they are not found to directly fix a problem facing organizations.

Instead, strategic communication research should uncover opportunities for equity and inclusion by welcoming different voices. Gender was welcomed in a postmodern strategic communication acknowledgment of the tensions and fragmentation of meaning making that dispute the attempt to achieve one overall organizational strategy, but the postmodern engagement of early publications has disappeared. Left is a scholarly endeavor that, by absence of recognition of the influence of race, sexuality, and class on communication strategy at the organizational level, maintains the hegemonic status quo.

FEMINIST APPROACHES

Organizational Structures Are Discursively Gendered and Raced

Several public relations and communication scholars argue that organizational structures are created through human discourse. Rakow (2014) called attention to the influence of organizational discourse on how public relations is structured and how public relations reinforced structure: "Organizations are both the result of systems of meanings and the generators of meaning through routinized and legitimated communicative practices involving deployment of human and environmental resources" (p. xiii). Discourses are the focus of rhetorical theory. Heath (2009) wrote that "rhetoric is the rationale for effective discourse" (p. 22). Structures created through discourses have been the work of critical scholars of public relations. Motion and Leitch (1996) used discourse theory as a means of critically interpreting organizations: "Discourse is a practice not just of representing the world, but of signifying the world, constituting and constructing the world in meaning" (Fairclouth, 1992). Applied to public relations, Motion and Leitch give the example of discourses that made meaning of organizations' production, distribution, and consumption of texts: "For example, the organizational routines that produce media releases, constitute discursive practices" (p. 299).

Rakow and Nastasia (2018) called out organizational discourses for creating and reinforcing patriarchal structures. They urged the use of ethnographies to reveal public relations discourses that create a patriarchal way of speaking (p. 268). They identified the discrepancies between official discourses (the "father tongue") about the social world and the experiences of everyday life (the "mother tongue") as a means of emancipating female and male public relations practitioners from oppressive institutional meanings (p. 271).

Research has shown that organizational decision-making articulates gendered discourse. Aldoory et al. (2008) identified gender differences in vocabularies of male and female public relations practitioners: the women's most frequent verb uses were to "express, discuss," and "voice concerns with management," while the men's most frequent verb uses were to advocate change with management, including "confront, combat, challenge," and "oppose" (pp. 745–746). "The men here seem to be representing a masculine discourse of power while the women may be very aware that if they chose to use similar terms, there would be negative reactions to them, given the learned social scripts in organizations" (p. 745). Unfortunately, the authors did not expound on how organizational discourse embeds racism and heteronormativity as well.

Edwards (2013), though, did examine how organizational discourse in the United Kingdom contributed to promoting and reinforcing sexism and racism. She used discourse theory to show how racism and sexism were legitimized in organizations. Through interviews and focus group research, Edwards (2013) named one challenge the "discursive subjugation," as exemplified in how an Asian female practitioner was viewed by dominant White public relations colleagues as an "exotic spectacle" (p. 250). "She was the only Asian person at a PR awards dinner and the only person wearing a headscarf. As the night wore on, her professional right to be there became obscured by curiosity about her 'abnormality' that White colleagues felt that they had a right to comment on" (p. 250).

From a poststructural feminist standpoint, discursive practices revealed how gendered and raced subjectivities become hegemonic. Certain definitions of masculinity and femininity constitute meaning and shift along lines of race, class, and other differences (Harter et al., 2010). Harter et al. centered their poststructural feminist analysis on discourses to explain the YWCA's contested single-sex mandate. Over a six-year period (2001–2007), the YWCA disaffiliated chapters from the national organization because they chose to admit men. Three key tensions emerged in the discourses of position statements, public reports, social commentary, and news reports surrounding these issues: inclusion versus exclusion of men when empowering women, symbolic versus material realities (male donors supporting women's programs), and local autonomy versus global solidarity for women.

Discourse theory provides the means to understand the backdrop of Creedon's (1993) infrastructure proposal—that of subconsciously reinforced societal sexism and racism. Discourse theory calls attention to the shared meanings of organizational actors whose language choices prioritize patriarchal and race barriers. By making conscious the language choices of organizational life through discourse theory, female and male public relations practitioners, the communication experts, would have different tools to create equitable structures.

Socialization: Cultural Barriers to Upper-Level Influence

Sociologists have led the way in theorizing how organizations are gendered and raced. Feminist public relations scholars have advanced an understanding of the organizational level with their research on the sociological concepts of norms, culture, and workplace environment. Organizational policies and practices are guided by masculinist norms, including norms of expression, decision-making, leadership, self-promotion, and humor (Ashcraft, 2006). "In other words, men's ways are expected and enacted in management behavior" (Martin, 2004, p. 148). Women do not fare as well in organizations because their socialized behaviors are not as valued as those of men (O'Neil, 2003). Female public relations practitioners must not only navigate a masculine organizational culture but also be the cultural interpreters for a masculine organization. A similar phenomenon occurs for people of color and LGBTQ practitioners: they are required to navigate organizational cultures that are predominantly White and heteronormative.

There are normative substructures of gender and race that successfully exclude marginal groups from understanding the rules of advancement. Accordingly, White male members of organizations will create and understand communication transactions with minimal supporting information, whereas organizational women and people of color remain cultural outsiders and will find it difficult to translate (Martin, 2004).

Rakow (1989) called attention to the "swinging back and forth between the organizational ideologies of masculinity and femininity that influenced the practice of public relations." She saw the positive of women entering public relations as a crisis of opportunity for the feminine that would favor "symmetrical relational cooperative forms of public relations" (pp. 294–295). However, she concluded that organizations could continue to favor masculine ideologies that primarily serve organizational interests (Rakow, 1989).

Culture, often called the workplace environment, refers to the ideologies, expectations, beliefs, values, and ethics that permeate a workplace. Culture is "the sum total of shared values, symbols, meanings, beliefs, assumptions, and expectations that organize and integrate a group of people who work together" (L. A. Grunig et al., 2002, p. 482). While structure references policies, norms, and practices put in place by organizational decision makers, organizational culture is a matter of a community reinforcing structural policies and practices with discourses and behaviors that judge worker appropriateness and worthiness. Agencies preferring male practitioners to make new business pitches, the lingering assumptions that if a woman leaves to have a baby she will not return to work, and women assumed to be primary caregivers and housekeepers are examples expressed by female practitioners of organizational cultural messages they have encountered at their workplaces (Aldoory & Toth, 2002).

Organizational cultures are not monolithic but are made up of subcultures, some dominant and others subordinate. Illustrative of this is L. A. Grunig's (1995) case study of a class action suit brought by female Foreign Service practitioners when a male-dominated counterculture was able to limit women's abilities for career advancement despite affirmative action guidelines to abolish sexual and racial discrimination.

Two studies of primarily White female public relations practitioners' perceptions of coping with work stress have built a deeper understanding of the impact of organizational culture on their lives. Jin et al. (2014) operationalized organizational culture along two variables: (1) the organizational cultural expectation that work and life were separate and (2) the importance of supervisory support for issues of work and life. In their survey of Public Relations Society of America members' coping with work-life conflicts in public relations practice, their probability sample of 565 practitioners (79 percent female), reported on the extent to which their coping was influenced by (1) an organizational culture promoting work as the sole priority and (2) the importance of immediate supervisor support. The authors found that organizational culture affected coping preferences. Female practitioners used a greater variety of coping strategies, such as emotional coping, positive thinking, denial, instrumental support, and avoidance, compared to the male practitioners in their study. These authors established that organizational culture not supportive of work-life integration reduced employees' positive thinking and led to the need for more supervisor instructions to help employees cope with workplace stress.

Jiang and Shen (2018) returned to their study of the organizational environment by focusing on "a family-supportive organizational environment." In their study of a probability sample of 650 Public Relations Society of America members (80 percent female), they used two concepts: "family-supportive organizational work environment" and "work-life enrichment." For their participants, trust and work-life enrichment were important mediators between a supportive work environment and practitioners' turnover intentions (p. 688).

Structuralist Perspective

In 2003, public relations scholar O'Neil introduced the structuralist perspective as a contribution to feminist theory based on the landmark book by R. M. Kanter,

Men and Women of the Corporation. O'Neil considered that power is embedded in the structures of organizations in such a way as to disadvantage women and people of color. Structuralists reject the notion that socialization nurtures inequities (p. 154), instead theorizing that women and marginalized populations have less influence than White heterosexual men because of exclusion from formal power structures (O'Neil, 2003). O'Neil defined power as "the capacity to effect (or affect) organizational outcomes" (p. 152) and influence as the exercise of power (p. 153).

The purpose of O'Neil's study was to test whether there are gender differences in influence due to differences in six measures of power:

- relegation to the technical role
- position in the hierarchy
- degree of employee support
- being a token woman among predominantly male-dominant senior management teams
- lack of mentoring and exclusion from networks
- lack of respect and value (p. 154)

Based on her structuralist propositions, O'Neil tested the relationships among power, gender, and organizational influence of public relations. O'Neil used three independent variables: (1) formal structural power, referencing employee support, organizational roles, hierarchical position, and gender ratio in the dominant coalition; (2) relationship power, composed of participation in the dominant coalition's networks, mentor relationships, and value and support received; and (3) gender defined by asking respondents their sex. Her dependent variable was perceived organizational influence.

Based on her quantitative analysis of a systematically randomized sample of 168 male and female corporate public relations practitioners' survey responses, O'Neil found that female public relations practitioners had a significantly lower amount of formal structural power than male practitioners (p. 168). She found no significant differences between men and women on any of the three measures of relationship power (p. 168). O'Neil found that "being female has a negative effect on their influence due to their reduced formal structural power" (p. 171). With the informal power perspective, "being female did not lead to reduced relationship power" (p. 171). She noted that this finding is at odds with prior research on the lack of mentoring, exclusion from influential networks, and feelings of subordination and devaluation (p. 173), but she speculated that perhaps women put a greater amount of effort into relationship power relative to men.

The structuralist perspective used measures of mentorship, role models, and networking within the organization as means of achieving power and influence. These may be more attractive to women in the workforce because they suggest individual agency where organizations' formal power structures are not as available for individuals to overcome. Relying on mentors continues to be an important solution found in many liberal feminist discussions of how women can advance.

There has been no scholarly elaborations on O'Neil's structuralist argument. Public relations industry statistics suggest that since 2003 women have advanced into public relations managerial roles (U.S. Bureau of Labor Statistics, 2019), but research hasn't advanced in understanding whether these positions have the formal power as conceptualized by the structuralist view.

Structuration Theory

Witmer (2006) added structuration theory to build a more complete picture of the organizational level of influence. Based on the work of Giddens (1984) and Banks and Riley (1993), Witmer summarized structuration as social structures formed by and through human interaction (p. 367). Structuration is conceptualized through agency and reflexivity, duality of structure, distanciation of time and space from praxis, and social integration. *Agency* and *reflexivity* refer to people knowing how to proceed in social interaction based on understood norms; individuals are self-reflexive in that they are able to articulate goals and motivations. *Duality of structure* refers to the recursive organizing of organizational structures as both medium and outcome. *Distanciation of time and space from practice* refers to structures existing only as actors' remembrances across time and geographic distances. *Social integration* refers to the interactive nature of systems (p. 368).

Also based on Giddens (1984) is adaptive structuration that moves beyond individual rational actors to explain group behavior. White (2012) defined adaptive structuration theory as "groups using behavioral control to create definitions and roles through initial actions, guiding and restricting subsequent actions" (p. 569). She illustrated the adaptive structuration process by describing the work of public information officers who "develop individual role expectations and duties and group norms and processes which inform professional conduct and perceptions of those outside their organizations" (p. 569).

Structuration theory explores the recursive nature of system interactions and environmental interfaces (Witmer, 2006, p. 368). As an example of adaptive structuration (communication), Rakow (2007) critiqued technology company marketing as recursive practices of stereotyping women as consumers, in the same ways they did with the typewriter, the landline telephone, and mobile devices. She called out the repeated claims of the new and newer technologies "that they reinforce political and ideological meanings about gender such as divisions of labor in the home and relationships such as the need for women to be safe, the need for women to coordinate home and work responsibilities, the need for women to have more time," rather than recognize that gender problems require economic, political and social reorganization rather than technology" (p. 406).

Structuration theory emphasizes the ways in which organizations create and reproduce social structures, contesting a systems view of genderless, raceless operations. Feminism adds to structuration theory by revealing how structures are built and negotiated through the construction of masculine and feminism, racist and classist norms. It focuses on the organizational actors whose central task is to articulate organizational goals of a traditional dominated workplace. Feminism argues that these human actors and their actions are not neutral but always embed gender and race implications.

CONCLUSION: FEMINISM DECENTERS STATUS QUO ORGANIZATION

The problematics at the organizational level are based on the assumption that public relations operates in a neutralized organizational zone that contributes to effectiveness, which helps to economically sustain the organization. Former studies of work-life integration, barriers to advancement, and the glass ceiling have shown that neutrality does not exist and that organizational norms and structures are sexist and racist. What is missing is scholarship that questions the capitalist enterprise in which organizational success is contested. The economic roots of public relations are not examined, and yet this level of analysis can help expose the political economy of public relations in organizational settings.

Having an organizational level of analysis for public relations means that organizational structures are a root cause of public relations' inequities. The dominant, mainstream theories of public relations mask marginalization and power inequities and continue to influence scholarship with their presuppositions of rational desire to explain parts of the organization that manage resources and processes. Systems thinking has led to policies and norms of decision-making that stifle the diversity of employees and of the environment in which organizations operate. Even some of the workplace initiatives identified in the literature, such as the individual coping around a relentless online environment, procedural justice, mentorships, and family-friendly workplace, carry with them beliefs in objectivity and coping "within the system."

One limitation of public relations scholarship is that organizations do not get examined very much as rhetorical spaces based on shared meanings of organizational actors. They are not critiqued enough for being political arenas that represent power struggles, especially to reinforce masculine values. The organizational level helps reveal a dominance of functionalist views in scholarship that generally ignore power relations.

Feminist approaches call attention to organizational culture perspectives—the expectations, beliefs, values, and ethics that permeate a workplace. Discourse theory can provide a critical examination of the meanings of institutional messages that carry power and inequity values. The sociological perspective emphasizes how dominant masculine ways of interaction reinforce societal ideologies in organizational norms, decision-making, and culture. O'Neil operationalized a power perspective contributing to how influence is gendered in organizational hierarchies. Structuration theory adds feminist thought to public relations practice with perspectives on the negotiation of structures through masculine norms and recursive practices. These approaches revealed outmoded social beliefs about caregiving and an interpersonal work environment dependent on supportive employer-employee relationships, leading to time-based, strain-based, and behavior-based stressors on female public relations practitioners.

IV

PROFESSIONAL LEVEL

Discursive Legitimacy and Professional Associations

7

Professional Level

Questions of Legitimacy and Value

OUTLINE OF CHAPTER CONTENT

- A profession: Contested definition
- Approaches to professionalism
  - o Traits
  - o Process
  - o Ethnographic
  - o Power
  - o Professional project
  - o Systems
- Issues tied to professional aspirations
  - o Encroachment
  - o Stereotyping
  - o Undergraduate education
- Postfeminism in professionalism
- Case study of Indonesian public relations
- Conclusion: Contributions of feminism to a professional-level view

The field of public relations has few laws, requirements, or mandates that define it as a profession. Only a handful of laws receive mention in public relations textbooks, such as the First Amendment, libel, and slander, but they are to assist practitioners with their jobs, not define what a public relations job is. In addition, regulatory bodies such as the Securities and Exchange Commission and the Food and Drug Administration oversee advertising/marketing messages and might tangentially include news releases, product descriptions, and technical publicity, but these are mandates on public relations products and outputs, not on the profession itself. Public relations is not licensed in most countries, nor do the associations act as governing bodies that are regulated.

Thus, what is and what is not the profession of public relations continues to be debated. Public relations practitioners lack agreement on what the meaning of a "professional" is and how to define public relations as a profession. Trade articles use the terms *professionals* or *pros* interchangeably with the term *practitioners* (Brown, 2020; O'Brien, 2020) to mean people who work in the industry. Kim and Reber (2009) summarized, "Discussions of professionalism in public relations are generally related to the expression of a need to improve it as an occupation" (p. 157).

While the boundaries of the profession stay blurred, there is clear evidence that public relations is a professional career and that the "professional project" continues to be an ongoing effort by the professional associations and several scholars. This chapter considers the public relations research on the professional level and summarizes public relations' efforts to maintain and grow its professional status. We interrogate the profession and its associations for their oppression of diverse voices and marginalization of populations of practitioners. We argue that the profession and its associations continue to exhibit racist, masculinist views to define legitimacy and reputation for the profession of public relations.

A PROFESSION: CONTESTED DEFINITION

The term *profession* has been defined and debated by sociologists for almost a century. It is a conceptually rigorous term yet also a "jumble of meanings and values from efficiency to wealth; from prestige through altruism to public service" (L'Etang, 2008, p. 37, referencing O'Sullivan, 1994, p. 244). Traditionally, it was agreed that an occupation would become a profession if it established training, formed professional associations, regulated practice through legal protection, and adopted a formal code of ethics (Wilensky, 1964). However, Molleda et al. (2017) claimed that these criteria have been criticized for failing to account for differing societal conditions and political challenges.

Even with criticism and debate, there tends to be four common, primary characteristics that define a profession. These are a standardized education and continued training, the development of ethics codes, an encompassing professional association, and a structured accreditation process (Meyer & Leonard, 2014; Molleda et al.,

2017; Sha, 2011). L'Etang (1999) defined a profession as a domain of expertise: "the establishment of monopoly in the market for a service based on that expertise; the ability to limit entry to the field through strategy; relationship with a client; a code of ethics; and a way of testing competence, regulation standards, and maintaining discipline" (p. 262, referencing Elliott, 1972, p. 5). Professionalism, the key construct for a profession, was defined by Johansen (2001) as an attitudinal predisposition toward focusing on the interpersonal/societal benefit of work rather than the intrapersonal/self-serving benefit. Coombs et al. (1994) examined professionalization in Austria and Norway as well as the United States and defined professionalism as the importance a worker attaches to the characteristics of their profession.

The public relations industry has been unable to meet all the demands of a profession. While we have a professional association and training, we have several codes of ethics, though there is no consequence if practitioners do not abide by them. We have an accreditation option, but not everyone has to become accredited to be a professional; thus there is no limit on who can claim to be a public relations professional. There is not one distinct expertise that would confirm what is public relations, and public relations competes with other communication-based occupations for market space. There is no means through which individuals get licensing or other regulatory standards to maintain discipline.

Hoffman and Hamidati (2016) suggested that professionalism in public relations has taken on two types of arguments. One represents arguments that professionals fulfill indispensable functions within society as a whole by applying certain skills in a responsible way. "This justifies autonomy and superior role within organizations and society" (p. 52). The second critical argument sees professions constraining practitioners due to power relations and exclusivity that monopolizes areas of activity driven by commercial or political moves (p. 52).

APPROACHES TO PROFESSIONALISM

L'Etang (2008) listed six key approaches to analyzing public relations professionalism and professionalization: traits, process, ethnographic, power, professional project, and systems. *Traits* refers to key characteristics such as specialized skill and service, intellectual and practical training, and ethics. The process approach focuses on the progression and history of the occupation. The ethnographic approach explores in-depth cultural and social factors affecting an occupation. A power approach believes that there are elite groups who seek "a great deal for themselves through exerting power and authority and controlling access to an occupation" (p. 39). The professional project approach observes efforts to use specialized knowledge to achieve social closure and elite status. The systems approach considers competition and context, comparing an occupation to its relationships with other systems, such as journalism and marketing. We frame research on professionalism using L'Etang's six approaches, honing in on what professionalism means for women and marginalized practitioners.

Traits

The trait approach, mostly developed in the 1970s before the influx of women entered public relations, predominates in scholarly and practitioner thinking (Hoffman & Hamidati, 2016). U.S. public relations scholars and leading practitioners generally agree on five traits of a public relations profession: specialized educational preparation of practitioners, a body of knowledge, a code of ethics, personal accountability, and public recognition that the occupation provides the community "a unique and essential service" (Broom, 2009, p. 120; see also summary of the evolution of criteria for professionalism in communication management by leading practitioners and scholars in Meyer & Leonard, 2014, p. 177). Hoffman and Hamidati, in their summary, identified three main dimensions of traits: (1) expertise, applying a body of knowledge that requires academic education; (2) autonomy, rather than politics or the market determining the practice, and governed by self-regulation associations; and (3) a value orientation, "claiming a strong normative orientation toward the common good" (p. 51).

The traits approach has had long standing in the public relations literature, yet the items themselves are so abstract that they permit multiple meanings. They are almost uncontested because practitioners from different standpoints can find some meaning in them. Meyer and Leonard's (2014) meta-analysis of the traits for professionalization of public relations from 1968 to 2008 concluded that over time the professionalization traits discussion reflected a deeper awareness of the connection of public relations and its impact on society (p. 377).

Van Ruler (2005) proposed a traits approach in devising three practitioner-preferred models of professionalism: the status, competition, and personality models. The status model uses the criteria of "internal systems of older professionals who inaugurate the younger generation and their strong sense of servitude to the power elite" (p. 163). The competition model views professional traits as offering something unique and effective to clients "that has nothing to do with strong associations of experts and job demarcation but rather individual competencies" (p. 163). The personality model emphasizes a "mentality shown in devotion, passion, and enthusiasm" (p. 164).

The status, competition, and personality models open up gender, race, class, and sexual orientation biases with these characteristics: think of the "good old boys' network" inaugurating the younger generation, client preferences for male account executives rather than individual identities vulnerable to stereotypes. The personality model opens the door to reinforcing stereotypical in-group meanings such as those associated with White males: efficiency, individualism, and competitiveness (Rakow, 1989) and of enhanced creativity because men aren't bound by rules (Hesmondhalgh & Baker, 2015). The more abstract the language used in the traits approach, the more it is problematic and exclusionary (Edwards, 2014, p. 326).

Fitch and Third (2010) found the professionalizing project of public relations to be a gendered construct. They argued that cultural constructs of masculinity are "at

best sidelining or at worst excluding women's work from the domain of the professional by repressing . . . those qualities culturally assigned to femininity" (Fitch &
Third, 2010, quoting C. Davis, 1996, pp. 669–672). The study of professional
traits, however, has done nothing to reflect lived experience related to race, class,
sexual orientation, or cultural capital "that would facilitate a more substantial recognition of their value" (Edwards, 2014, p. 330).

Process

The process approach toward professionalism is most clearly illustrated in J. E.
Grunig and Hunt's (1984) four models of public relations: the publicity model, the
public information model, the two-way asymmetrical model, and the symmetrical
model. Presented as a means of describing the history of the field, each model proposed an advance in professionalism, from one-way communication and unethical
practices to two-way communication or symmetry as the most ethical of practices.
The process approach toward professionalism dealt very little with the progress
toward public relations becoming a female-intensive occupation. If anything, the
feminization of the field made promoting progression toward professionalism more
difficult because of revealing industry issues of salary inequities, structural barriers,
and labor stratification along gendered axes (Fitch & Third, 2014).

Ethnographic

The ethnographic approach to analyzing professionalism eschews the discussions
of abstract professional traits and instead looks at the actual cultural and social practices of the field (Pieczka & L'Etang, 2006, p. 267). Practitioner discourses reveal
cultural and social constraints or preferences for masculine norms and routines.
Documented are conversations of female practitioners who negatively code gender
through their descriptions of the field as "a sexless trade" (L'Etang, 2015), "a real
job" defined as one that would be a good job for a man in Russia (Tsetsura, 2011),
or women as "natural born communicators" (Frohlich & Peters, 2007). While some
expressions were meant as self-deprecating humor, they instruct an understanding of
how female practitioners dealt with microaggressions to stop their desire to be public
relations professionals.

Two articles published in the Public Relations Society of America's trade publication, *The Strategist*, illustrated continuing gendered stereotypes: the devaluation of
women speaking and the motherhood penalty. Mason (2019) challenged the absence
of female public relations professionals as thinkers and speakers for organizations:
"We are disproportionately the experts in the room, but the absence of women's
voices, ideas and insights is the elephant in every room" (np). Vogt's (2020) article
attested to "how motherhood made her a better pro" to offset the perception of a
"motherhood penalty" for female public relations practitioners who have children.

Power

The power approach to defining professionalism considers market control, social closure, and elite status. Power is viewed as efforts of occupations to win social approval and to control their work: "a distinctive and special way of controlling and organizing work and workers with real advantages for both practitioners and clients . . . an occupational value" (Evetts, 2011, p. 406 in Meyer & Leonard, 2014).

Pieczka and L'Etang (2001, 2006) linked power and professionalization in public relations with research dealing with gender and roles. Theirs is not a feminist critique of the gender issues and power, but it insinuates that the field's lack of interest in achieving power in an organization was based on the feminist value of dialogue rather than competition. They conclude that "the strong normative drive present in public relations theorizing focuses on proving that dialogue is the best way in which to enact work relations or even all relations" (p. 271) and reference a feminine contribution to best practices for the field by L. A. Grunig and colleagues (L. A. Grunig, 1991; L. A. Grunig et al., 2000).

Studies of power and gender in public relations practice have illustrated differences in how male and female practitioners construct their status and control opportunities and their claims of professionalism. Aldoory et al. (2008) found in their examination of discourses of male and female practitioners that women voiced a desire for greater access to domains of power, while men perceived themselves as already having access but as constrained by the devaluing of public relations; thus, they used claims of professionalism as a source of influence, such as public relations knowledge, expertise, and use of research data (p. 747).

Lee et al. (2018) revisited gendered assumptions of practitioner power in a survey of 150 Public Relations Society of America practitioners. They concluded that despite work roles, overall, male practitioners perceived that they had higher levels of power than their female counterparts (p. 196). Male practitioners perceived greater power than reported by the female practitioners on coercive power and expert power. No differences were found between the male and female practitioners on legitimate power and referent power. They suggest that "it takes an official objective title or a charismatic personality trait for both male and female practitioners to sense that they hold an equal influence in their organizations" (p. 196).

Professional Project

The global public relations industry has been growing and with it a desire to acquire a greater level of professionalization, which means attaining an exceptional standard of practice and specialized knowledge via the "professional project." This project involves efforts to address the respect, prestige, and public image of a profession. An example of a study that represents the professional project was conducted by Molleda et al. (2019). Researchers completed a survey in 2009 and 2015 of public relations professionals in Latin America to measure the evolution of professionalization in their target countries and to examine the impact of contextual factors, such as economic performance, political system, and press freedom. Their survey covered nine countries and had 674 participants, 61 percent of which were female. Race of participants was not included in the published findings. Countries were Argentina, Brazil, Chile, Colombia, Costa Rica, Dominican Republic, Mexico, Peru, and Venezuela.

Findings from the Molleda et al. (2019) study showed that the profession of public relations in their sampled Latin American countries was "in flux" (p. 1091). Three indicators of professionalism were considered priorities: formal education, ideology and ethical principles for the good of society, and a scientific body of knowledge. Specialized status, in organizations and in the marketplace, was not as important. Participants also did not value the role of professional associations to assist with the professional project. The younger the participant, the more critical they were of the legitimation efforts of the professional associations. Finally, the study indicated that economic performance of a country was important for evaluating whether a profession had legitimacy. The political system and whether there was freedom of the press were less influential factors.

The professional project approach includes the concern that the feminization of the field will be a detriment to legitimacy and perceived status for the profession. The literature is silent, though, about how White the profession remains and whether this is perceived as a factor of legitimacy and status. Fitch et al. (2016) argued that professionalization processes were in part a response to feminization: "Certain kinds of public relations activity are marginalized by an exclusive occupational identity that hinges on a narrow conceptualization of (professional) public relations" (p. 282). For example, strategic management roles noted professionalism, while the nonprofessional technical activity included publicity and promotion (Fitch & Third, 2010). The authors coded certain sectors of public relations, such as corporate communication and public affairs, to be more "professional" and were more conducive to the development of careers for male professionals. By stratifying the tasks of public relations and usage of labels, the male professionals increased their aspirations toward social closure and elite status (Fitch & Third, 2014).

Systems

The systems approach to defining professionalism uses the term *jurisdiction* to mean that the occupation has a knowledge system that differentiated itself from other occupations and also from jurisdictional competitors (Pieczka & L'Etang, 2006, p. 269), such as journalists and advertising and marketing practitioners. Hoffman et al. (2007) argue against the systems and traits analysis of public relations professionalism because public relations is part of the "management of interdependence within and for organizations, requiring a balance among professional identity, organizational alignments and structural openness" (p. 125). They referenced the influence of how organizations structure their public relations work rather than individuals with special jurisdiction, found more typically with law and accounting, who are granted more organizational autonomy or monopoly because they have specific skill sets, licenses, or certifications.

One skill set that may contribute to professional aspirations of higher status has been tied to social media expertise. Smith and Place (2013) found in their qualitative interviews that social media expertise enabled public relations practitioners to demonstrate their value to organizations. In a follow-up study, Lee et al. (2018) hypothesized that social media expertise would be an equalizing gender force in the practice. They found in a survey of public relations practitioners that social media expertise was perceived equally between the female and male participants.

The professional level allows a space for diving deeper into what has been missing from the legitimacy discourse. Viewing professional status as a model that includes traits, process, ethnographic, power, professional project, and systems begins to detail the areas of conflict. While most writings on professionalism and public relations remain silent on sexism and racism, for example, there have been some feminist analyses to contest the "neutrality" of professional public relations literature. To add to the jurisdictional approach to understanding a professional-level view, we turn next to the issues tied to professional aspirations for a unique set of skills differentiated from other communication disciplines, such as discrimination and education. We finish this professional view with comments on postfeminism and how feminism contributes to a professional-level view of public relations.

ISSUES TIED TO PROFESSIONAL ASPIRATIONS

There are some key areas of concern that have the potential to limit the public relations profession's reputation and legitimacy.

Encroachment

Bourne (2019) calls more than a century of public relations efforts to achieve professional status "a project marked by a struggle with adjacent professional fields for market control, social closure and elite status" (p. 1). She argued that an exploration of the public relations profession, from a socially constructed viewpoint, must include jurisdictional disputes. These disputes or boundary work include encroachment or the process by which professionalism from adjacent fields of marketing, investor relations, law, human resources, risk management, or engineering assume the organization's senior public relations role. Encroachment forces public relations professionals into technical functions or into servicing other departments. Jurisdictional losses have led to the fragmentation of activity into subfields, such as strategic communication, the subfield included in the analyses of this book given its growing influence. Additional tussling occurs with human resources and management consultants over who owns crisis communication (Bourne, 2019, p. 4). Furthermore, encroachment has led to public relations practitioners abandoning the name of public relations.

Encroachment threatens to perpetuate the glass ceiling, in particular for practitioners of color. Female public relations managers compete with outsiders brought in by top management and with male practitioners who can surpass women for higher levels of management (Pompper & Jung, 2013). However, practitioners of color are even more vulnerable to encroachment, as the field offers a larger pool of capable White personnel to usurp their access to advancement. Women are pigeonholed in technician jobs or not seen as management material, and encroachment allows organizational leaders to select more leadership-appropriate men from outside the public relations department, sometimes from departments seen as having similar activities. This outcome also exacerbates the idea that no formal training is needed to perform the public relations function (Gesualdi, 2019). Thus, the profession becomes devalued.

Stereotyping

There is a wide range of stereotypes that affect the perception of public relations as a legitimate profession. For example, the profession is predominately White, and stereotypes about practitioners of color hurt chances for recruitment and diversity goals. Unfortunately, people of color entering the field of public relations have to make accommodations to be in the industry (Wills, 2020). Edwards exemplified the denial of a practitioner's status by describing both the individual's race and gender: "Through a single statement, her professional status is denied and she is re-placed into a junior and less visible position that allows her Black female identity to remain subjugated" (p. 250). Edwards uses the term *professional pragmatics* (from Cottle, 1998, p. 296) to mean that public relations practitioners who are Black, Asian, and otherwise of color have to "focus on practice to produce high-quality programs that could fit within mainstream thinking rather than specialist program categories. A practitioner's race requires professional distance from the communities they represent in their output" (p. 246). People of color's choice represents the double-bind of orienting toward the dominant understandings of professional public relations practice, thereby reducing the complexities of cultural representations. "Professional pragmatics" may also lead them to adopt strategies that ensure professional success and recognition, using their ethnicity structurally when it may enhance perceptions of their skills and abilities but also limiting the degree to which it defines their expertise" (p. 247).

Ageism, a form of discrimination based on age, devalues the professionalism of public relations because youth and a female majority in public relations is equated with lack of qualifications for advancement in the field. Pasquarelli (2018) reported Bureau of Labor Statistics data on the age of communication workers: "In 2017, the majority, or 63 percent of workers in advertising, public relations and related services were under 45 years of age. The median age in this category was 39.2—roughly the same as a decade earlier" (p. 20). Hon (1995) reported women recalling how glad they were to turn thirty. In Hon's focus groups, one participant stated, "When she was in her 20s, and in a maternity dress, people did not take her seriously" (p. 56). Another participant wondered when she would be considered "old enough. She joked there may be just a 3-year slot during which women are considered the appropriate age" (p. 56).

LGBTQ discrimination limits the professional aspirations of the field of public relations because of inequities faced by LGBTQ practitioners. Industry assumptions of practitioner heterosexuality have resulted in homosexuality being variously rendered invisible in public relations practice, marginalized, or stereotyped. Pejorative stereotypes retarding the professionalism of public relations included gay men reporting they were "one of the girls," presumed to have special insights regarding interactions with women (Tindall & Waters, 2012, p. 461). Tindall and Waters (2012) identified the stereotypical gay role "of being the cool, creative employee who can navigate both mainstream and LGBTQ campaigns" (p. 459). A practitioner in Tindall's (2013) study said that the gay male stereotype focused only on their sexual behaviors. She said that "lesbians were less scary than gay men because women are less scary, especially sexually. Everybody thinks about sex when they think about gay men. That's all they think about, I guess because that's all men think about" (p. 33).

LGBTQ discrimination is a violation of civil rights in the workplace. Yet researchers have found harassment and reluctance to provide protection for LGBTQ individuals. Tindall and Waters (2013), in their edited book on LGBTQ issues, reported on harassment experienced by LGBTQ individuals, including social exclusion in the workplace and inequitable advancement opportunities. Ciszek (2020) called out organizations that sought LGBTQ individuals to be cultural intermediaries to build relationships with LGBTQ publics to "get their ducks in a row . . . by having established inclusive and equitable and internal policies that protect and empower employees who identify as sexual or gender minorities" (p. 5).

"Lookism," or discrimination based on appearance, has been linked to a lack of professionalism (Frohlich & Peters, 2007). Hon (1995) identified lookism as a form of sexual harassment. From focus group research, Hon reported participants being called "bimbo" and "sex kitten" (p. 54). One participant called lookism "the ultimate power play by men to demean women's professionalism" (p. 55).

Frohlich and Peters (2007) reported that women are guilty of discriminating on the basis of women's appearance as well. The Frohlich and Peters findings suggested the "PR bunny" stereotype—representing a denigration of women for "hopping around at parties," also called PR girly, and "Barbie doll" (p. 241)—was used by the female participants as a sign of lack of professionalism in other female practitioners. Their participants thought "PR bunny" was part of women's natural weapon and simply part of professionalism itself: "PR sluts! (laughs). We call ourselves that! And I don't have a problem with it. We are service people. And you have to play the game of service don't you" (p. 242). In a popular culture study, Fitch (2015) described the stereotypical female public relations practitioner as "single, White, childless, middle class and attractive" (p. 610). Little research exists about how males experience lookism. However, in the Pompper and Jung (2013) study of men working in a "feminized" field, their participants reported "threats on their masculinity" (p. 504). Lookism exists because of professional anxiety over the field's feminization (Fitch, 2015).

Undergraduate Education

Most of the criteria for claims of public relations professionalism include the requirement for an expertise applying a body of knowledge obtained through academic education (Hoffman & Hamidati, 2016; Meyer & Leonard, 2014). However, "then the numbers of women graduating with public relations degrees began to appear problematic for the status of the industry" (Fitch & Third, 2014, p. 262).

The public relations body of knowledge has no standard curriculum as delivered to the hundreds of undergraduate public relations majors, sequences, tracks, or concentrations through which thousands of students prepare for public relations careers (see Public Relations Student Society of America, 2020; Sha & Toth, 2005). The body of knowledge obtained in undergraduate public relations education is lacking in preparation for future practitioners to learn how to enter a raced and gendered, heteronormative world of work.

Two organizations represent the most influential effort to standardize undergraduate public relations education: the Commission on Public Relations Education (CPRE), founded in 1973 as a consortium of most academic and practitioner associations, and the Public Relations Society of America (PRSA) Certificate in Education for Public Relations (CEPR). CPRE issues benchmark standards for what should be taught to public relations students. The CEPR program uses the CPRE curriculum standards in addition to criteria on resources, faculty, Public Relations Student Society of America chapters, and placement in internships and public relations jobs to award a certificate of merit similar to the Accrediting Council in Journalism and Mass Communication's government-sanctioned journalism accreditation. Neither of the commission's 2017 reports of standards, *Fast Forward: Foundation + Future State. Educators + Practitioners* (2017) nor the *PRSA Certification Guidelines* (2020) mention standards for gender studies or the reality of gender issues in the workplace. Both the CPRE report and the CEPR guidelines address diversity and inclusion. The CEPR requires documenting enrollment demographics. The commission's diversity chapter mentions gender only in a list of differences.

The few studies we have of student perceptions of gender issues reinforce the lack of formal preparation for the gendered workplace and the belief that the lack of men in the classroom devalues their education. Both findings disquiet aspirations to public relations professionalism. Sha and Toth (2005) found in a survey of Public Relations Student Society of America members that perceptions were already formed on issues of gender. The male students agreed less than the female students that men are promoted more quickly and that it is more difficult for a woman than it is a man to reach the top in public relations. The men agreed less than the women that juggling work and family needs is harder for women than men. The men agreed less than the women that employees with children living at home would have more difficulty being promoted. The men also disagreed that women are paid less than men for comparable jobs. All these findings suggest that the male students tended to believe that gender discrimination in public relations had been eradicated. It is concerning that the male public relations students would take these perceptions with them into the practice.

Public relations students have also carried into the workplace perceptions that gender plays a negative role in their education. In interviews with early career public relations practitioners, Waymer et al. (2016) reported negative implications of the underrepresentation of men in the classroom. One female participant reported that her fiancé, one of the few men in her class, experienced some effects of being part of a minority. Another man stated that he and other men felt alienated: "I have witnessed female colleagues intentionally leave out top tier male students. As a male, I felt as if I was discriminated against" (p. 125). Another reported "seeing females try to overpower an idea or suggestion a male has by getting more females to agree with them" (p. 125). A White woman wanted more men in the classroom in order to better prepare for working with men in the business world.

The discourses from the Waymer et al. (2016) study are taken at face value as descriptors of the socialization and precareer development of public relations practitioners. The authors didn't question whether the alienation attributed to the few men in the public relations classroom reflects the disruption of prior socialization of male privilege. A feminist reading of the male respondents' complaints of being left out or overpowered by women suggests a reading of male expectations to always be in power.

Another disquieting reflection from a participant in the Waymer et al. study was, "I feel that my development will be hindered in order to show how 'equal' the PR industry is becoming (since men still hold many of the leadership positions in the field" (p. 125). This opinion suggests that the beginning practitioner wanted more men in the classroom rather than be misled about gender inequities in the industry. Some of the participants suggested that the programs should prioritize recruiting more male students with courses of interest to them, such as "sports."

The Waymer et al. (2016) study reinforces the gendered nature of public relations education. Our body of knowledge and expertise is hindered by the lack of knowledge regarding how perceptions of careers are driven by gender socialization. Male and female public relations students would be better served to understand the theories behind sex roles. They would be better prepared to negotiate their future workplaces and make them more egalitarian in salaries, advancement, and work-life issues.

University studies have multiple examples of concentrations of men, such as in science, technology, engineering, mathematics, and business programs, and concentrations of women, such as in education, nursing, dance, and communication programs. There are no artificial college barriers in place prohibiting students from choosing specific majors. The socialization processes causing men and women to stay in their respective lanes is the missing knowledge that they will be welcomed in all occupations.

POSTFEMINISM IN PROFESSIONALISM

Fitch and Third (2010) argued that public relations has entered an era of postfeminism, a period of assumed equality and a backlash against feminist arguments. The postfeminist position "assumes that explicit consideration of 'the gender question' is no longer necessary" (Fitch & Third, 2010, np). "Post-feminism is a step backwards from the arguments for systemic change to the celebration of personal responsibility, individualism, and autonomy" (Fitch, 2016). An example of this is a search of PRSA's articles using the terms *gender issues* or *women's issues* and finding only two that were related to gender inequities (Vogt, 2020; Mason, 2019).

Postfeminism represents exhaustion with the strictures of the public relations profession, a resignation to the spaces women have been given in the profession. Yet the drive toward professionalism cannot ignore oppressive processes and issues of power evident in this field (Fitch & Third, 2010). Female public relations practitioners continue to be marginalized by the field's association with "women's work" or "emotional labor." They work in an industry that expects them to adopt masculine values that reinforce gender stereotypes.

Postfeminism is grounded in a traditional view of feminism as antimale and radical. Feminism today advocates antiracism as well as equity for all marginalized voices. Feminism has evolved to counter not only masculinist narratives in a profession but racist and homophobic ones as well. Thus, feminism remains a valuable lens by which to critique the missing voices in the public relations profession. By increasing the equitable inclusion of marginalized voices, the profession of public relations will actually represent a more idealized version of effective communication.

CASE STUDY OF INDONESIAN PUBLIC RELATIONS

An example of how professionalism does not acknowledge issues of gender, or issues of colonialism and national culture either, for its workers or for its work with publics is found in a study by Hoffman and Hamidati (2016) that dismisses gender in the practice of public relations in Indonesia. Seeking to theorize why Indonesian public relations practices were achieving professionalism at a snail's pace, Hoffman and Hamidati surveyed heads of corporate communications in three countries, resulting in 211 completed questionnaires. Although the authors report several demographic characteristics of the participants, such as education, age, and membership in professional associations, they do not report the sex, race, or national heritage of the participants. Curiously, the authors drop items pertaining to gender egalitarianism, from Hofstede's (2001) cultural dimensions, because they stated the variables did not significantly correlate with one another. The authors instead used two new dimensions: personal influence and saving face (p. 56).

Hoffman and Hamidati (2016) argued that the professionalism of corporate communication in Indonesia should not be compared to the professional standards of Western societies in part because their participants contrasted the cultural context in which they work in distinctly different ways than their Western counterparts in Austria and Australia. The authors found that culture in the other Western countries was not as impactful on corporate communication practice as it is a "mirror of the social status quo." They argued instead that there's a strong alignment to corporate contexts that can impede the development of new professional ideals.

Hoffman and Hamidati (2016) did not reference Simorangkir's (2011) Indonesian study of feminization of the public relations industry. Simorangkir (2011) prefaced her qualitative study of practitioners with a history of Indonesian patriarchal culture and its societal oppression of women. Simorangkir found that Indonesian women in public relations were more likely to be relegated to the technical tasks of public relations practice and tended to occupy supportive types of management positions, such as personnel training or marketing, rather than critical operating or commercial functions (p. 36). The female practitioners reported that feminization of public relations had led to a degradation of the industry due to the perception that practitioners had low intelligence. Furthermore, male practitioners were regarded as gay. Gender discrimination in this study led to encroachment: "Encroachment can bring serious consequences when the organization's power elite place men with general management credentials from other departments to direct public relations efforts" (p. 41). Appearance was a job prerequisite as well, showcasing the "lookism" that guided professional success.

These two studies offer a case analysis of worldviews of public relations professionalism in the same country. Hoffman and Hamidati discounted gender and globalization as factors in their study, while Simoranghir emphasized the role gender played in negative perceptions by organizations and the profession.

CONCLUSION: CONTRIBUTIONS OF FEMINISM TO A PROFESSIONAL-LEVEL VIEW

We find that the literature that analyzes the field's "professional project" has seldom addressed the exclusionary and marginalizing norms, routines, and role inequities. It has proposed abstract value standards and criteria for professionalism that invite multiple meanings that maintain and reify dominant values of White patriarchy. Whether viewed through lenses of traits, progress, power, or systems, practitioners with intersectional identities and standpoints are disadvantaged and remain voiceless in the dominant view of these approaches.

We encourage building on the work of feminist scholars who contribute different worldviews on the norms and ethics of public relations' professionalism. Rakow (1989) called attention to valuing the feminine. She saw the opportunity in public relations to achieve the ethic of social responsibility with a feminine alternative value system that thinks in terms of relationships, preference for cooperation, and collaborative styles as opposed to the masculine ideology of rationality, autonomy, competitiveness, efficiency, and individualism.

Connected to aspirations of public relations professionalism, L. A. Grunig et al. (2000) argued that feminist values parallel the effective, ethical practice of public relations (p. 49). They offered altruism, commitment, equality, equity, ethics, fairness, forgiveness, integrity, justice, loyalty, morality, nurturance, perfection, quality of life, standards, tolerance, and cherishing children (p. 58). The authors argued that public relations ethics should represent the values of diversity, justice, sensitivity, and cooperation, and research and education offer promising directions for the field to realize these important values (p. 63).

Fitch et al. (2016) contribute the feminist intelligences or modalities to understanding the professionalization processes of public relations. A feminist intelligence "examined the assumptions of public relations practice and 'common sense' meanings may be revealed as highly gendered social constructions" (p. 285). Feminist intelligence means active politicization of issues to guide public relations practice to new ways of configuring gender and race relations. These feminist authors open up new ways of discussing public relations norms, routines, and ethics in understanding the professional-level body of research.

The concept of public relations professionalism is embedded in a specific historical and cultural construction of masculinity and a masculinist vision of professional work (Fitch & Third, 2014, p. 250). Their study focused on Australian female public relations practitioners' 1980s work experiences because "the 1980s represented a period for the Australian public relations industry in which women entered public relations practice in greater numbers" (p. 247). Based on in-depth interviews with six Australian female practitioners who worked in the 1980s, they found that women were excluded from specific parts of the industry and included in others. Similar to the U.S. research findings of the 1980s by Cline et al. (1986), masculinity played out in the management vs. technical function, with the managerial functions being considered more professional as the industry sought to be known as "strategic" while women performed the emotional labor, "such as negotiation and smoothing of relations thought natural for women" (p. 257). "Whereas men did the so-called 'serious' work of corporate affairs, strategy development, media management and dealing with external stakeholders, women tended to perform internal and community relations, marketing, promotion and public education roles and only later in the 1980s media relations" (p. 257).

Fitch and Third (2014) found that because of the constraints women experience in working in public relations, they sought to negotiate professional identities in several ways. Some embraced their promotional girl identity by dressing in feminine ways at the office. Some tolerated the inappropriate behavior of male colleagues. Another strategy was adopting a more masculine identity by being directly confrontational. Some moved to greener pastures when they perceived a lack of recognition or financial reward, some opted out by starting their own agencies, and some joined professional organizations to achieve more professional identities by winning national awards and networking with other practitioners to share professional knowledge.

We believe that public relations is a female-intensive occupation with little professional support. The practice of public relations and its professional aspirations still come with the same cultural preferences for masculine norms and routines. How the masculine norms constrict the professional project is embedded in how we approach analyzing public relations professionalization.

8

Professional Level

Interrogating Difference
in Professional Associations

OUTLINE OF CHAPTER CONTENT

- Assessment of associations' commitments
- Arthur W. Page Society (established 1983)
- Association for Women in Communications (established 1909)
- Hispanic Public Relations Association (established 1984)
- International Association of Business Communicators (established 1970)
- National Black Public Relations Society (established 1998)
- Public Relations Council (established 2000)
- Public Relations Society of America (established 1947)
- General theme: Gender as cis woman and heterosexual
- General theme: Antiracism and equity
- General theme: Feminism and codes of ethics
- Strengths and weaknesses of professional associations
- Case: Task Force on the Status of Women (1989 to 2017)
- Conclusion: Questionable value of professional associations

Industry associations have been identified as an important criterion to claiming professional status for an occupation. Public relations' professional associations, of which there are several, such as the Public Relations Society of America, the International Association of Business Communicators, the Arthur Page Society, and the Global Alliance (Global Alliance, 2020), offer codes of ethics to their members. However, these codes reach membership numbers that do not come close to the more than 270,000 people who report to the U.S. Bureau of Labor Statistics (2019) that their occupation is public relations. Potentially, these and other associations have resources for their members and help set standards for how to legitimize and authenticate public relations as an occupation. Associations potentially strengthen their hold on what their industry delivers in contrast to other competitors. Associations may confer status on their members.

Industry associations create exclusionary structures through membership selection and/or annual dues, creating a form of closure through their formal programs, called "professional development" activities. Industry associations reinforce occupational identity "to underpin claims of occupational legitimacy and thereby justify the social recognition an occupation receives" (Edwards, 2014).

The reality on the ground regarding public relations associations is that their total combined memberships do not reflect the numbers of people who call themselves public relations practitioners. The combined membership total of the two largest public relations associations, the Public Relations Society of America and the International Association of Business Communicators, is approximately thirty thousand members. The U.S. Bureau of Labor Statistics (2019) reported public relations workers in two occupational categories: public relations and fundraising managers and public relations specialists. The estimate undercounts the numbers of public relations practitioners because those who work in public relations align themselves with other job titles. Public relations associations thus do not speak on behalf of the thousands of people who work in public relations but are not labeled public relations practitioners.

Associations of public relations practitioners should be interested in issues that potentially damage the reputation of the field, such as stereotypical assumptions, racism, and homophobia. This chapter investigates a range of public relations associations and whether they have addressed the marginalization and underrepresentation in the field. Of interest was to learn whether they are cognizant of their obligations to address these concerns for their members and to help construct a different public relations profession in order to advance ethical, diverse, and equitable norms and practices.

ASSESSMENT OF ASSOCIATIONS' COMMITMENTS

In our assessment, we considered three criteria. First, we questioned how the association defined discrimination and underrepresented members. We define gender and race as socially constructed meaning systems arising from communicative acts and legitimized through policy and rules of a profession—professional associations codify these constructions and what is considered valued. In general, we found that while sex (not gender) has been included in association discourse, it is devoid of identities shaped by race, ethnicity, sexual orientation, class, and geography. Second, we searched for whether public relations membership associations acted to advance equity. We looked for information about the actions of groups to inform, educate, advocate, or seek solutions. Such actions would suggest an advocacy role and a commitment to changing the public relations field and society at large. Third, we searched for membership associations' codes of ethics, reasoning that if an association publicly supported values for the field that stood for antiracism, feminism, and equity, it would include these values in its ethical codes of conduct.

From a trade association list of over seventy associations, clubs, and societies "that work toward the growth of the public relations industry" (O'Dwyer's, 2020, np), we chose to review seven national public relations membership associations: the Arthur W. Page Society, the Association for Women in Communication, the Hispanic Public Relations Association, the International Association of Business Communicators, the National Black Public Relations Society, the Public Relations Council, and the Public Relations Society of America.

We limited our assessment to associations that admitted members based on whether they were employed in public relations work, that charged annual dues, and that had a formal leadership structure of volunteers and paid staff. Membership associations with elected representative leadership structures and paid staffs should have as their mission to advance the needs and interests of their members. Eliminated from review were groups that were affiliated at the state or local level with the national public relations organizations and groups with wholly separate strategic communication functions, such as advertising, marketing, and technical information. We eliminated associations organized around specialties under the broad umbrella of public relations, of which there are many, such as investor relations, lobbying, public affairs, and government.

We conducted a qualitative content analysis of the websites of the seven organizations during the one-month period of June 2020. We note that in June 2020, COVID-19 continued to seriously threaten public health and nations' economies. Simultaneously, the Black Lives Matter movement affected all aspects of society. Public relations associations responded with website messages to their members on these public health and social issues. However, the seven associations' websites also continued to reflect their standard programs and services to members. Websites are the outward-facing means of explaining to the public as well as their members what an association's mission, activities, and ethics are. All associations had home pages and sections such as "about us," membership, chapters, events, advocacy, resources, and awards. We reviewed each section that was publicly accessible. Our search started with identifying the background and mission of each organization to qualify it as having a central focus on public relations. While our approach was primarily thematic, we used principles of discourse/rhetorical analysis to take a broader view of the text and images presented on the websites, reflecting on the "ideological, shaped by and shaping social structures, norms and values; deconstructed further to reveal representations of identity and purpose of the occupation" (Edwards, 2014, p. 324).

We looked for text and images that provided an understanding of how the association addressed issues of marginalization and underrepresentation. We searched for the words *gender, women, men, race, LGBTQ, diversity,* and *inclusion*. We looked for actions in support of equity, such as advocacy initiatives, special interest groups, partnerships with other associations, professional development activities related to women or practitioners of color, and articles in the association's media. Then we reviewed codes of ethics and conduct statements, looking for obligations of members to achieve equity, assuming that statements of ethics reflected the values these associations supported. Below we summarize the findings from our analysis, according to association (in alphabetical order).

ARTHUR W. PAGE SOCIETY (ESTABLISHED 1983)

The Arthur W. Page Society (Page), named after one of the public relations industry's first chief communications officers (American Telephone and Telegraph), is an association of eight hundred senior public relations and corporate communications executives and educators (Arthur W. Page Society [Page], 2020a). Page's mission is to strengthen the leadership role of chief communications officer (Page, 2020a).

The Page website lists programs for membership development: conferences and international exchanges; a knowledge base composed of white papers, podcasts, and videos; and the *PageTurner* blog. Page's four membership development programs are Page-Up, an ongoing membership organization for potential chief communications officer successors; Future Leaders Experience, a two-year executive education program; Diverse Future Communication Management program, "to build a pipeline of diverse communication executives" (Page, 2020d); and a student case study competition.

A review of the *PageTurner* blog between 2016 and 2020 yielded only one discussion that addressed gender issues: a Hot Topic feature entitled "Diversity & the Future of Work" (Page, 2020b). In a section of "take-aways," the discussants defined diversity as "broader than gender or ethnicity. It encompasses the distinctions that make us human" (Page, 2020b, np). Examples were given related to how the changing conditions of COVID-19 are affecting young employees, office physical proximity, and women practitioners: "Are women under greater stress given the higher likelihood they're balancing work with additional family care duties? (They are.) In what ways can we make sure this doesn't disadvantage them professionally?" (Page, 2020b, np).

The Page Society has no official code of ethics, but it addresses ethics with seven Page principles to guide actions and behavior (Page, 2020c). Two ethical principles address the importance of stakeholders and employees but discuss them only generally as respect for diversity and inclusion in the workplace:

> Conduct public relations as if the whole enterprise depends on it. Public relations should encourage the enterprise's decision-making, policies, and actions to consider its stakeholders' diverse range of views, values, experience, expectations and aspirations; and realize an enterprise's true character is expressed by its people. It is the responsibility of corporate communications to advocate for respect, diversity, and inclusion in the workforce and to support each employee's capability and desire to be an honest, knowledgeable, ambassador to customers, friends, shareholders and public officials.

The Page Society mission is to advance best practices of corporate communication. No actions were found on its website concerning the issue of a feminized field.

ASSOCIATION FOR WOMEN
IN COMMUNICATIONS (ESTABLISHED 1909)

The Association for Women in Communications (AWC) was the only national industry association with an identified gender focus on female communicators (men are welcome to join). It began as an undergraduate women's journalism sorority around a new journalism program at the University of Washington. AWC became a professional women's organization in 1972 with a name change to the Women in Communication (WICI). In 1991, WICI was dissolved and the organization renamed itself the Association for Women in Communications.

The Association for Women in Communications, with 1,100 members, champions the advancement of women across all communications disciplines by recognizing excellence and promoting leadership (Association for Women in Communications [AWC], 2020). The AWC promotes women's careers in the breadth of communication fields through twelve professional chapters and seven student chapters. Member benefits include networking, professional development, leadership opportunities, and national and local recognition through its Clarion Awards and national membership awards. Benefits also include national exposure through its *Trending* blog and writing opportunities through its newsletter, *Communique*. It offers employment searches through a job board, members-only affinity program (discounts), and website resources.

Early in AWC's history, it advocated for women's rights, first reporting on the lack of female journalism educators. In the 1970s and 1980s, AWC lobbied for the Equal Rights Amendment. Its 1984 national president, Denise Gray, a Black public relations practitioner, led AWC in efforts to tell more stories about Black people through the media (AWC, 2020). Website information reinforces female members' solidarity, with the home page phrase, "Behind every successful woman is a tribe of other successful women who have her back."

AWC had two goals to advance the professionalization of the communications occupations: working for First Amendment rights and responsibilities of communicators and recognizing distinguished professional standards throughout the communications industry. AWC has no code of ethics; however, the website lists six value statements: tradition, community, respect, integrity, intellect, and mentorship.

HISPANIC PUBLIC RELATIONS ASSOCIATION (ESTABLISHED 1984)

The Hispanic Public Relations Association's (HPRA) goals include "to serve as the voice of professionals working in the Hispanic communication field nationwide; to empower its members through support, resources and education; and to offer guidance and assistance to students pursuing careers in the field" (Hispanic Public Relations Association [HPRA], 2020, np).

The HPRA national website home page provides information about the vision and mission of the association as an organization focused on supporting the needs of Hispanic public relations practitioners. Its About Us section references the creation of HPRA because "other PR organizations' well-intentioned efforts to embrace multiculturalism were more geared to serving the needs of the organization than they were Hispanic practitioners" (HPRA, 2020).

The HPRA provides members professional development and leadership growth through exchanges and networking with other Hispanic marketing professionals; obtaining diversity insights and global marketing intelligence; the educational benefits of conferences, workshops, and industry events; access to industry data; job board opportunities; and scholarship opportunities.

The organization's structure includes chapters in Los Angeles; Miami; New York; the Carolinas; and Orange County, California; and a student chapter at the University of Florida. In its fifth year, the Bravo Awards program showcases Hispanic public relations and emphasizes the importance of the Hispanic market in the United States. The HPRA website contains no gender references or activities. The HPRA website provides no code of ethics.

HPRA advances a cultural identity not available in other associations of public relations practitioners. The website emphasizes jobs, networking, and chapter exchanges to help Hispanic practitioners; HPRA is a means to make members more visible to recruiters searching for diverse practitioners. Secondarily, the HPRA signals with the Bravo Awards program how companies and agencies can achieve better marketing to the burgeoning Hispanic customer base.

INTERNATIONAL ASSOCIATION OF BUSINESS COMMUNICATORS (ESTABLISHED 1970)

The International Association of Business Communicators' (IABC) About Us page promotes innovative thinking, shared best practices, in-depth learning, and career guidance (International Association of Business Communicators [IABC], 2020a). A global-level organization, IABC provides its nine thousand members extensive professional development programs including a career roadmap, the IABC world conference, certifications through the Global Communication Certification Council, the Gold Quill Awards competition, a job center, webinars, and an online community for members to network and share information.

The IABC website references no membership demographics (IABC, 2020c); however, IABC membership is likely to be primarily female. In a history of IABC, Gordon (2002) noted that in 1997 IABC's membership was 82 percent female. Taft (2003) reported that the IABC Profiles annual report for 2002 estimated a 76 percent female membership.

IABC has one hundred chapters worldwide and numerous national-level special committees and taskforces, although none of these groups' titles suggests a focus on race or gender issues. IABC has a task force on diversity and inclusion charged with developing recommendations on how to integrate diversity and inclusion into IABC's organization and culture. IABC developed a diversity and inclusion statement and a code of conduct to which members are to abide. The IABC statement on diversity and inclusion is, "Regardless of your race, culture, faith, sexual orientation, disability, skin color, gender, gender identity or expression, national origin, age or experience, you are an equal and valued part of our global community" (IABC, 2020b, np).

The IABC code of conduct addresses discrimination under its section titled Unacceptable Behavior. It states that participants should refrain from bullying, demeaning, discriminatory, harassing, and otherwise inappropriate behavior. Examples of harassing and inappropriate behavior may include, but are not limited to, sexist, racist, homophobic, transphobic, or otherwise discriminatory jokes or language; physical intimidation, stalking, or following; verbal abuse; posting or displaying sexually explicit or violent material; unwelcome sexual attention, which includes sexualized comments or jokes; inappropriate touching, groping, and unwelcomed sexual advances; and advocating for, or encouraging, any of the above behavior (IABC, 2020b). Acceptable conduct in the IABC code includes the principle "I am sensitive to other's cultural values and beliefs" (IABC, 2020b, np). The remaining ten principles deal with issues of accuracy, freedom of speech, and industry practice values such as honesty, confidentiality, and obeying laws and public policy.

NATIONAL BLACK PUBLIC
RELATIONS SOCIETY (ESTABLISHED 1998)

The National Black Public Relations Society (NBPRS), with four hundred members, advocates for Black professionals in public relations. Its goal is to address "the diverse needs of its members through programs and partnerships that provide cultural and competitive advantages" (National Black Public Relations Society [NBPRS], 2020a, np). Its membership profile, illustrated graphically with a Black woman, is 71 percent female and 35 percent between the ages of thirty-five and forty-four years; 75 percent have graduate degrees, 60 percent started in public relations, and 13 percent speak a foreign language (NBPRS, 2020b).

The NBPRS home page promotes to educators, students, and practitioners the PRSA Foundation's *Diverse Voices: Profiles in Leadership*, a book of contributed experiences by the public relations industry's Black, Hispanic, Asian, and gay leading practitioners. NBPRS's home page also features a partnership with Communication Match, an employment search platform, and a job bank. A separate pull-down on the home page links to the 2015 NBPRS State of the Industry white paper calling for efforts to increase diversity in the public relations field and to strengthen partnerships with smaller firms (NBPRS, 2020b).

NBPRS member offerings include networking, programs, and partnerships; a career center for job seekers to post profiles and for potential employers to list positions; a monthly newsletter; and special members-only webinars. Affiliate NBPRS chapters are in Los Angeles, New York, Atlanta, Chicago, Detroit, Philadelphia, and Washington, D.C. No actions related to gender topics or a code of ethics were found on the NBPRS website.

PUBLIC RELATIONS COUNCIL (ESTABLISHED 2000)

The Public Relations Council (PR Council), a public relations trade association, comprises 110 public relations agencies "to help grow talent, revenue, profit and reputation for member agencies and the industry" (Public Relations Council [PRC], 2020a). The PR Council website categorizes initiatives under the following headings: resources, programs, advocacy, and thought leadership. Its resources to members include annual studies of the agency industry, webinars, and case studies. The PR Council's two programs were a certificate for undergraduates and new college graduates and SHEQUALITY.

The SHEQUALITY program sponsors regional networking dinners, workshops, and events to "build women's skills, advocate for an environment of equality regarding gender pay, career opportunities and financial backing/funding, as well as to create more champions for women in the PR workforce" (PRC, 2020e). Noted in a video was that women represent 70 percent of those who work in public relations agencies (PRC, 2020e). The council sponsored four SHEQUALITY workshops: the 2017 Acting Operations: Financial Management for Rising Female Executives workshop; the 2018 Sorry, Not Sorry: Breaking through Bias and Behavior that Gets in the Way workshop; the 2019 From the Ground Floor to Breaking the Glass workshop; and the 2020 HERSTORY: Sharing Lessons Learned workshop. SHEQUALITY provides forty podcasts from female public relations industry leaders.

The Public Relations Council Advocacy category contains two policy statements that reflect feminist values: a pay equity statement and an antiharassment and nondiscrimination statement. The fair pay statement is, "We encourage our Member agencies to adopt policies that ensure fair pay for all PR professionals, and to utilize consistent criteria when determining initial and subsequent compensation decisions. Consistent review of compensation will not only narrow the gender pay gap, but also boost productivity and benefit our Members and their employees" (PRC, 2020d, np).

The nondiscrimination statement is "We expressly affirm our commitment to ZERO TOLERANCE for any form of harassment or discrimination in our company's workplace and any work-related situation" (PRC, 2020b, np).

The PR Council has a Diversity Awards program and advocates for diversity and inclusion with a pledge listed in its code of ethics and principles: "We value diversity and inclusion in our profession. This statement references helping clients speak with regard to race, color, religion, national origin, sex, sexual orientation, age, veteran status, disability and any other basis prohibited by applicable federal, state, or local law" (PRC, 2020c, np).

PUBLIC RELATIONS SOCIETY OF AMERICA (ESTABLISHED 1947)

The largest association of public relations professionals in the United States is PRSA, at twenty-one thousand members (Public Relations Society of America [PRSA], 2020e). PRSA offers professional development programs leading to certifications through online courses and webinars, a job center listing and career resources, the Silver and Bronze Anvil awards, a national newsletter and member blogs, international and section conferences, an advocacy commitment to speak out on issues affecting the public relations field, a code of ethics, and an accreditation credential (the APR, Accreditation in Public Relations).

A search of the PRSA website using the search term *gender issues* led to one announcement of a webinar on diversity and inclusion in the LGBTQ and Latinx community (PRSA, 2020c). This $200 seminar was marketed to help public relations professionals understand the issues facing the LGBTQ and Latinx communities.

The PRSA membership is approximately 70 percent women and 30 percent men (Mason, 2015 in Place & Vardeman-Winter, 2015, p. 7). This estimate reflects several surveys of PRSA members done over the years. In a 2006 sample of PRSA members totalling 289 respondents, 69.9 percent were female (Kim & Reber, 2009, p. 161). In 2011, Sha reported on a sample of PRSA members' perceptions of accreditation, that of her 1,377 respondents, 997 or 72 percent were female (p. 124). In 2014, in a study of coping in strategic management of work-life conflicts on public relations, the authors reported that of a sample of 565 randomly selected PRSA members, 79 percent were female (Jin et al., 2014, p. 73). The preponderance of percentages reported across studies confirms that PRSA is greater than majority female.

Structurally, PRSA oversees 110 chapters across the United States. It has fourteen member sections representing interests in such areas as finance, counseling, technology, health, and education. PRSA has national committees but none related to gender issues. Its Diversity and Inclusion Committee, while not addressing gender issues per se, mentions sexual orientation and gender differences in its charge: "build consciousness by increasing visibility of D&I [diversity and inclusion] standards, resources, and best practices for racial, ethnic, religious, sexual orientation and gender differences, as well as diverse skill sets, mindsets and cultures at all levels of the organization" (PRSA, 2020b). The plan for 2020–2022 seeks to position PRSA as a leader in diversity and inclusion with several objectives and strategies to advance awareness and advocacy. Neither in the committee description nor in the plan itself is diversity and inclusion defined.

PRSA's code of ethics identifies six core professional values and six provisions of conduct but none that address gender or race. Its values are advocacy, honesty, expertise, independence, loyalty, and fairness. Its provisions for conduct are the free flow of information, healthy and fair competition, open disclosure of information, safeguarding confidences, avoiding conflicts of interest, and enhancing the profession. PRSA members pledge to adhere to the articles of the member code of ethics and accept that the consequence of misconduct may be membership revocation, but emphasis on enforcement of the code has been eliminated (Wilson et al., 2019, p. 317).

The Public Relations Society of America provides its members a credentialing program, the Accreditation in Public Relations (APR), as a means of designating professional distinction in the field. However, as of 2012, only 18 percent of PRSA members had earned the credential, raising the question of whether there was professional distinction in earning the APR (Penning & Sweetser, 2015).

Penning and Sweetser (2015) used secondary data collected in 2012 by the Universal Accreditation Board of public relations practitioners after they had taken the computer-based APR exam to learn how participants valued the APR credential. Of the 150 participants, 121 of whom were female, the most frequently selected reason was personal satisfaction (80.7 percent), followed by desire to be a better practitioner (80 percent) and to have greater confidence in strategic management (70 percent). Respondents were less motivated by job promotion or the ability to obtain a new job (p. 136). The authors found only one statistical difference in motivation for accreditation based on gender. The men in the sample were more likely than the women to be motivated by "greater respect from employer/clients" (p. 135). The authors interpreted this finding to mean that the men in the sample felt that their male peers in other professions received more respect (p. 137).

GENERAL THEME: GENDER AS CIS WOMAN AND HETEROSEXUAL

The term *gender* appeared infrequently on association websites. However, when it was used it implied cis women who were heterosexual. The dominant construction of gender on these association websites was that of women and women's issues. For example, women had family obligations (rather than women and men). In the Page Society Hot Topic blog post about diversity and the future of work, gender was questioned but was used to mean women: "Gender. Are women under greater stress given the higher likelihood they're balancing work with additional family care duties? (They are.) In what ways can we make sure this doesn't disadvantage them professionally?" (Page, 2020b).

The Association for Women in Communications addressed women and provided members services such as networking, professional development, and leadership opportunities to advance women's careers. The Public Relations Council's SHEQUALITY project built women's skills and advocated for an environment of equality regarding gender pay, addressing the women's pay disparity in the agency field.

An example of an action directed toward solving the gender issues of public relations is the SHEQUALITY series of activities advocated by the Public Relations Council. Directly related to the gender inequities of preparing women who work in public relations agencies to advance, the SHEQUALITY leadership instituted regional dinners for agency women, annual workshops, and a podcast series. All these programs are ongoing opportunities for women to learn from panels of women and individual female leaders who share information about what female agency practitioners need to know: finance and management, breaking through the bias, breaking the glass ceiling, and sharing lessons learned from their experiences.

In all but one case, professional associations did not directly or specifically speak to gender minorities or LGBTQ communities. The one exception was IABC, which had a code of conduct that included sexist, racist, homophobic, or transphobic jokes or language as unacceptable. Also unacceptable were the actions of posting sexually explicit or violent material and engaging in unwelcome sexual attention, including making sexualized comments or jokes, inappropriate touching, groping, and unwelcome sexual advances. IABC's statement on diversity and inclusion separates its demographic categories into sexual orientation, gender, and gender identity and expression. The IABC code of conduct referenced gender separately and advocated against homophobic and transphobic categories.

GENERAL THEME: ANTIRACISM AND EQUITY

The associations included statements of diversity and inclusion, and associations were developed for purposes of carving out a voice for Black and Latinx public relations practitioners. Two other examples of equity efforts were found: one with the Association for Women in Communications and one with the Public Relations Council. The AWC, which has a long track record of helping female communicators break into the communications fields, advocated for more attention to Black practitioners. Diversity and inclusion efforts were found in the IABC's Diversity and Inclusion Statement, the PR Council's Diversity and Inclusion principle, and the PRSA's Diversity and Inclusion Committee's charge "to build consciousness by increasing visibility of D&I [diversity and inclusion] standards, resources, and best practices for racial, ethnic, religious, sexual orientation and gender differences" (PRSA, 2020b, np).

GENERAL THEME: FEMINISM AND CODES OF ETHICS

Five of the seven associations had codes of ethics or value statements: the Arthur W. Page Society, the Association of Women in Communications, the International Association of Business Communications, the Public Relations Council, and the Public Relations Society of America. These codes were generally directed to individual practitioner behavior. Only IABC addressed unacceptable behavior around gender.

Statements of ethical principles and their underlying values communicate a great deal about the professionalism of an industry. They become the standards by which behaviors of individual public relations practitioners as well as the whole industry are judged. Members of associations look to codes of ethics for a professional identity; and for critics of communication fields, statements of ethics and values influence broader societal perceptions about the work of public relations and whether it is worthy of being called a profession. This analysis found little in the codes or principles of these organizations to address gender equity. The exception was in the IABC code of conduct listing of unacceptable behaviors. These statements addressed specific gender issues: bullying; harassment; unwelcome sexual advances; and sexist, racist, homophobic, and transphobic language.

STRENGTHS AND
WEAKNESSES OF PROFESSIONAL ASSOCIATIONS

This interrogation of public relations associations revealed both strengths and weaknesses in the associations and their role in changing the profession for women and people of color. Against the reality that the numbers of people practicing public relations are far greater than those who have joined public relations associations, when practitioners of an occupation organize to speak to issues of difference in their public statements of conduct, it has the ability to elevate the professional aspirations of the field. In some cases, association positions moved past the oversimplified focus on sex and elevated the importance of equity and inclusion. Actions themselves, such as the Public Relations Council's SHEQUALITY programming, potentially inform and prepare women to lead the field and change society's image of public relations as a legitimate profession. However, the associations are not living up to our expectations that they serve as professional advocates for the dismantling of power differentials due to gender, race, ethnicity, sexual orientation, and class.

One concern is that race and gender are only treated as demographic characteristics. Diversity is more complex than just categories of race and ethnicity. The professional associations ignore the value that intersectionality brings to the field and how celebrating and encouraging intersections could result in greater legitimacy for the field. As L. A. Grunig (2005) said, "Diversity is broader than categories of individual difference such as class, race, sex, age, physical abilities and appearance, sexual orientation, creed, and so forth. It is a social construction that reflects the intersection among those characteristics and the resultant power differences" (p. 27).

There was a reason for the creation of associations for women, Black practitioners, and other marginalized groups. The AWC, NBPRS, and HPRA filled a gap for public relations practitioners who wanted to acknowledge their gender, race, and ethnic identities. The Association for Women in Communications had a clear mission of helping female practitioners. The NBPRS and the Hispanic Public Relations Association believed that race and ethnic identities of their members should be more visible to the larger public relations profession. Unfortunately, these associations rarely work together where universally accepted professional standards could increase value for practitioners.

The Page Society, Public Relations Council, and IABC moved in the direction of feminist values to act responsibly toward stakeholders and publics. The Page principles included "listening to stakeholders" and "considering stakeholders' diverse range of views, values, experiences, expectations, and aspirations" (Page, 2020c, np). The PR Council encouraged practices that increase society's confidence in the practice of public relations. The IABC promoted sensitivity to diverse cultural values and beliefs.

However, with general pithy phrasing, diversity and inclusion statements diminished the possibility for any real, applied change that that would help legitimize the profession while dismantling the status quo. The rhetoric used to denote support for diversity is abstract; thus, those in power need not act in ways to alleviate power differentials. This is disheartening when the responsibility to achieve diversity goals in public relations falls to a White female majority not in the more influential positions of public relations management.

Finally, public relations associations do little to address intersectional and standpoint dimensions of identity. Practitioners should recognize their own and others' multiple identities and their understanding of how race, class, sexuality, ethnicity, and gender influence practice (L. A. Grunig et al., 2000, p. 62). These early ideas have found more recent resonance in critical race theory and standpoint theory but deserve more attention by associations.

CASE: TASK FORCE ON
THE STATUS OF WOMEN (1989 TO 2017)

This is a case of how gender became the focus of some work by the largest association, the PRSA, and how the association eventually halted the work due to the perception that the problems were resolved. In 1989, the Public Relations Society of America headed by president John Paluszek formed the Task Force on the Status of

Women after members objected to an article Paluszek wrote in the *Public Relations Journal* expressing the belief that there were no problems for women in public relations (L. A. Grunig et al., 2001, p. 1).

The task force published, with PRSA National Board and PRSA Foundation funding, several surveys describing salary and role disparities among PRSA members (see Gilkerson et al., 2018, for a review of these studies). In 1990, a joint project with the PRSA National Research Committee resulted in a 1991 monograph, *Under the Glass Ceiling: An Analysis of Gender Issues in American Public Relations* (Wright et al., 1991). This sparked enough interest by the association to encourage further examination of gender discrimination among its membership. Thus, PRSA and the PRSA Foundation funded a series of gender surveys of its membership in 1995, 2000, and 2005. Using PRSA participation, articles advanced understanding of such gender issues as role disparities (Toth & L. A. Grunig, 1993; Serini et al., 1998), job satisfaction (Serini et al., 1997), sexual harassment (Serini et al., 1998), theories of discrepancies (Aldoory & Toth, 2002), leadership (Aldoory & Toth, 2004), and work-life integration (Aldoory et al., 2008; Jiang & Shen, 2018; Jin et al., 2014). In addition, Sha and Toth (2005) produced findings on Public Relations Student Society of America member perceptions of how gender influenced their perceptions of future careers.

In 2005, PRSA and the PRSA Foundation stopped funding the gender work of the task force. While data continued to show perpetual discrimination and significant disparities, the association did not support ongoing research. PRSA did permit its research committee access to membership lists for any subsequent studies, though funding had lapsed. This may be evidence of a backlash to feminism in public relations or a resignation that the problems are intractable. In 2001, the task force became the PRSA Committee on Work, Life, and Gender Issues, but it was disbanded in 2017.

Through initial funding and continued access to membership, a body of work documented entrenched inequities. Although unrecognized by PRSA, the Committee on Work, Life, and Gender Issues played an influential role in uncovering gender disparities and eventually published its research findings in academic publications. Unfortunately, the task force did not highlight the racism and homophobia that also existed among PRSA membership. It was myopic in its focus on women, and while survey samples did include women of color, their voices were not recognized for having unique experiences due to the compounded impact of racism. In addition, without association backing, there was limited association-level promotion of the findings about gender and no association-wide advocacy for change.

CONCLUSION: QUESTIONABLE VALUE OF PROFESSIONAL ASSOCIATIONS

This chapter interrogated the professional association interests in feminist issues. Public relations associations have influence because of their resources and can be the mouthpiece for the field. The associations have their primary foci on serving members' needs, especially in networking, professional development, and job searches. They do not exclude practitioners on the basis of identity, although some organizations are invitation-only (Arthur W. Page Society), and other barriers include a complicated application process and cost. The dominant White culture of the profession has led to forming more race-specific associations. Some associations have advocated for gender issues through codes of conduct, statements of principles, and mentorship. We found statements of diversity and inclusion principles, though without antiracist intent. There was no evidence of associations working together to confront power inequities of the profession.

Public relations associations have seldom moved outside their members' interests to advocate for the industry as a whole. Even though their member demographics are reflective of an industry that is 60 percent to 70 percent female and even though they have advocated for their members' social equities, they appear to reinforce a dominant reading of patriarchy that supports networking, special interests sharing best practices for individual success, and job opportunities.

Scholars of public relations values have provided frameworks for feminist thought on both masculine and feminist values that provide a framework for assessing the values of public relations associations. Rakow (1989) detailed a list of masculine values that represent the development of large impersonal organizations in the era of industrial capitalism: efficiency, rationality, individualism, and competition. These masculine values appear in the PRSA and the IABC codes of ethics in terminology about healthy and fair competition, safeguarding confidences, and avoiding conflicts of interest. Feminist values posited by L. A. Grunig et al. (2000) were altruism, commitment, equality, equity, ethics, fairness, forgiveness, integrity, justice, loyalty, morality, nurturance, perfection, equality of life, standards, tolerance, and cherishing children (p. 58). These values are evident in AWC's and the PR Council's value statements of integrity and also in PRSA's core value of loyalty. These value sets are worthy of further consideration in determining whether public relations associations provide leadership in achieving equity.

V

PRACTITIONER LEVEL

Lived Experience and Identity

9

Practitioner Level

The Lived Experiences of Same and Difference

Over many years of study, feminist public relations scholars have documented the "lived experiences" of individual public relations practitioners. This chapter is the longest in the book because most of the published literature addressing feminism, gender, and race is about individual practitioners and their experiences with discrimination. A meta-analysis by international scholars found that most of the feminist literature comes from the United States, and most are framed within a liberal feminist perspective (Topic et al., 2020). The self-reports have detailed women's and men's public relations career investments despite the perceived barriers. Scholars have explored how individual practitioners have sought to overcome existing power structures by enhancing their skills, obtaining master's degrees to offset perceived inadequacies, or opting out of the profession altogether.

Researchers have asked practitioners to explain how their identity has influenced their salaries, roles, and professional advancement. Research has for the most part exposed the norm of the "standard White woman in public relations" and corresponding sexism and racism due to the preponderance of White female practitioners in the United States and Europe. Quantitative studies have relied on demographic data of practitioners who self-identify as male or female. Qualitative research revealed perceived inadequacies and discrimination in public relations practice.

To begin unpacking the experiences and identity of the practitioner in public relations, we start with their numbers in the field, and in the United States and most of the world, the numbers primarily reflect female, White, and Western racial and cultural backgrounds. Reskin and Roos (1990) were the first organizational researchers to document how public relations was an occupation experiencing a rapid gender transition in the 1970s. Roos and Stevens (2018) updated the occupational census analysis and showed that in the years 2000 to 2014, public relations was documented as a continuing example of a predominantly female industry. This is not only in the United States. Moreno (2018) reported that "the feminization of the profession is verified with 59.6 percent of women versus 40.4 percent of men in European communication roles and 66.6 percent versus 33.4 percent in Latin America in the samples from 2017 European Communication Monitor and the Latin American Communication Monitor" (np).

In 2019, the U.S. Bureau of Labor Statistics reported that 82.8 percent of public relations specialists were White, 10.7 percent were Black/African American, 3 percent were Latino, and 3 percent were Asian. The bureau estimated that 274,600 people were employed in this labeled profession, and it was defined as people who "engage in promoting or creating an intended public image for individuals, groups, or organizations. Many write or select material for release to various communications media" (U.S. Bureau of Labor Statistics, 2019). The professional associations in North America similarly reflect this White majority. The Public Relations Society of America (PRSA) board of directors and officers in 2019 included eighteen individuals listed, and one was Black. Its membership was 94 percent White. In 2019, the International Association of Business Communicators had an executive board that included people from North American and European countries, and all twelve were White. Ford and Brown (2015) surveyed Black practitioners and indicated that, in participating organizations, 53 percent had no Black male communicators employed, and 86 percent had no Black female communicators employed. Similarly, Applebaum et al. (2015) reported that most of the Black and Latino professionals in their study said that people of their racial and ethnic backgrounds comprised a small percentage of employees in their organizations.

These figures offer just a snapshot of the profession at an individual level of analysis. While there is a female majority, the power still resides in the hands of masculine authority, and the position of White privilege here should not be understated. These are base causes for ongoing salary disparities, role differentials, sexual harassment, and microaggressions, which plague the organizational and professional space.

SALARY DISPARITIES

The public relations field has a well-documented history of salary disparity, beginning in 1979 (Dozier et al., 2019). Landmark studies in 1986 and 1989, the *Velvet Ghetto* reports (Cline et al., 1986; Toth & Cline, 1989), provided empirical findings showing that women make less than men. Follow-up surveys in the 1990s and 2000s continued to confirm pay disparities (Aldoory & Toth, 2002; Dozier et al., 2013; Taft, 2003; Wright et al., 1991). In 2010, women in public relations earned seventy-eight cents for every dollar earned by men (Sha & Dozier, 2011). When income was statistically adjusted for professional experience, the pay gap was still eighty-six cents on the dollar. When income was further adjusted for enactment of manager and technician roles, women in public relations earned only eighty-seven cents on the dollar earned by men (Sha & Dozier, 2011).

Place and Vardeman-Winter (2015) summarized the salary gap data across a ten-year period. Using survey data from PRSA members and annual *PRWeek*/Bloom, Gross & Associates surveys, Place and Vardeman-Winter reported that 2004 data showed a salary gap of $27,027, and in 2013 the gap was $44,500 (Daniels, 2017). In 2015, that gap was $42,000 (Daniels, 2017).

Salary disparities have continued. Ford and Brown (2015) reported perceived salary disparities between Black practitioners and their White peers. One participant said, "[My] compensation may not be equal to my peers of other races." The 2017 *PRWeek*/Bloom, Gross & Associates Salary Survey reported that for practitioners with five or more years of experience, women earned median salaries of $95,000, while men earned median salaries of $135,000 (Daniels, 2017). The 2018 survey found a $35,000 gender gap in median public relations salaries: "By my math, that's 72 cents to the dollar" (Strong, 2018, np). Across Europe and Latin America, the same disparities exist. Moreno (2018) found that, on average, 70 percent of European and Latina female practitioners have lower salaries than their male counterparts.

As early as 1985, critics argued that it was just a matter of time before women gained the necessary professional experience to achieve parity with men's salaries.

Over thirty years of research finds that the pay gap between men and women persists. Dozier et al. (2019) reviewed the salary reports of female and male PRSA members over four decades, in 1979, 1991, 2004, 2010, 2014, and 2015. They concluded that over the thirty-five-year span, men in public relations earned higher annual incomes than women in public relations (p. 13). The authors reported that the gap is shrinking "but at glacial speed" (p. 13). They reported that in the 1979 PRSA sample of members, women earned fifty-eight cents to every man's dollar. In 2015, women earned eighty-two cents to every man's dollar. The eighteen-cent gap in 2015 ($17,738 a year) amounted to $709,520 over a forty-year career (Dozier et al., 2019, p. 13).

There is also research that indicates that both men and women are aware of the salary disparity that exists in the profession. In one study, men and women said they found out male counterparts were doing the same tasks as women but for more money, with some suggesting their managers and human resources departments made excuses as to why men were paid more (Dubrowski et al., 2019, p. 10). In a follow-up study, "forty-six percent of the female respondents believed that men in public relations make a higher salary than women in a similar cohort vs. 10 percent of the men; and 56% of the men felt that 'men and women in a similar cohort make approximately the same salary' as compared to 26% of the women" (McCorkindale & Rickert, 2020, np).

The most recent data continue to confirm a pay gap. Data show that the difference is statistically significant after controlling for professional experience (Dozier et al., 2019). In a 2020 survey, 52 percent of the women had experienced pay discrimination versus only 6 percent of the men (McCorkindale & Rickert, 2020, np). Dozier et al. (2019) concluded that the persistent pay gap, spanning thirty-seven years and their six surveys of 2,695 PRSA members, "should be blamed, in part on gender" (p 16).

Almost all the PRSA and International Association of Business Communicators salary data account for disparity among White practitioners. The data by race revealed similar salary disparities as were found between White women and White men, but with compounded effect. The *Holmes Report* provided information on gender and race salary disparities (Shah, 2017). Based on 5,580 responses from employees at fifty-one agencies in North America, non-Whites made $9,302 less in average annual salary than Whites when other variables such as sex and years of experience were held constant (Shah, 2017, np).

Importantly, race and sex discrimination is multiplicative, not additive, meaning that the pay gap is most pronounced for non-White women. In 2017, non-White women had a baseline average salary of $45,910. Non-White men earned an average of $51,982 in annual salary. White women earned a $55,212 average salary. White men in public relations earned a $61,284 average annual salary (Shah, 2017). In other words, non-White women earn a whopping $15,000 less than White men in average base salary. The salary disparity by sex shows similar patterns in that non-White women earned $6,000 less than their male counterparts, and White women earned $6,000 less than their male counterparts. But when race is accounted for, there is a stark difference.

Of course, salary disparity is part of the sex and race discrimination patterns found in all occupations around the world. This does not lessen the impact that discrimination has on women and people of color. As in other industries, women in public relations are more likely to also be responsible for children and elderly parents (Dozier et al., 2013, p. 2). Public relations pay inequity hurts the field's ability to attract the best and the brightest. "Why would people choose to enter a profession whose salaries appear lower than they should be?" (Dozier et al., 2013, p. 3). Pay equity is a matter of fairness and social justice.

On a professional level, salary has been an indicator in the past of an occupation's status. The higher the earnings in an occupation, the higher its status in society. Early theory suggested that as women entered an occupation in significant numbers, they would drive down status (Bates, 1983; Joseph, 1985; Lesly, 1988). This may be the case, but with little evidence that the salaries of men in public relations have been reduced to match their female counterparts.

Researchers have explained that women have lesser salaries because they are working in lower-paying specializations within the profession. They also have fewer years of professional experience because they are more likely to have career interruptions. Workplaces are structured to require the sacrifice of career for family. For people of color, salary compression starts early due to racism. Authors agree that sexism and racism are causes of salary disparities (Dozier et al., 2012; Dozier et al., 2019).

The salary disparity research findings and interpretations stay within a neoliberal perspective favoring free-market capitalism. Explanations for the pay gap value individual agency in making life choices. "The messages are always the same: If women would just change some or all of those behaviors (children, family time, lack of confidence doing too much office 'housework') they can shrink the pay gap," said Nick Corcodilos, author of the Ask the Headhunter series. "Women don't cause the pay gap, employers do" (Corcodilos, quoted in Shah, 2017, np).

ROLES DISPARITIES

Roles research represents a long-running stream of gender studies in the public relations literature. A search of the Employment, Social Policy, Health and Consumer Affairs Council database identified over three thousand articles related to the search terms *public relations* and *roles*. Social psychologists have conceptualized roles as the job assignments, duties, and positioning that are central to understanding organizations (Katz & Kahn, 1966, 1978).

Historically, public relations scholars used the roles concept for several reasons. Roles were a means of identifying the skills and knowledge practitioners must have for organizations to hire them for communication work. Roles were a means of signaling the influence of public relations in organizational decision-making by where they are located in the organizational hierarchy. Roles correlated to salaries, a major capitalistic form of value. Finally, public relations roles were most conveniently studied through the individual perspectives of female and male practitioners.

Although there have been several depictions of what public relations practitioners do for organizations, there were four roles that dominated the U.S. literature, developed by Broom and associates in the 1970s (Broom & Smith 1978, 1979; Dozier & Broom, 2006). Broom and Smith conceptualized the roles of expert prescriber or organizational expert on all public relations matters, communication facilitator or "go-between" for an organization and its publics, problem-solving process facilitator or assisting organizational leaders to solve the public relations problems of organizations, and communication technician or person to provide the communication materials needed to carry out programs developed by others.

In follow-up surveys of public relations practitioners, Broom (1982, 1986) found that the first three roles were distinct but highly correlated with each other (p. 20) but were not correlated with the technician role. In continued quantitative studies, there emerged two dominant public relations role categories: the communication manager, enacting the activities of the expert prescriber, communication facilitator, and problem-solving process facilitator; and the communication technician (Dozier & Broom, 2006, p. 139). Although throughout roles research, scholars reported that public relations practitioners perform the activities of all four roles, Dozier and Broom found that their public relations participants' responses reflected a predominant role—that of either manager or technician (Dozier & Broom, 2006).

This resulting dichotomy of manager or technician categories has meant there was a parsimonious way of building public relations theory. "The four-way and two-way typologies have proven efficacious and stimulating to intellectual debate" (Dozier & Broom, 2006, p. 142) and were reaffirmed in scores of research studies to follow. The two roles typology had a central place in European and Latin American studies as well as in U.S. and global excellence studies (L. A. Grunig et al., 2002). Excellent public relations was equated with the managerial role rather than the technical role.

In a landmark turn for the field, Broom and Dozier's public relations roles research linked gender to public relations roles. Broom (1982) wrote that female practitioners were less likely to enact the managerial role and more likely to take on the technician role (Broom, 1982; Broom & Dozier, 1986). They reported that salary was related to roles as well as sex, and women were most likely to work in the technical roles. Later, Dozier (1988) wrote, "Typically, women in public relations play the technician role predominantly whereas men play the manager role predominantly" (p. 7).

Later studies found that more women were taking on managerial roles, though this advancement was slow and still not at parity. Ford and Brown's (2015) study of Black practitioners found that about 62 percent of the participants did not have any Black men in communication leadership roles in their organization, while 37 percent of the participant organizations did not have any Black female communication leaders (p. 13). Moreno (2018) reported that 70 percent of European and Latina female practitioners held lower positions in the field than their male counterparts.

Furthermore, the managerial role when occupied by women had a lower salary than when occupied by men (Dozier et al., 2019). The effect of the managerial role on salaries found support in the 1979 to 1991 surveys "with the greater dominant manager role enacted by men showing as a significant contributor to the income gap" (p. 14). However, in 2010 and 2014, their longitudinal analysis found the female public relations practitioners were closing the manager role enactment gap, but women achieving the managerial role made no contribution to the gender income gap (p. 14). The income gap adjusting for professional experience and dominant managerial role enactment "actually increased in the 21st century" (p. 14). As women closed the gender gap with regard to indicators of professional growth (e.g., professional experience and manager role enactment), the gender income gap remained stubbornly persistent (Dozier et al., 2019, p. 15).

Why women were more likely to be in the technical roles of the field has been debated and challenged ever since the initial roles research. Early on in the back-and-forth debate, the theories centered on women's lack of investment in educational preparation, years of experience in the field, and professional development opportunities (Aldoory & Toth, 2002, p. 107). Different factors for women's ghettoization in technical positions came from the structural demands of organizations on individual women: balancing work and family, lack of attention to women's needs for skills and knowledge, and such variables as negotiation tactics and assertiveness (Aldoory & Toth, 2002, p. 124).

Researchers such as Ashcraft (2006) found that both men and women were complicit in reinforcing gendered norms through communication processes that disciplined those who don't conform to the societal stereotypes of women supportive of men in the workplace. Women in public relations have reported that they prefer to work for men, and they have called out women as "queen bees" who enact managerial roles in ways that do not meet societal expectations of gender (Wrigley, 2002).

The dominant dichotomy of male public relations professionals in managerial roles and female public relations professionals in technical roles may have run its course. In 2014, public relations roles correlated with male and female practitioners through quantitative methods turned up no significant gender effects with regard to roles. Authors Vieira and Grantham (2014) reported that their findings were the results of a sample that was two-thirds women and one-third men. The 2019 longitudinal analysis of gender and roles (Dozier et al., 2019) reported that women are "closing the gap in terms of professional development and manager role enactment" (p. 15). Because the gender income gap persists, the authors conclude that their theoretical and conceptual understandings of role enactment and practitioner status need to evolve.

In addition to the effects of too few men in the samples reporting on role activities, what individuals are reporting as their managerial titles may have more to do with technical than managerial tasks. The measures of public relations management in twenty-first-century practice referenced in the Bureau of Labor Statistics Occupational Outlook Handbook's description of public relations does not mention the expert prescriber or the problem-solving process facilitator. The handbook even merges the public relations occupational category with fundraising managers: public relations and fundraising managers as those who "plan and direct the creation of material that will maintain or enhance the public image of their employer or client. Fundraising managers coordinate campaigns that bring in donations for their organization" (U.S. Bureau of Labor Statistics, 2020). This language of planning and directing the creation of materials or coordinating campaigns suggests that the managerial role has become more technical than strategic. One effort to move beyond role conceptualizations that may have run their course is the current research on women and leadership.

Manager Role Morphs into Leadership Research

The concept of management used in public relations research will be most identified with Broom and Dozier's (2006) four typologies of expert prescriber, communication facilitator, and problem-solving process facilitator. Other definitions of the managerial role include the four manager roles delineated by Moss et al. (2005): monitor and evaluator, key policy and strategy adviser, trouble shooter/problem solver, and issues management expert. Vieira and Grantham (2014) used the negotiator and policy adviser role categories as managerial in scope.

Broadly speaking, discussions of public relations management generally include the ideas of communication expertise; advising on cultivating and maintaining key relationships; and the direction, planning, and implementation of actions to cultivate relationships. The 2011 member-sourced PRSA definition of public relations does not use the term *management* (Public Relations Society of America [PRSA], 2020a). Instead, PRSA continues with a lengthy definition of public relations as a management function:

> As a management function, public relations encompasses the following: Anticipating, analyzing and interpreting public opinion, attitudes and issues that might impact, for good or ill, the operations and plans of the organization; counseling management at all levels in the organization with regard to policy decisions, courses of action and communication, considering their public ramifications and the organization's social or citizenship responsibilities; protecting the reputation of an organization; researching, conducting and evaluating, on a continuing basis, programs of action and communication to achieve the informed public understanding necessary to the success of an organization's aims; planning and implementing the organization's efforts to influence or change public policy; setting objectives, planning, budgeting, recruiting and training staff, developing facilities; and, overseeing the creation of content to drive customer engagement and generate leads. (PRSA, 2020a, np)

Beyond these studies and descriptions, interest in women and management has lost ground. Indeed, Place and Vardeman-Winter (2015) grouped management and leadership together into one category, "women's managerial/leadership roles," but with only a few exceptions their bibliography of studies focused on leadership.

The importance of managerial enactment and women's advancement in public relations took a turn toward leadership in Aldoory and Toth's (2004) survey of gender and leadership styles in public relations practice. They observed that women are slowly moving into management roles but queried whether women with certain leadership styles might better break through the glass ceiling. They argued that little had been written about the importance of leadership in public relations practice, "although public relations researchers had emphasized management, strategy, and relationship building, three concepts potentially integral to leadership" (p. 158). They hypothesized that in public relations, leadership styles will be gendered in ways that disadvantage female practitioners. Aldoory and Toth directed female practitioners to envision using different leadership styles in different situations (p. 179).

This theme of leadership, not management, as a way forward for women's advancement took on currency and was promoted as the next possible solution to gender inequities in the field. Called the leadership gender gap by Bronstein and Fitzpatrick (2015), a refocus in gender and public relations dialogue has been on achieving not managerial positions but the top leadership roles in organizational governance positions. They attribute this gap to "pervasive stereotypes that characterize leadership as a male trait and the lack of female leaders as role models and mentors as well as psychological and social barriers" (p. 79).

Studies of public relations management and its attending gender connections saw a shift in interest to leadership's impact on practice with the establishment of the Plank Center for Leadership in Public Relations at the University of Alabama in 2005. Plank Center leadership was defined as "the capacity of individual practitioners to exert their influence in an organization" (Meng & Berger, 2013). Leadership meant affecting organizational decision-making, but more specifically, it was a "dynamic process that includes a complex mix of individual skills and personal attributes, values and behaviors that consistently produce ethical and effective communication practice. Such practices fuel and guide successful communication teams, help organizations achieve their goals, and legitimizes organizations in society" (p. 143).

The Plank Center surveys of nationwide senior communications and public relations and communication professionals and a second group of entry- and medium-level practitioners resulted in an excellent public relations leadership model with six dimensions: self-dynamics, team collaboration, ethical orientation, relationship building, strategic decision-making capacity, and communication knowledge management capacity (Ming & Berger, 2013, p. 141).

The center has issued three report cards, in 2015, 2017, and 2019, on whether and how male and female practitioners are exemplifying the best practices of public relations leadership. They reported significant gender differences in industry leadership performance. Participants in the 2017 survey were mostly experienced high-level leaders and managers. Of the over one thousand respondents, 53 percent were women, most White (87 percent of the sample total). The authors found that the women were significantly less engaged, less satisfied with their jobs, less confident in their work cultures, less trusting in their organizations, and more critical of top leaders than were men (Berger et al., 2017).

The 2019 Report Card concluded that the gender gap deepened in every survey subject area. According to the authors, women's perceptions of shared power in decision-making, two-way communication, and the valuing of their opinions differed significantly as reflected in trust in the organization, culture, and engagement issues. "Women said they want more involvement in strategic decision making, they want their opinions to count more, and they want a communication system that places greater emphasis on two-way communication" (Meng et al., 2019, np).

The Plank Center research has been forthright in calling attention to gendered perceptions of public relations leadership and the leader-employee gap in their work experiences. Their article does not draw conclusions about why these perceptions exist, but they do express concern for the reduced levels of engagement when they posit that top leaders and front-line managers can strongly influence engagement through their leadership performance.

Place and Vardeman-Winter (2018) called the state of women and leadership in public relations "lackluster leadership presence" (p. 173). Rather than a glass ceiling in public relations, a more apt meaning revolves around influence in management positions, or "unequal gender assumptions about role enactment" (p. 173). Perhaps this is why the research on women has turned to "leadership."

PIGEONHOLING, CODE SWITCHING, AND MARGINALIZATION

Pigeonholing became a concern in the United States and other Western countries at the end of the twentieth century as a growing number of Black, Latino, and indigenous practitioners entered the public relations profession. This was the situation where a person from a marginalized community was assigned tasks that related only to that marginalized group. While the number of practitioners from marginalized groups was increasing, the percentage of people of color in any one organization was small, and thus those practitioners tended to get assigned to special markets or committees that represented diversity or mirrored their own racial and ethnic backgrounds. In Applebaum et al.'s (2015) study, half of the employers from the survey supported this notion. They viewed specific knowledge about culture, neighborhoods, and ethnic media to be a positive quality among African American and Latino entry-level practitioners that they hire.

This pigeonholing, while still a concern to be reckoned with, has not been as evident in the twenty-first-century literature. Tindall (2009a) interviewed eleven female African American practitioners who did not perceive themselves to be pigeonholed. The author concluded, "Pigeonholing, although a genuine and documented phenomenon, was not a reality for these practitioners" (p. 444). Two-thirds of the participants from Applebaum et al.'s (2015) study of Black and Latinx practitioners reported that they were satisfied with their jobs. They were just as likely to work on mainstream projects as projects related to ethnic markets. However, patterns of difference occurred between the men's and women's experiences at work. "The women are more likely to report satisfaction with the job, more likely to regularly work with Caucasian fellow workers, and more likely to say they oscillate between their ethnic culture and mainstream culture" than did the men (Applebaum et al., 2015, p. 20).

Marginalization awareness was an experience particular to practitioners of color. Applebaum et al. (2015) reported that young professionals believed that racism existed in their work sites and that their race marked them as different and prevented them from being perceived as equal to White peers. One in six said that they could not pursue their career without making race or ethnicity an issue. Only one in ten felt that their contributions were less valued when not directly relevant to an ethnic topic. Seven in ten felt they were "representing their race" in both their successes and shortcomings, with all the women and African Americans expressing this more so. Applebaum et al. (2015) presented perceptions from Black and Latinx practitioners where they were very aware of their race in the workplace. One participant said, "For most of my nine to five working life, I can never forget what I look like. My ethnicity is always going to be somewhat of a hinderance" (p. 22). Another said, "I have not felt valued at work, especially at the entry level. I don't want to say this is because I am Black, but you start to notice that there are just certain events that you just won't be able to go to" (p. 23).

Applebaum et al. (2015) reported that the Black and Latinx professionals were strongly satisfied with their careers, but they voiced reservations related to marginalization. Forty percent said they were not treated with respect by their colleagues. They gave examples of feeling marginalized or treated unfairly. A similar percentage believed that they had to be more qualified than a White person in the same situation. One-third believed that they spent longer in an entry-level position than their White counterparts. Six in ten said they were not afforded the same opportunities as their White peers, and one in four said they had to show themselves as if they were separate from their ethnicity or race (p. 33). One participant remarked, "Sometimes I get frustrated when I see firms that say they (value) diversity. But then you look within that firm and you see that it's because they only checked the boxes of what's required to say they are diverse" (p. 11).

In response to being marginalized and treated with disrespect, practitioners of color may subscribe to and practice code switching. Parrish and Gassam (2015) defined code switching as people of color performing in certain ways to appease dominant cultures (p. 188). In the public relations field, practitioners may assimilate their voice, vernacular, and other external traits to maintain good standing within their organizations. Code switching can also work as a defensive factor for the individual practitioner, where one study in the related field of advertising showed that it helped dissociate from negative stereotypes (Boulton, 2016).

DOCUMENTED MALE RESPONSES TO SEXISM

Much of what we know about experiences related to sex discrimination have come from publications that focused on female voices or on quantitative data that merely compared salary statistics or job duties. There are a couple of studies that dug deeper than this and documented male reactions to sex discrimination. One was the Mind the Gap research, where men's perceptions of organizational structures, policies, and mentorship were included (Dubrowski et al., 2019; McCorkindale & Rickert, 2020). These studies provided space for senior-level and midlevel men to share their exposure to discrimination and their opinions about it. No men said they had personally experienced discrimination in the workplace. They were aware of a pay gap that favored men making more money than women doing the same tasks. They agreed with the women that "it was important to join together to increase equality and inclusiveness in their organizations and the industry" (Dubrowski et al., 2019, p. 11). However, they perceived that female practitioners were favored to serve on corporate boards (p. 7).

In the survey, men and women reported taking similar steps to advance their careers. These included taking on additional responsibility above their day-to-day role (men = 98 percent; women = 98 percent), raising their visibility (men = 91 percent; women = 91 percent), and leaving the organization to pursue better opportunities (men = 66 percent; women = 67 percent) (McCorkindale & Rickert, 2020). With one exception, the men's top personal challenges to being promoted were the same as those reported by the women: "honesty, reliability, authenticity, and interpersonal communication" (p. 18).

However, there were many more documented differences between the men and women in the Mind the Gap survey. The men were more likely to receive a competitive offer to increase their salary/benefits or standing with the organization (men = 43 percent; women = 33 percent). The men were less likely to ask for a promotion (men = 55 percent; women = 65 percent) or to seek training and professional development (men = 91 percent; women = 95 percent). On a five-point scale, the men expressed more ambition when asked if they would like to be a top communications leader in their organization (men = 3.74; women = 3.62). They were less apprehensive about moving up in the ranks (men = 2.37; women = 2.70). They were more content in their current roles (men = 3.13; women = 3.08) and less interested in being promoted to a more senior-level position (men = 4.01; women = 4.08).

Pompper and Jung (2013) provided important insights into male practitioner perceptions about gender discrimination in the field. They collected data through in-depth interviews (n = 16) and focus groups. They also conducted a survey with 428 male respondents. Their results explored the "tensions and complexities of gender identities and the gender order" (p. 540). Two-thirds of those surveyed agreed or strongly agreed that public relations is a "feminized" field. More than half agreed that men hold the highest senior-level positions in public relations. Those who saw the field as feminized agreed that the field was becoming an "old girls club" (p. 502).

There was agreement that they modified their behavior in response to working with women. They also said they felt excluded from social settings and from important decision-making. They experienced face-to-face contact avoidance by female colleagues who preferred to communicate in writing and experienced being stereotyped as "cocky, bossy, disoriented, or not detailed oriented" (p. 502).

The men in Pompper and Jung's study also perceived themselves as victims of "reverse discrimination." They found their sex to be a detriment. They believed women were more likely to hire other women and spoke of being "on guard" and "careful" because women would rather not work with men. These feelings were more pronounced among younger men "who report attacks on their masculinity" (p. 504). The men were split on whether and how women would advance to top leadership positions because of the inequality in the workplace and "old White men set in their ways will die off before more diversity arrives" (p. 503). They were concerned about feminization because they believed it hindered their aspirations to senior-level management (p. 503). This study explored the fault lines between men and women in public relations. It showed that men wished to protect their masculine identities either by "defining themselves as superior to women, by concentrating in sub-specialties" or by leaving the field all together (p. 504).

These reports on male responses to discrimination used predominantly White samples and did not explore differences by race or sexual orientation. We did not find a public relations study that focused on non-White men's perceptions of sex discrimination. However, there is a group of studies that focused on gay men's experiences in public relations (Tindall, 2013; Tindall & Waters, 2012, 2013). Based on in-depth interviews, focus group research, and telephone interviews, Tindall and Waters (2012) gave voice to the experiences of gay men who worked in public relations. The participants discussed how they played different roles and navigated a culture of heteronormativity and how power in the workplace influenced perceived identities. They reported being assigned as their organization's cultural interpreter for the gay community. One participant said, "People started asking me to explain what different symbols and icons meant to the gay community. . . . I wasn't hired to explain what it meant to be gay to everyone else, but I guess if it's helping people understand our differences, it's worth it" (p. 458). The participants reported feeling isolated in a culture of heteronormativity, self-censoring themselves from discussing their personal lives related to topics of dating, serious relationships, and health care. Participants also felt pressured into taking on extra assignments because they didn't have "a wife and children waiting for them at home" (p. 461).

Gay men fear repercussions if they reveal their orientation and thus hide it or resort to subterfuge in an effort to keep their jobs and earn a living. In Tindall and Waters's (2012) study, the participants downplayed their sexuality and conformed to expectations prescribed to them. For example, one said, "Do you think the old White men in suits want a flamboyant gay man at the decision-making table? They're fine with a gay guy working on accounts and coming up with ideas, but they want them left out of the management of the organization" (Tindall & Waters, 2012,

p. 461). Tindall (2013) described this downplay of sexuality as a necessity to get through a lavender ceiling, a barrier to promoting those in the sexual minority to power and leadership roles.

SEXUAL HARASSMENT IN THE WORKPLACE

Public relations practitioners face sexual harassment in the workplace just as frequently as any other worker in any field. This affects job satisfaction, job performance, perceptions of the workplace, and mental health. Thus, while not a unique public relations problem, it cannot be ignored as an influence on the public relations practitioner. Given the frequent organizational context for sexual harassment, the power dynamics of it, and the accepting organizational culture that may allow it, we considered placing this discussion in the organizational level of influence. Strayer (2015) reminded practitioners of their organizational role to combat sexual harassment with best practices that companies can issue through policies, reporting systems, and management letters. However, sexual harassment also occurs outside of organizational settings, the culprit is an individual, and the research on it has been at the practitioner unit of analysis. Therefore, we decided to add our discussion of sexual harassment to the practitioner level of influence.

However, public relations research has had little to say about sexual harassment in the workplace. One early survey of PRSA members published in 1998 asked practitioners to weigh in on whether they perceived sexual harassment in their organizations. Of the 678 responses as part of a larger survey, 53 percent of the men and 45 percent of the women in the sample denied that sexual harassment existed in their organizations, although 22 percent of the women and 19 percent of the men agreed that it did exist across the field (Serini et al., 1998). After 1998, the line of research on sexual harassment was all but abandoned.

Sexual harassment research findings appeared again more than ten years later, when Simorangkir (2011) reported data from in-depth interviews with thirty-five female and eighteen male Indonesian practitioners and educators. Participants viewed sexual harassment policies in Indonesia as necessary only once a crisis had happened (p. 44). Even though Simorangkir's female participants reported harassment from clients, sexual advances from journalists, and discomfort with male office conversations, she found little interest in creating programs or policies dealing with sexual harassment or how to create a harassment-free environment at work (p. 45).

There have been more recent attempts at discussing the frequency and impact of sexual harassment in public relations. Pompper (2016) gave voice to a Latina agency executive who regretted attending sexual harassment and diversity "political correctness workshops, because 'Latinos have lived a lifetime of failing to take women seriously considering it [the workshop] the biggest joke imaginable'" (p. 77). In 2018, K. Robinson reported on sexual harassment issues from qualitative interviews with fifteen female and six male practitioners in U.S. organizations across industry sectors. She sought to learn how public relations employees perceived their organization's stances toward sexual harassment and how internal communication affected their attitudes toward sexual harassment reporting systems. Among her findings was the importance of organizational culture on whether these practitioners would utilize reporting systems, citing reluctance to use systems because of a lack of knowledge on next steps given a complaint's implications: "Cultures characterized by supportiveness, stability, and social responsibility were discussed as having influenced employee's reporting feelings" (np). The Mind the Gap survey indicated that 32 percent of the women reported experiencing sexual harassment as compared to only 10 percent of the men (Dubrowski et al., 2019). Strayer (2016) reported on one study that showed that one in four women in the workplace have witnessed someone else being harassed, and 23 percent reported they have experienced sexual harassment. "With 74.6 million women in the labor force, making up roughly 47 percent of all workers, that represents more than 18.5 million women experiencing sexual harassment of some form" (Strayer, 2016, np). Gaille (2017) reported that one in ten men experienced sexual harassment in the workplace. With the #MeToo movement's impact in the United States (K. Robinson, 2018), we doubt that any practitioner is immune from sexual harassment, and we believe that the national statistics are reflective of the public relations workplace.

MICROAGGRESSIONS

Like sexual harassment, microaggressions are a concern at the practitioner level, though organizational norms and expectations can create a climate of acceptance for them. The term *microaggression* was originally used in the 1970s to refer to the subtle racist insults directed at Black Americans (Sue, 2010). Since then, microaggressions have been found to occur against any marginalized group in society. Microaggressions are defined as brief, often subtle, verbal or behavioral actions that are derogatory or insulting toward a member of a marginalized group (Sue, 2010). Whether intentional or unintentional, they are representative of racism, sexism, homophobia, and classism. They are often indicative of workplace culture and norms, though they are communicated person to person and often occur outside of any organizational setting. Applebaum et al. (2015) found that Black and Latino practitioners identified microaggressions in their work sites and perceived them to be a prevalent issue for practitioners of color.

As Sue (2010) explained, there are critics who have argued that identifying and claiming microaggressions make a "mountain of a molehill" because the comments are typically unintentional, minor, and seemingly trivial (p. 6). However, the frequency and insidiousness of microaggressions cannot be ignored. In our time, when overt racism and sexism in the workplace is viewed as politically incorrect, microaggressions have become more commonplace and more damaging. While one microaggression itself may not cause harm, their cumulative effect can have detrimental consequences. As Sue (2010) listed, microaggressions "assail the self-esteem of recipients, produce anger and frustration, deplete psychic energy, lower feelings of subjective well-being and worthiness, produce physical health problems, shorten life expectancy, and deny minority populations equal access and opportunity in education, employment, and health care" (p. 6).

While the general body of knowledge about microaggressions is growing, almost no research in the communication field can be found that focuses on microaggression experience. Most of the research that specifically analyzes microaggressions are in college settings and in psychology and counseling (Harris et al., 2019). There have been a few studies focused on the workplace and on organizational leadership that may have relevance for public relations (Constantine & Sue, 2007; Holder et al., 2015). One study, for example, identified seven microaggression themes found among White supervisors when they spoke to Black supervisees: (1) invalidating racial-cultural issues, (2) making stereotypic assumptions about clients/audience, (3) making stereotypic assumptions about supervisees, (4) reluctance to give performance feedback for fear of being viewed as racist, (5) focusing primarily on weaknesses, (6) blaming clients of color for problems stemming from oppression, and (7) offering culturally insensitive recommendations (Constantine & Sue, 2007). In another study where Black female senior-level corporate professionals were interviewed, the authors found several coping strategies, including religion, support networks, mentorship, and self-care (Holder et al., 2015).

A handful of communication studies on microaggressions have been done from an interpersonal lens, examining language use and speech acts (see, e.g., S. M. Davis, 2019; di Gennaro & Brewer, 2019). One study found that microaggressions were not only from Whites to Blacks but also from those perceived as the same racial background. West African immigrants experienced these types of negative communications from African Americans (Otusanya & Bell, 2018). Another study examined microaggression experiences of immigrant professionals in the United States. The participants reacted to these communication exchanges by rationalizing the intent, creating alternative selves, and taking blame (Shenoy-Packer, 2015). A special issue of *Southern Communication Journal* in 2019 was devoted to microaggressions. The editors wrote in their introduction that their goal was to explicitly address the role of communication in "perpetuating, identifying, processing, and responding to race-based interpersonal transgressions" (Harris & Moffitt, 2019, p. 67).

One project was found in public relations that included a discussion of microaggressions among marginalized public relations practitioners (Applebaum et al., 2015). Findings indicated that microaggressions were common occurrences among practitioners of color, especially among African Americans. Due to these and other racial biases at work, retention and job satisfaction of practitioners of color were lower. Participants in the survey told their friends to reconsider public relations as a career choice. The authors recommended education programs for employees to increase awareness of their microaggressions and double standards at work (p. 10).

EXEMPLAR INTERNATIONAL PRACTITIONER STUDIES

Across all chapters in this book, we integrated literature from various countries, though most of the scholarship on such concerns as sexism, racism, and marginalization of practitioners has been written by dominant, mainstream scholars in the United States, Great Britain, Europe, Australia, and New Zealand. Within these cultural contexts and outside of them, a few particularly relevant and critical studies have contributed significantly to our understanding of feminism in public relations at the practitioner level. We wanted to highlight some of the studies across the globe that have explained the lived experiences of female practitioners from different countries (Vanc & White, 2011). The descriptive studies described below are by no means meant to generalize or imply that this is a comprehensive view of the work that is constitutive of the practitioner-level scholarship. These studies provide important comparisons to the U.S. experience with regard to the roles and perceptions of the feminization of the field. They contextualize how public relations as an industry and profession has constructed oppressive norms that marginalize practitioners across different national cultures.

Germany

Frohlich and Peters (2007) focused on whether German female public relations practitioners perceived differences in men's and women's suitability for the technician and managerial roles of public relations practice. They theorized that female public relations practitioners constructed beliefs about their abilities because of societal expectation and self-selection or self-stereotyping. The authors asked thirteen female public relations experts if they knew of hidden threats of stereotypes that derailed opportunities for advancement. Their participants described "women's exceptional communication skills as the main factor in explaining the female majority in public relations" (p. 240) but also had led to discriminatory difficulties because of gender stereotypes. "'Naturally suited communicators' led to the stereotype of PR [public relations] bunny," a term that the authors coined to represent such participants' descriptions: PR clone, PR auntie, PR waffle or girly, and PR Barbie (p. 241). Participants recoded female exceptional skills to a marginalization of female practitioners because of physical attributes of sexism, lookism, and ageism (referencing Hon's 1995 study). The participants also perceived the PR bunny stereotype was of other female public relations practitioners rather than themselves, thus reproducing the "bunny" stereotype.

This study of German female practitioners is one of only a few published works that asked female public relations practitioners to construct their beliefs and experiences with how they think of their abilities and skills and how they judge other female public relations practitioners.

Russia

Tsetsura's article on how Russian women socially constructed public relations practice provides an additional example of female practitioners navigating the public relations field's gender beliefs. Tsetsura (2011) characterized the Russian field of public relations as one of the fastest-growing markets in Eastern Europe with agencies and clients all over the world. She situated her "ground-up research" on the perceptions of female practitioners within a transition from a female majority field that men were not interested in until the "demand for public relations services grew and men could advance quickly, make money, and build managerial careers" (p. 7). Her research question was how female public relations practitioners had constructed public relations as a "real job" or a "woman's job." She interviewed twenty-five Russian female practitioners that either were female owners or senior executives or female mid- and entry-level practitioners in the summer of 2003 with member checks in 2006 and 2007 to confirm that the results of the interviews still represented female practitioners' perceptions of the field.

Tsetsura found that Russian women constructed their professional identities in gendered ways that limited their career opportunities (p. 1). Her participants spoke of their public relations jobs as "real" because their jobs were interesting and enjoyable, exciting and challenging (p. 11). These female practitioners were proud of the income earned as their primary means of support. They distinguished between agency work as a "real" job in comparison with the status of public relations work in companies, referring to agencies as legitimizing the profession, thus making it "real." However, Tsetsura reported that her participants perceived that "outside of the agency, public relations could be dismissed as not a real job" (p. 14).

Tsetsura's participants defined a "real job" as one that would be good for a man (p. 14), suggesting they were concerned that public relations was viewed as a woman's job. On the other hand, her participants liked the flexibility of public relations agency work "because it is often considered a woman's job" (p. 17). They reported that corporate public relations could be defined as a woman's job because it was more accessible for women entering the field, whereas men went into political public relations, such as working in government or lobbying. Tsetsura contrasted her results with studies of American female practitioners' issues with work-life integration rather than concerns over positioning public relations as a real job rather than a woman's job. Her study contributes to further constituting what the public relations field is in countries where the industry is still developing (p. 18).

Chile

Mellado and Barria (2012) studied the roles of public relations practitioners in the Chilean context. They argued that as in other Latin American countries, Chilean public relations was strongly linked to journalism, "creating a hybrid and ambiguous definition between the two professions" (p. 447). The authors gathered 577 survey results from a population of 1,630 practitioners, asking them to judge the importance of thirty functions of public relations. On average, 63 percent of the participants were female, with the highest percentage of women working in the education sector (75.3 percent) and the civil society sector (69.4 percent). By contrast, 61 percent of the sample's women worked in private companies, and 52 percent worked in the public sector. The authors' statistical analysis found role differences by gender, with women giving more importance to a long-term strategic role than men. The authors concluded that "since the number of female PR professionals has dramatically increased in the last few years, surpassing the number of men, it is possible to think that they have begun to gain power and assume important roles in the planning and development of organizations' strategic vision" (p. 450). The authors also posited that the women were more "socialized to have greater proximity, planning and empathy, versus the reactive and immediate logic associated with men" (p. 450). Their data found that female public relations practitioners gave greater importance to the "active-vigilant role" identified as a role dimension in which practitioners gave importance to controlling the output and accuracy of messaging. The authors concluded that female public relations practitioners, more than men, gave more importance to this professional role of the public relations practice, "to use communication as a way of control and vigilance of their organizations" (p. 451).

India

While not in a public relations journal per se, we found an article that used a feminist lens to analyze the voices and experiences of women working in "technical and professional communication" in India. Matheson and Petersen (2020) conducted semistructured interviews with forty-nine women from three cities in India: Chennai, Hyderabad, and Pune. Their goal was to understand how female communicators perceived professional legitimacy and their success at reaching their own goals within a globalized system. According to the authors, their feminist lens allowed them to "observe how workplaces discipline and govern women's bodies amid the globalized, networked distribution of uncritically negative responses to the term feminism" (p. 377).

In particular, the authors wished to highlight forms of resistance to sexism and marginalization that the women in India may face at work. They explained that, in their analysis, they avoided defining their participants as victims of the system and instead examined how they resisted, challenged, and subverted power processes. The field of professional communication in India is predominantly female and has thus been feminized and devalued, as in the United States and European countries. Unique to Indian professional communicators, however, is the global nature of the work, where Euro-Western rules and norms are transplanted to Indian organizations "without regard for cultural norms" (p. 378).

Findings from the study supported the perspective that the participants did feel devalued and did perceive oppression in their work. The middle-class Indian women interviewed explained that they were among the first generation of their society to balance careers with motherhood, and they were expected to continue to uphold traditional Indian households while working. They also pointed out that since they are the first working generation, they had no role models of older women to help support them. However, the participants also emphasized that they pushed back against devaluation. One example was a woman who created opportunities for new research where she could control the subject matter and how the findings could be used in later communication. The authors discovered five types of tactics used by the participants to resist their organizational systems of oppression: asserting technical skill, using constructive rhetoric, patience, persistence, and politeness.

CASE: "THE FEMINIST FALLACY" AT THE PRACTITIONER LEVEL

The feminist fallacy refers to the fallacious rhetoric in media content that masks a very different reality for women in the workplace (Ferguson, 1990). This is illustrative of the feminist fallacy in the practitioner-level perspective that there are no more problems for female practitioners in public relations. Arenstein (2019), for example, interviewed female leaders who expressed that women can and should be able to overcome barriers to senior positions.

The top female public relations leaders spoke to the opportunities for women to advance in the field. Lina Baena, Group VP, Public Relations, COMM Group, said, "These are great times for women in public relations and marketing." Laurie Goldberg, Group EVP, Public Relations, Discovery and Science Channel, agreed: "In my years, I've seen a lot of progress for women in PR and communications." Caroline Guscott, director, Communications and External Relations, The Cleveland Museum of Art, also supported this by saying, "By sheer determination to share our talent and be key contributors to successful workplaces, women continue to gain a more impactful presence across all disciplines and industries" (Arenstein, 2019, np).

The "onus is on us and the industry to close the leadership gap" according to Arenstein's headline. Advice from the female leaders included the following list:

"Believe in yourself."
"Don't be the same, be better."
"Support one another."
"Stay ahead of the curve in a digital savvy world."
"If you are not at the table, I'd encourage every female leader to master the art of translating their value to the C-Suite in language it understands: Hard metrics that drive business goals."
"We as women have a responsibility to speak up and seek leadership positions. Sometimes it's you have not, because you ask not."

Some of the women profiled mentioned the responsibilities of the industry to establish standards and practices in the field of public relations, such as pay equity and equal representation. However, their advice serves to reinforce the fallacy that with "grit and determination" alone, individual female practitioners can achieve leadership roles in the public relations industry.

This is a discouraging yet cautionary case example of how feminism can be easily co-opted and designed to be against women's better selves. This case shows the invisibility of influences of class, education, race, and gender while also assuming a success story for women.

CONCLUSION: ABUNDANCE YET MYOPIA

Understanding the impact of gender on the practice of public relations is enriched with the perceptions of individual practitioners. Their reports of salary disparities, advancement issues, role enactment, and navigating the workplace have been instrumental in identifying the gendered nature of public relations practice. Indeed, the preponderance of research on gender and public relations has come from the individual level and clearly demonstrates sex discrimination and how it affects the lived experience of mainly White female practitioners.

This large body of knowledge, though, has its problems. It lacks diversity and thus offers a myopic vision of the lived experience of different practitioners; thus it furthers the marginalization of practitioners of color in particular. At the same time, the frequent use of individual-level analysis reinforces the narrative that individuals have the agency and responsibility to build their own careers. Research on individual practitioners has embedded in it what the individual should do. This message communicates that "it is all on you" to take charge of your career. This bias toward the "positive" is only natural from individuals who have invested their work lives in public relations. Finally, the interpretation of the individual level of analysis appeals because of its storytelling nature. It is compelling but limited and should be considered within the other levels of analysis we've put forward.

10

Practitioner Level

Theory-Driven Approaches to Understanding Identity

OUTLINE OF CHAPTER CONTENT

- Human capital theory
  o Occupational sex segregation
- The unidimensional approach
  o Gender = White cis woman
  o Racial identity as invisible
  o Queer theory: Multiple and variant genders
  o Critique of the unidimensional approach
- The multiples approach
  o Power studies
  o Co-constructed difference
  o Intersectionality
- Conclusion: The centrality of identity

This chapter summarizes the theorizing about why and how disparities persist at the individual level of public relations. First, human capital theory comes from the field of occupational sociology that has singled out public relations as an exemplar occupation experiencing rapid gender disparity. Of specific interest are the underlying false assumptions of equity in men and women's career investments, choices, and opportunities. Second, much of the research done in public relations derives from a unidimensional approach that focuses on a single practitioner identity; the standard White woman has come to be the prototype for the public relations worker. Third, a few public relations scholars have pushed for a multiples approach to examining constructs that affect all practitioners. This includes intersecting more than one demographic category and intersectionality, which has contributed to a richer and more realistic understanding of the lived experiences of practitioners.

HUMAN CAPITAL THEORY

L. A. Grunig et al. (2001) introduced human capital theory as an underlying assumption of early thinking about public relations gender disparities. Comments such as "it is just a matter of time before women catch up to male pay" or "but women choose to work in less well-paid areas of public relations, such as nonprofits and education" assumed that women and men had equal opportunities to invest in their education, job training, and job seeking and have equitable investment opportunities on the job to advance or obtain work continuity, such as family leave.

The theoretical basis of human capital theory focused on the variables of "demand" and "supply" in the marketplace. Workers made investments in order to negotiate the value of their work based on the scarcity of skills wanted by employers. Early theorizing on gender and public relations was that, in time, women would accrue the education, job training, and tenure on the job comparable to what men in the field had invested and would receive equal pay because of their investments.

To test the efficacy of human capital theory to explain the gender disparities of public relations, Aldoory and Toth (2002) theorized that by comparing equivalent years of experience, job interruptions, age, and education level, the practitioner pay between men and women should be equivalent. Instead, they found that holding all these variables equal, "gender still made a significant impact on salary, where men made more than women" (p. 115). Thus, human capital theory failed to support claims that gender bias didn't exist in public relation practice—that is, that it was just a matter of time.

Human capital theory has received little attention since the early research of Aldoory and Toth (2002). However, it didn't disappear from public relations literature despite its lack of utility. In the following two examples, there remains the assumption of equal gender capital investment experiences. Jin et al. (2014) mentioned human capital in theorizing that a family-friendly workplace was a possible human capital organizational resource to offer its employees (p. 70), with no mention that family-friendly would be socially constructed differently between male and female public relations employees. Human capital theory also appeared as a means of measuring the influence of gender on career success in Taiwanese public relations agencies. Chen (2011) tested human capital as a means of explaining the relationship between public relations career success and gender in Taiwan. She defined human capital as educational level, area of education, career tenure, rank in the agency, and career motivation measured in the number of hours worked a day in the previous week (p. 437).

Chen theorized that individuals who built investments in their human capital were more likely to develop professional expertise, increase productivity at work, and achieve positive rewards from organizations than those with fewer investments (p. 431). She defined objective career success as compensation and subjective career success as job satisfaction and career satisfaction. Chen measured human capital with two variables: rank in the agency and career tenure. Based on a nonprobability sample conducted in 2006 of 150 public relations agency practitioners, of whom 87.3 percent were women, Chen (2011) hypothesized that gender moderates the relationship between social capital, human capital, and career success. However, human capital as a predictor failed to make her results. Chen only reported that gender did not predict career success, concluding that "we can probably say that public relations, which is demonstrated by females in Taiwan, is a female-friendly business. The public relations practice does not seem hostile to women" (pp. 443–444). As with the Aldoory and Toth (2002) study, human capital theory as conceptualized has tempting assumptions of gender equivalences but little evidence as yet of explanatory power.

Occupational Sex Segregation

The occupational sex segregation theory is a variation on human capital theory. Reskin and Roos (1990) argued that many differences in wage and promotion based on gender were tied to specific occupations, specifically naming public relations as such an occupation. "Women seemingly crowd certain occupations bringing down their wage value because there is an oversupply of women to fill these positions" (p. 46). Their theory identified a dual-queuing process called labor queues and job queues. "Labor queues order groups of workers in terms of their attractiveness to employers; job queues rank jobs in terms of their attractiveness to workers" (L. A. Grunig et al., p. 46). Reskin and Roos theorized that employers turned labor queues into gender queues when they used such variables as educational attainment, experience, group membership, and stereotypes that prioritized the masculine because they are unable to discern who will be productive employees. Then, when women started entering an occupation, employers were concerned with male employees' negative responses to female coworkers. Employers were willing to pay higher wages to retain men, who could "vote with their feet" and seek more attractive occupations still closed to women. When employers shifted their preferences because of a dearth of male workers, then women could make inroads into male occupations.

Reskin and Roos (1990) advanced the concepts of occupational segregation by sex by looking beyond human capital theory to noneconomic factors—preferences of employers and employees for working conditions, autonomy, prejudices, stereotypes, and custom. Queuing with its focus on employers' preferences for male workers explained better why women entered formally male occupations, such as public relations, and became ghettoized within them (Reskin & Roos, 1990).

Hesmondhalgh and Baker (2015) reinforced public relations as an occupation experiencing sex segregation with a feminist standpoint analysis of how gender dynamics drive patterns of work segregation. They argued that feminists (both men and women) should be concerned with work sex segregation. Work segregation by sex is strongly linked to inequality in pay. Work segregation by sex limits the autonomy, freedom, and recognition given to women and men. When occupations are considered "male" or "female," it is more difficult for the opposite sex to enter them. Third, work segregation by sex limits an occupation's flourishing because people are inhibited from using their talents to make the occupation better. Fourth, sex segregation both draws on and contributes to social stereotypes that limits both genders' opportunities (p. 26).

THE UNIDIMENSIONAL APPROACH

The unidimensional approach refers to theoretical explanations based on one identity category, giving it primacy. The bulk of public relations scholarship on gender and public relations practice has detailed the experiences of American female public relations practitioners. This research has been instrumental in identifying salary inequities and issues of gender in the workplace, but it has been limited to American female public relations practitioners, who are the largest demographic group of those practicing public relations. However, scholarship limited to one gender has led to the primacy criticism of the "standardization" of White female practitioners' experiences (although race was never articulated) to represent all female practitioners, what Vardeman-Winter and Place (2017) called "a lily-White field" (p. 236) or what Grimes called "the invisible norm" actively upholding White privilege (2002, p. 381). With these limitations in mind, unidimensional theories that contribute to understanding gender barriers are gender identity and masculinity theories followed by a critique of the unidimensional approach.

Gender = White Cis Woman

Gender identity as an explanation of inequities contributed theory at the individual level because of its psychological and sociological dimensions. Sha (2006) highlighted the work of Cross (1987) on the individual's self-concept, made up of a combination of personal identity and group identity. Personal identity referred to the characteristics of persons as individuals with building blocks such as gender mediating how much of this variable is present across cultures of different groups of people (p. 51). Sha (2006) introduced the terms *avowed identities* and *ascribed identities* to pursue why individuals make the choices they do. Avowed gender identity referred to how much an individual identified with her gender; ascribed gender identity referred to how much identity the referent group assigned to a woman (pp. 153–159). Pompper (2016) argued for work on gender identity dimensions because of their importance in reinforcing privilege and disadvantage.

Pompper identified the negative effects of gender identity as between- and within-gender issues. For example, a Caucasian/White male participant preferred working for a male boss because men are less sensitive (p. 75). Within-gender issues was illustrated with this example: "Women shared painful outcomes of operating within patriarchal structures that pit women against women" (p. 76).

Pompper also found that social identity dimensions beyond gender, those of age and ethnicity, reinforce privilege and disadvantage. "Women across ethnic identities lamented that they are not only discriminated against by older men at the top but defied by younger men at entry levels" (p. 76). Pompper also found in her analysis ways that practitioners were navigating barriers associated with social identities in the public relations workplace: launching their own careers, staying the course, networking, enhancing skills, volunteering at high-profile charities, and doing more coursework. Men assumed an even playing field (pp. 73–80). Pompper's theoretical views of the social and interactive dimensions to gender identity underscore the importance of unpacking gender identity and the practice of public relations as a means of uncovering gender biases and oppression. Writing from a postmodern and critical theory perspective, Yeomans (2016, p. 88) quoted Alvesson and Billing (2009), who argued that "gender identity is an ongoing project of the self, prompted by social interaction and subject to flux and change," hence the term *identity work* (p. 98).

Yeomans (2016) challenged us to consider the gendered public relations performance and identity work in public relations consulting relationships. She was interested in how the demands of performing emotional labor tasks, such as face-to-face interactions, interacted with ascribed gender roles. For example, was this interaction between roles and gender identity an explanation for segregation of men into the senior high-status positions and women acting in gendered support roles (p. 89).

Drawing on empirical work to explore male and female public relations consultants in the United kingdom, Yeomans identified discursive strategies that reinforce gender segregation in the public relations firm, with "men adopting a more confrontational style and re-defining their practice as discursively masculine" (p. 104). Further, she argued that both female and male practitioners consider the professionalism project of the field to require masculine identities "in doing so to reject the 'fluffy' PR stereotype" (p. 104).

Drawing on masculinity research, Pompper and Jung (2014) sought to find a more nuanced understanding of why men in public relations perform specific identities. Their 2014 literature review considered works that identified effects on men's self-concepts when working in women-concentrated fields, such as stereotyping, marginalization, and low self-esteem, and how men bolstered their identities to help maintain workplace advantages over women. Pompper and Jung referenced the research showing men using "gender privilege for horizontal job segregation by forming male dominated sub-specialties or by riding the glass escalator surpassing women to higher levels of pay—although effects varied for men of color" (p. 498).

As with the Pompper and Jung themes, Ashcraft (2006) built a case for studying masculinities in occupational identity—gender differences in the division and hierarchy of actual labor that constitute the tasks and jobs of occupations. She argued to move beyond professional communication that favors masculine orientations, engendering difficulties for many women, such as the double-bind and glass ceilings (p. 99). Gender inequity is not merely binary—that is, men/masculinity over women/femininity—but entails dynamic hierarchies among men and women (i.e., dominant and subordinate masculinities/femininities" (p. 105). In other words, there are multiple masculinities at work in men's occupational identities as opposed to hegemonic masculinity, and these should be explored rather than neglected.

Theories of the masculine in occupational identity, such as public relations, come with two important presuppositions: (1) gender is an organizing principle of occupational identity, (2) which in turn is a vital means of reproducing the division and hierarchy of labor (Ashcraft, 2006, p. 111). But beyond these assumptions, our public relations gender scholarship has produced little that explains the performative masculine identities of men in public relations.

Racial Identity as Invisible

Public relations literature about White women does not address the race of the women. In rare instances do authors and participants center the racial privilege of being White as a public relations worker in a highly racialized professional and typically organizational space. Instead, public relations literature only ascribes "race" to practitioners who are Black, Latino, or Asian, or generalizes the experiences under the terms *practitioners of color* or *non-White*, which we have done throughout this book when generalizing groups of practitioners. When the literature does center the racial identity of practitioners, the priority concerns of the practitioners relate to their race and not their gender.

Studies by Applebaum et al. (2015) and Ford and Brown (2015) provide perceptions of practitioners who experienced racial biases and barriers to their careers. Another potential source that includes the biographies of practitioners of color, *Diverse Voices: Profiles in Leadership* (Spector & Spector, 2018), gives some indication of the importance of racial identity in the avowed and ascribed experiences shared by the public relations field's notable practitioners. We found an older study by Tindall (2009b), who interviewed Black female public relations professors, not practitioners. The issues the women faced, though, were similar to those in the practice and emerged due to what they believed was their racial identity, not their gender identity. The nine interviewed participants said that mentorship by professors of color was lacking, that their workload was more than other faculty because they often had to "represent" diversity, and that what they chose to study and discuss was perceived as always under a microscope.

In sum, identity research in public relations has begun with studies of the lived experiences of practitioner groups based on gender, race, ethnicity, and sexual orientation (Sha, 2018). These were important milestones in feminist contributions to understanding public relations practice because they moved us beyond the White woman/White man perspectives to considerations of cultural and subcultural influence on public relations practice.

Queer Theory: Multiple and Variant Genders

Queer theory enriches our understanding of the individual practitioners' sexuality and its place in understanding gender and public relations. The categories that dominate gender research on public relations practice are demographic, such as female/male, and the homogeneous heterosexual impression that such a binary gives. Rarely have practitioners been asked to self-report their own sexuality. Public relations research has assumed invisible heterosexual norms and expectations around gender, marriage, and sexuality. Heterosexuality expectations in gender research on public relations are "taken for granted" understandings so that those who construct their identities differently are marginalized into the categories of LGBTQ: lesbian, gay, bisexual, and transgender (McDonald, 2015).

While little research exists on the individual practitioner's sexuality and gender, Tindall and Waters (2013) have edited a volume on LGBTQ issues in public relations theory and research. Their contributing chapter authors address gay practitioners' observations of how their sexuality advantages and disadvantages their public relations careers (Tindall & Waters, 2012). LGBTQ and heterosexual categories were part of the study of millennial practitioners by Gallicano et al. (2012), but no public relations research has included transgender perspectives.

Queer theory is contributing to an understanding of the normative expectation of heterosexuality as natural, given, and taken for granted (Yep et al., 2003, p. 3). Queer theorists focus on institutional critiques and practices that oppress LGBTQ people but also examine "how those categories are defined, by whom and through what processes, what boundaries they set on what we know, and how and whom we desire and so on" (Gamson, 2003, p. 386). Queer theory approaches sexual identities as multiple, unstable, fluid social constructions (Gamson, 2003; Yep et al., 2003). Ciszek (2018) adds that "queer analysis is a critique of practices and discourses that produce sexual knowledge and how they structure social life, focusing on how such knowledge and practices repress differences" (p. 135).

Queer theory and feminist theory are similar in their examinations of power and oppression as the basis of social oppression. They both interrogate gender and sexuality as vectors that create social norms. Ciszek (2018) argued that queer theory answers Golombisky's (2015) call to strengthen feminist public relations theory with contributions to theory building in performativity, queer of color critique, and multiplicity. Queer theory contributes to the performativity of gender by moving beyond the binary female/male enactments of gender to the nonbinary considerations. Queer of color critique "brings together queer theory and critical race theory to engage with race, gender, and sexuality and in institutions that produce and sustain them" (Ciszek, 2018, p. 141). Both intersectionality theory and queer theory remind us of the challenge of learning from the individual public relations practitioner outside the postpositivist preferences of social science research. Both theories urge consideration of the fluidity and multiplicity of individual identities. Identities are neither fixed nor static, but they can be points in time for assessments of the conditions, contributions, and issues of public relations practice.

Critique of the Unidimensional Approach

The unidimensional approach fails to explain the complex identities of individuals by focusing on one characteristic. For example, the Applebaum et al. (2015) study of young African American and Latinx practitioners centers on the race of the participants in their responses to their work and careers in public relations. Yet over 80 percent were female. The study seemed to miss entirely that the documented perceptions were those of diverse women whose lived experiences are not so identified. Only in the implications section does gender appear as a category, labeled "the need to understand the impact of gender" (p. 49). The authors stated, "The results of this study suggest significant male-female disparities in the experiences of young professionals" (p. 49). Yet there is no report of gender disparities in the fifty-five-page report. The unifying category imposed by the written report is the one category of race/ethnicity.

A second critique is on past gender research where gender appeared as "sex," an empirical binary where the source or production of difference is of little interest. It is when difference studies look past the biological "sex" category and toward gender identity that there can be greater implications and connections between the symbolic and empirical—that is, socially constructed images of femininity and masculinity and the "real-life behaviors of women and men" (Ashcraft, 2006).

A third critique of the unidimensional site of difference in gender brings in the organizational level and moves away from individuals and their interactions in organizational settings. The organizational structures themselves formed a meta-communication about gender relations and the recognition that gender relations are deeply institutionalized. Gender difference is an organizing principle of personal identity but also an organizational system design (Ashcraft, 2006, p. 102). Ashcraft references the "tenacity of job segregation or women's work" (p. 103). Scholars have explained this tenacity of women's work that in the final consensus across the literature is that women are disadvantaged—at least economically—by their subordinate status in both horizontal and vertical integration (p. 105). Men's work has been explored for the doing of identity that men use to code masculinity, such as "professional" figures who appear as refined masculine subjects who rein in bodily excess to perform the higher-order work of the mind (p. 105). In fact, researchers have proposed that professional masculinity is vulnerable to feminization given its bureaucratic sterility, suppression of the body, self-imposed discipline, and obligatory ingratiation (Bederman, 1995; Ferguson, 1984).

As with the gender scholarship in public relations, Ashcraft (2006) warned of unidimensional studies at the individual level as "reifying a model of gender wherein differences appear as a stable, binary phenomenon" (p. 99). Ashcraft noted also that these studies were mostly examining White, middle-class professionals. Despite these flaws, Ashcraft contributed to understanding how gender affected occupations such as public relations finding favored masculine orientations, engendering difficulties for many women, and marginalizing men (p. 99).

THE MULTIPLES APPROACH

In this approach to theory building, research examines more than one category, for example, gender and race/ethnicity, in relationship to one another. An example of this is found in Pompper's (2012) study comparing the voices of female public relations practitioners of color with those of Caucasian women to characterize their working relationships with other women in her development of a theory of internal public relations. Pompper argued that power was at the heart of workplace inequities (2016, p. 81).

Power Studies

Two studies support the theory that male and female public relations practitioners understand and explain power differently as it influences how they navigate their jobs. The first study, by Aldoory et al. (2008), merged power relations and gender theory in public relations to provide a metatheory analysis of three studies that found gender differences in practitioner responses to power-influence in public relations. Using the definition of power as influence, their results indicated that the majority of the 869 participants in their studies defined influence as "having a seat at the table and a voice in decision-making" (p. 740). However, secondarily, the men adopted a masculine discourse of power as "winning" (p. 740). The men in the sample identified personal relationships and professional experience as their most valuable power sources, while the women in the sample were more likely to indicate level of reporting position and access to decision makers as their most valuable power sources. This difference suggested that female practitioners still sought access to power through higher reporting relationships, while the men may have perceived that they already had formal power in their organizations. These data also reinforced the different strategies taken by male and female practitioners—choice of influence tactics, perceptions of constraints on practice, and vocabulary of dissent—all in line with gendered ideologies and preferences for masculine means of achieving and exercising power. The men in these studies perceived that they were powerful, while the women were still in search of power.

The second study is by Lee et al. (2018), who theorized that gender differences in public relations could be equalized through social media expertise. Using the definition of power as influence, they surveyed the perceptions of 113 Public Relations Society of America members about their roles, level of decision-making ability, perceived public relations expertise, and perceived public relations accountability. They found that the female practitioners' perceptions of power increased with years of experience. The male practitioners perceived no difference in perceptions of power relations based on years of experience. In addition, the men moved away from using social media expertise, possibly equating social media with the technical rather than the managerial role of public relations. The Lee et al. (2018) study of power reinforced the theory that male practitioners see themselves as more comfortable with positions of power earlier in their careers, whereas women perceived power to come only after years of experience.

Co-constructed Difference

Ashcraft (2006) examined sites of gender difference as bringing difference into sharper focus. Her foci benefitted from research on politics, performance, and masculinity. She welcomed feminist standpoint theory as underscoring "the location of particular gendered identities and rejected the notion of gender as an isolated theoretical construct or empirical phenomenon" (p. 99). Feminist standpoint theory brought into research the political, material, temporal, and special characteristics of identity positions as well as intersections among gender, race, and class (p. 99). Ashcraft adds a turn toward poststructuralism "to conceptualize gender as an ongoing, local performance that yields agentic, yet also precarious subjectivities" (p. 99).

Ashcraft's perspective challenged researchers to look at social constructions of gender in particular interactions between men and women in the workplace and how these performances and/or challenge gender dualism (p. 99). She moved from "doing gender" to doing co-constructed gender difference in various work contexts. She welcomed the arrival of scholarship that looked at co-constructed masculinities and femininities in the context of organizing. She stated, "The doing co-constructed difference approach underscores "how we are all held accountable to gender" (p. 100).

Public relations gender research is missing an examination of co-constructed gender as, for example, in the dynamics of workplace hierarchies among men and women (i.e., dominant and subordinate masculinities/femininities). For example, in a study of an advertising firm, analysis of the complex interplay among masculinities and femininities indicated how local constructions of gender can depart from global images; it also suggests a looser connection between the domination of masculinities and the domination by men" (Ashcraft, 2006, p. 107). This portrait of the co-constructed identity work of men and women provides a theoretical avenue that could make transparent the efforts of control and resistance that move beyond the privileges of men in a feminized profession. Ashcraft challenges us to look beyond "doing gender" to doing difference in gender.

Also, we should be open to the costs of job segregation for both men and women, especially marginalized men and women who strategically utilize hegemonic masculinity (Ashcraft, 2006, p. 114). We had some hint of this in the Taiwan study in which the women were more satisfied with their careers than were the men, who were concerned with the tangible material consequences of desegregation (Chen, 2011, p. 114).

Criticism of the multiples approach centers on the comparisons made between groups, such as White women and Black women, men and women, even if they are co-constructing difference together. White privilege and masculine privilege inevitably enforce a standard by which one group is deficient in some way.

Intersectionality

Other than as ideology, intersectionality is most discussed as individual identity. Intersectionality contributes to our understanding of practitioners' salary disparities, advancement opportunities, job satisfaction, identity, and experiences with sexual harassment and microaggressions. Intersectionality is "used to explore interconnections of multiple and overlapping social identities to ensure that rich complexity is not diluted and that dimensions are not considered as separate, unrelated categories" (Pompper, 2016, p. 68). Dill and Kohlman (2012) defined intersectionality as emphasizing the interlocking effects of race, class, gender, and sexuality, highlighting the ways in which categories of identity and structures of inequality are mutually constituted and defy separation into discrete categories of analysis (p. 154). Vardeman-Winter et al. stated, "Identities are not additive and irreducible to the individual identities because they are nested within each other" (p. 392).

In what he described as "thick intersectionality," Yep (2016) offered four defining characteristics of intersectionality for use in communication analyses. First, intersectionality should struggle against coherence and premature closure by focusing on identity as "an ongoing process of *becoming* rather than *being*" (italics in original). Second, it embraces the messiness of everyday lived experiences associated with performing identity. Third, it focuses on the emotional investment of identity performance. Last, it views identity as part of cultural and sociohistorical contexts and not as an abstract social category (p. 116). By examining communication practitioners and how they make meaning of professional and personal identity, we thus must consider these characteristics that ultimately will help create "enfleshed knowledge," a term Yep and Lescure (2019) used to describe a critical process of sense making through attention to "thoughts, perceptions, affects, sensations, social practices, and bodily actions" (p. 116). In other words, public relations scholarship at the practitioner level must recognize the complex intersectional identities of individuals involved at their particular cultural and sociohistorical moment.

Vardeman-Winter et al. (2013) theorized that intersectionality in public relations is an explanation for persistent social inequality among practitioners: "Intersectionality is universal and produces simultaneous privileges and subjugations" (Vardeman-Winter et al., 2013). Conceptualizing the multiple identities that represent people's lived experiences sharpens our understanding of the gendered nature of public relations practice because we begin to account for diverse views, those practitioners who live as women but will experience different positionality in practice and how these differences influence or are influenced by public relations practice.

White American female practitioners as a group are not monolithic, so to generalize female public relations practitioners based on White women alone oversimplifies the experiences of public relations people living as women. Generalizations from one race/nationality of women do not recognize the diversity of women's experiences. In order to advance feminist thought in public relations, scholars need the lived experiences of women in the minority—not merely minority women but women whose standpoints differ because of race, age, class, sexual orientation, and so on—not only to sharpen the conceptualization of the individual practitioner but also to include their perspectives and understanding of public relations practice. Golombisky (2015) called the need for revealing the distinct experiences of female practitioners a paradox of feminist research and said that documenting the status of women's equality must critique not only gender but also the "social justice implications of interlocking oppressions and privileges for all people" (p. 390).

Public relations scholarship has taken steps to diversify the studies of the individual public relations practitioner with a stream of research on gender, race, and ethnicity, despite the inability to statistically document the numbers of public relations practitioners by gender, race, and ethnicity (Vardeman-Winter and Place, 2017, p. 330). Pompper provided important qualitative research on African American female practitioners' and Latina female practitioners' experiences (2005b, 2007, 2012). Other research on diversity of women include women by age, nationality/geography, ability/disability, and sexuality/sexual orientation or gender orientation.

Golombisky (2015) called for a theoretical adjustment of feminist theories of gender and public relations by searching out and recognizing the diverse standpoints of practitioners through the lens of intersectionality as "a method and habit to get past binary difference" (p. 389):

> Key dimensions of intersectionality are: (1) An individual's many identifications interlock so that one's experiences of gender are predicated upon one's simultaneous experiences of gender identity, race, ethnicity, economic and social class, sexuality, ability, nationality and religion, for example: (2) An individual's identifications likely include privileges and oppressions interlocking concurrently. (3) There are important differences between avowed and ascribed identifications, which trace power relations. (4) There is multifaceted interaction among (a) the individual's sense of self, (b) the individual's memberships in various social groups from household to community and citizenship (e.g., local, virtual, and imagined) and (c) the individual's systematic conscription into the social order's institutions. (5) Extant categories of identification, such as gender and

race, are constructed and provisional, and therefore do not oblige between invisible, hybrid, mixed, liminal, and interstitial positions. (6) Labels within categories of identification, such as woman/man and gay/straight, tend to default to positive/negative binaries and do not oblige between indivisible, hybrid, mixed, liminal and interstitial positions. (7) The dynamics of power may be specific and institutionally authorized and/or diffuse, productive, and thus classically hegemonic. (8) Intersectional analysis by definition engages in the work of social justice. (Golombisky, 2015, p. 403)

An intersectional approach at the individual level of analysis means that research examines multiple categories equally, questioning their interrelation rather than presuming an order of importance. In their summary of the state of workforce diversity in public relations, Vardeman-Winter and Place (2017) call for the use of intersectionality theory in understanding the diversity of the public relations field but find no "generalizable intersectional research that considers multiple identities as interlocking and indistinct" (p. 331). The single example in public relations research seems to be the use of intersectionality theory to segment publics around health decision-making. Vardeman-Winter et al. (2013), in in-depth interviews with fifty-nine women of different races/ethnicities, classes, and ages, argued that there were interlocking political, structural, and representational identities that constrained women from acting on health information. Applying intersectionality theory to women in public relations challenges us to consider multiple identities of female public relations practitioners simultaneously and whether these interlocking identities reveal different experiences in public relations practices.

CONCLUSION: THE CENTRALITY OF IDENTITY

This chapter contributed theoretical perspectives that contextualize the individual level of analysis and focus on identity. We began with a view from the occupational sociologists who examined census trends but also introduced into their work feminist standpoint theory. Public relations scholars have contributed to individual practitioner theorizing by discussing the importance of identity to explain how practitioners shape and accept public relations practice. Identity is reviewed through psychological, sociological, postmodern, and critical perspectives. Public relations scholars have examined individual public relations work through comparisons of different groups, such as women of color and White women, but primarily in looking at the experiences of women and men in public relations. Queer theory helps reveal the unspoken assumption of heteronormativity and the fluidity of sexuality that is part of the individual practitioner experience. While these comparisons are biased toward the masculine, Ashcraft (2006) argued that co-constructed difference is an important breakthrough against positioning women as deficient to the standard White male model. We welcome intersectionality for looking at individual practitioners as a means of learning what interlocking identities have meant to public relations.

Theories of individual practitioners' identity carry with them limitations. Although they should help individual practitioners understand ideologies in order to help navigate their career choices, theorizing emphasizes agency that is limited by organizational structures and societal worldviews. Theories of individual practitioners should break down built-in gender, race, and sexuality biases and view the multiple identities that construct meaning.

VI

DIALOGUE AND FUTURE DIRECTIONS

11

Dialogue with Scholars and Practitioners

Co-Constructing Meaning of the Model

OUTLINE OF CHAPTER CONTENT

- Feminism and intersectionality
  - o To identify or not to identify
  - o Contested intersectionality
- Challenges for women and people of color in public relations
  - o Racism, xenophobia, and misogyny
  - o Western, White bias in research
  - o Lack of resources
  - o Distinct experiences of women of color
- The model: Ideological level
  - o Missing pieces in public relations
  - o Defining public relations
  - o Intersectionality
- The model: Organizational level
  - o Organizational norms and expectations dictate status
  - o Organizations obstruct change
  - o Lack of organizational accountability
- The model: Professional level
  - o Professional associations not reflecting diverse reality
  - o Greater advocacy needed by professional associations
- Recommended revisions to the socio-ecological model

Part of developing our feminist, socio-ecological model includes feedback and critique by others who may voice differing perspectives about the model and its appropriateness and value. We agree with Fitch et al. (2016), who said that talking back, interrogation, and disruption should "open up public relations scholarship and practices to new ways of configuring gender relations" (p. 285). To that end, we invited women from different backgrounds and different countries, who represented a range of experience and expertise in public relations, to participate in a facilitated dialogue. The dialogue took place over two days and covered general concerns regarding feminism and public relations as well as specific content areas addressed in this book.

We started the conversation with broad, thematic questions, and then we honed in on the book's content and the socio-ecological model. For example, we asked the participants how they defined feminism and what they believed were the biggest challenges for women and people of color in public relations. We also asked about the socio-ecological model and if they recommended revisions to it. A large portion of the conversation was devoted to ideology, the model's organizational level, and problems with the profession and the professional associations.

The dialogue took place via video conferencing and was recorded. The recording was professionally transcribed for purposes of using some actual quotes in this chapter. The quotes included below have been edited for brevity and clarity. Also, some of the participants' first language was not English, so we translated some words for purposes of clearer understanding.

Participants in the dialogue included, in alphabetical order, Kate Fitch, PhD, senior lecturer, Communication and Media Studies, Monash University, Australia; Denise Hill, PhD, associate professor, School of Communications, Elon University, United States; Ángeles Moreno, PhD, professor TU, Group of Advanced Studies in Communication, Universidad Rey Juan Carlos, Spain; Katie R. Place, PhD, associate professor, Department of Strategic Communication, Quinnipiac University, United States; Candace Parrish, PhD, director and assistant professor of Strategic Communication and Public Relations online master's program, Sacred Heart University, United States; Lana Rakow, PhD, professor emerita of communication, University of North Dakota, United States; Bey-Ling Sha, PhD, professor and dean, College of Communications at California State University Fullerton, United States; Martina Topic, PhD, senior lecturer in public relations, Leeds Business School, Leeds Becket University, England; and Jennifer Vardeman, PhD, associate professor and interim director, Jack J. Valenti School of Communication, University of Houston, United States.

This chapter by no means covers the entire dialogue that took place, as it lasted for hours. We pulled from the conversations the main topics that were addressed and selected quotes that helped cover the range of perspectives shared. We also wanted to ensure all participants' voices were included in this chapter, even though some participants talked less or more than others.

FEMINISM AND INTERSECTIONALITY

To Identify or Not to Identify

Moreno: I'm proud to use this term [*feminism*] really. I call myself a feminist and in my country in recent times, there is a strong ideological attack to the term. And I think it's very important to defend the term *feminist*, because we have been working for that for a long time. We have—I think we have a debt—to women who preceded us and worked for feminism. And I understand feminist is a part of diversity, but when we go from feminist to diversity in a broad approach, I think we lose something too. I think we win something, because we are taking new views. But depending on how much the identity is challenged, who is first and what is first in the agenda? For example, in Europe, the problem of race is not even the problem of leadership. We are just in the first step, attracting people to the field, or making the field in the way that people can feel interested to be in. For me, it's important to maintain, to be researching feminism still, because we have not gotten what we wanted to achieve, so we still have to work on it.

Place: I can tell you that it is almost this assumption that public relations, gender, and feminism, it's all fixed and it's all just done. There is feedback from reviewers and others in power saying, 'oh, not another feminist [work]. We had one last year, why do we need another one, it's the same old stuff.' Trying to address these misunderstandings about, well, it's not just another gender/feminist [work], we need to have this conversation every single day of our lives, and it's really important. So, lots of pushback . . . , I can tell you, it's a tough fight.

Vardeman: My definition of feminism . . . is all about change, and it's a complicated word just because there is so much critique around feminism largely within like the intersectionality movement. I've been struggling with this because I still call myself a feminist, and I have no problem with it, but it's so incomplete. Whenever I do bring up issues like this . . . I never say I'm a woman; I always now say I'm a White woman. And I try to do that to signal to students who maybe haven't taken any classes in this stuff is that there is a race to every one of us and that White should be acknowledged . . . and not just White but educated American citizens. So, I still use *feminism*, but I definitely think it's a very complicated term, and it's almost—it's very hard for me to just use by itself now. I do believe that feminism is fundamental. It means change, an effort to change, a recognition of change toward better equality and equity. But it's very limited, and so I don't even use that term that much anymore, especially in my writing.

Rakow: When we talk about feminism, I really have to get to the place of understanding my own privilege and what it means to be a White woman. And what it means to be a White feminist trying to do work in feminism and in feminist theory, and having a platform to speak, which sets an agenda that isn't my place to set or not my place to set it for everyone. And so, I got to the point, really, of my career where I was saying I think I need other people to speak about feminism, and I think that it's actually easier to change the world than it is to change gender and race.

I came to the place of thinking that we need to really figure out what the solution is and that it has to do with enabling all of us to participate in developing the meaning systems we want, about what it means to be women, people of color, of various identities, how we want to construct a society and how we're going to function together, which is why I went into the area of public democracy participation, because to me all those voices need to have a way to participate and be part of decision-making. What I want to throw out here is the notion of White privilege, of how we figure out how this can work for all of us without some of us setting the agenda, and yet do we really need some transformational changes in how we function as a society if we're going to get there.

Topic: I like the approach that you make with this, socio-ecological approach. Because it moves away a little bit from liberal feminism. I think there is nothing wrong with liberal feminism, it's just not my feminism. I define normally as an ecofeminist, which I see as the intersection of radical and socialist feminism, so I'm more on the far left politically. That's why I've been looking also in the structural reasons and how society works, in arguing that inequality is inherent in capitalism. So, I think [this book] is more a bit on that liberal feminist side than this side of the argument, which is fine.

Place: We have to stop thinking of gender, everything, sexuality, as a binary; we have to think of it almost as this infinity. Any one of us at any point can represent any infinite representation of race, gender, sex, class, I mean on and on, and on. And so, I think once we begin to really smash some of those forms of binary thinking we can reenvision all sorts of ways we make meaning of race, class, gender, and really move forward in our organizations and our profession.

Contested Intersectionality

Vardeman: I think looking at not just public relations work, because we really haven't done a great job of understanding intersectionality, but doing a deep dive into Crenshaw, plus also different feminist scholars that don't come anywhere near communication. I think critiques of intersectionality have been really good, and what I mean by that is not just saying all the time that intersectionality is the approach . . . intersectionality is more of like a theory, and it has a lot of issues with applying it and with studying it. There is part of it that is almost always impossible to achieve.

Topic: I don't subscribe to intersectionality theory. And this is again, my personal socialization. When I first heard about the approach and the theory, I went and I read. But that actually pushed me towards starting to do more research on social class, which coincides with the fact I live in England, a class society—not formally, but in practices. So, you have working-class people who can't progress, who can't get jobs, who don't get to the best universities, who have all this inequality that follows you from early age to, well, end of your life basically. It's very difficult to achieve social mobility here. Almost it's easier for me as a foreigner than it was for the English, which is absolutely ridiculous, I think.

And then, . . . reading that intersectionality theory actually made me remember my upbringing, which was in Croatia during the time when Croatia was in Yugoslavia, so it was socialism. It was a working-class regime, basically, that enforced this equality policy that meant if you were a racist you would go to prison. And I know families who some members went into prison because they expressed racist views. . . . The lack of privilege that I see pushed me toward far left even further, so I started to advocate this class research, that we need to focus on class first, and then everything would fall into place. If we sorted out the class inequality. . . . To me, living in capitalism it's inherent that you are unequal because there is always some sort of class system in place.

Sha: In the United States right now we're having a lot of conversations about racism and racial hierarchies, but it all comes back to this notion of caste and the social hierarchies, whether it's grounded in class or whether it's grounded in race, and that ultimately it all does go back to capitalism, right, because that's just kind of the structural inequities that we live in.

To your original question about intersectionality, I don't even know what intersectionality theory is, because in the original schema set up by Crenshaw, intersectionality is an analytic frame, and I think what's happening now is it's become a substitute word for people who really are talking about diversity but want to sound hipper or more woke, and so they substitute the word *intersectionality*. It's like, oh, let me talk about intersectional identity, I'm a female and I'm an Asian, and I'm a professor, and I'm a this and I'm a that—that's not intersectionality, that's just multifaceted identity. . . . It would be great if we did it correctly, which is to use intersectionality as an analytic frame.

Vardeman: Intersectionality has been co-opted by feminists, because it was largely [originally] about race. Crenshaw talked about poor Black women, and it wasn't just about race, it was really about like Black women and the importance of centrality of Black women's experience, poor Black women's experience in America, and how problematic that is and how it shaped so much of our political, economic, and regulatory systems. It still very much has to stay grounded in what Crenshaw was originally saying, which was that it is about Black women's experience. In America, race and class are intricately tied, so it's almost inherent that she's talking about low-income Black women—and I think that's lost in the intersectionality discussion.

CHALLENGES FOR WOMEN AND PEOPLE OF COLOR IN PUBLIC RELATIONS

Racism, Xenophobia, and Misogyny

Fitch: I'm going to start by talking about the experience I've had in terms of public relations scholarship this year with [a professional conference]. . . . I think it is relevant. So, I put forward a proposal . . . and the panel was on women researching public relations in the Asia-Pacific region. My panelists included people from Indonesia, Malaysia, New Zealand, Australia, and an indigenous Australian. And the proposal was rejected, which was not particularly surprising, it's a competitive conference, but it was rejected with comments—and I'm going to read this so that I get it right: "Gender was a hot topic in the '80s of the last century. Even though the topic is on women in public relations, it will be innovative approach to include male scholars discussing this topic from men's perspective, and first of all, this proposal lacks regional and gender diversity." So, I entered into a very polite dialogue with the division [head] who defended [the decision]: "I agree with these comments, they're from three senior scholars in the field." So, I guess my concern here is what is this arch conservatism within the PR field that is not in tune.

I don't know who the [reviewers] are. Obviously, it wasn't blind peer reviewed because they knew who we were, but who are these senior scholars who think those comments are appropriate and who are not aware of the kind of very good work being done around gender and diversity within public relations.

Vardeman: I was talking with a journalism professor and he—we were talking about my scholarship, and he just basically said feminism and gender studies are just an interest group. And I think that—at the time I didn't really have like my way to explain things, you know, he was an older male scholar and I was just brand new, and I think that's largely part of the problem is that we have not made equal the idea that every single discussion that we're having in public relations is gendered and it is raced, because there's still so much Whiteness in the field both scholarly and practice. . . . I'm constantly trying to explain every aspect that we talk about in public relations, whether it's ethics or crisis or relationship management, it is gendered and it is raced, there's always an argument for that.

Moreno: I will say that even between feminist researchers, you find this problem. For example, you go to certain academic journals, and you want to publish certain kinds of approaches, and you can be rejected because you are too liberal or even don't be sent to review because you are too critical radical. I mean, we are in a certain point, where feminism is trying to open, but on the other hand, there are some feminist groups who are more powerful and have the control. For instance, White women in a certain age are trying to define and restrict the agenda of what is important for feminism. I think we have to encourage and refresh these discussion in our work.

Place: I mean there's just so many structures in place that devalue. That disempower people regardless of race, sexuality, gender. Jen and I did a publication recently about women in public relations. And a reviewer actually asked us to address why is this area of research so marginalized and why do we not do research on women. And so, we had to actually insert a section into our paper about that, and really talk about it.

Parrish: I also experienced that same thing with—I think that some subjects are just hard even with our names erased off the paper, that reviewers have biases once they read your title. And when they go into the paper, they're reviewing it with that bias as like a microscope, and I think that's one of the things we have to talk about in the field, because I've submitted a paper and got really harsh criticism. And I mean literally to the point where I had to cry to let that energy go. And then I sent it to a mentor and they were like, wow, I've never gotten these, like, questions before. But that just let me know—and then I started to talk to other people doing some similar research on race, gender, and they were like, yeah, and even some people that I consider to be really senior in different fields of research have considered just leaving.

If the area of research we are doing is not going to be published or is going to be overly critiqued, and you'd rather I do the fifty millionth social media study, then we have some areas of improvement here. If I can't get that through then I won't even make tenure, so why would I continue to chase the wheel? And I think that's one—we all understand why like blind review, peer review is important, but I think that's one of the things we need to talk about in peer review is just bias.

Hill: There are certain reviewers who are just going to keep pushing back because the way that they do it is the way that it's always been done, and they don't want to give up that power and share different types of scholarship. Power has to do with gender, race, and class, and those who have the power apparently feel like there's just not enough to go around and are not giving it up.

Western, White Bias in Research

Vardeman: [In research,] . . . when you do consider gender or race it is nothing more than a forced option on one item on the survey, so there's no interrogation whatsoever. That's the institutional and methodological linkage at how that completely continues to make identities very unexplored and undervalued, so that we have all of this amazing scholarship coming out right now about crisis in social media, but it's completely barren of any kind of consideration about how all of those areas are, in fact, extraordinarily gendered and raced.

Fitch: We've talked about race and gender, perhaps not class, . . . I think that's got a lot of currency—certainly in the UK and, to a lesser extent, in Australia—but in terms of PR scholarship I think we don't have enough voices from the global south. And I've got empirical evidence to support that, you know, I'm on a journal editorial board, and I did a quick count, it was a very quick count of all the authors that have been published between 2012 and 2019. Out of—basically, about 1 percent were from the Asia/Pacific and about 1 percent from the African region. We've got a real geographical bias in our scholarship, and I don't think we have enough empirical work coming from outside Europe, Australia, New Zealand, and America.

Lack of Resources

Vardeman: I had heard a lot of students talking about their experiences with learning about the gender pay gap. And that they were saying, you know, I've heard women don't negotiate, I've heard that they don't know . . . I didn't have the discussion, I didn't know this when I was an undergrad, so I didn't know what I didn't know. I had to learn along the way that, men that work less and maybe not as qualified are making more than me, and that doesn't seem right. I didn't know to negotiate, I didn't know to even do the research ahead of time, that I should go in with a number and ask for a number, and negotiate. I think at least for younger practitioners, that's possibly what it is, that there's a lack of undergraduate education on gender and building their skill set of confidence plus being able to market themselves. Do the research ahead of time to know what their value is, and then be able to ask for their value. I told them you're never going to make more than what you ask for. And so really having those kinds of hard, but important, discussions early on.

Topic: I would just add I agree with everything you said, and especially this comment, I didn't know what to know. I didn't know the information, I didn't know I'd have to fight for a bigger salary, that there were conditions. I think this leads me back to what I've been exploring in my research, it's cultural masculinities. We are all expected to act like men when we do things, but we are not socialized that way. . . . If you look at this gender socialization when you grow up, there is no chance for you to even build these skills when you are raised differently. So, I think it just all goes back to the society and the parents, the families, the peer networks . . . and why we don't know what we should know.

Sha: The biggest challenge that we still face is not the gendered pay gap or that people don't negotiate, but the biggest challenge is just the insidiousness of the patriarchy—and how patriarchal attitudes and expectations are embedded in our systems, in our practices.

Moreno: I fully agree. A clear manifestation of patriarchy is the big problem of work-life conflict. This is the big break for professional practitioners, individual practitioners, because we find in our empirical researches that the variable that has more weight toward restraining the practitioners—the female practitioners to advance in the profession—is that problem of work-life balance. Of course, it's based on ideological and social factors, it is one of the factors that came from the ideological even though it is seen in the organization and in the profession and finishes in the individual identity of practitioners. I think that's a big, big challenge that we have to look at closely.

Distinct Experiences of Women of Color

Hill: I'll speak first from a practitioner standpoint. The field being predominately women, I think we also need to say this is a field predominately of White women, so that's our groundwork. There is the perception that within the group of women that there is a camaraderie and a synergy, however, that does not carry over into race in organizations, and I'm speaking generally. You have a racial divide among women. That's something that's impacting the profession. One thing that has always impacted the profession and still does to this day, there's just more attention to it, especially more attention has been paid to it in the last six months, is the issue of attraction. So, attracting people of color into the profession and then retaining them, and then people of color in leadership positions, and then add women to that.

There are more women leaders, obviously, than there were twenty years ago; however, we still have issues where a lot of leadership positions—a lot of the chief communication officers—are men. Compounding that is race. And so, if a woman is going to be judged in a certain way, a person of color has those two judgments. When you show up in the boardroom as a White woman, you are not showing up as an employee, you're showing up as a White woman. A man shows up as an employee. The White woman walks in, she is a White woman. The Black woman walks in, she's a woman that's Black, so she's got to prove herself twice. So, we have to attract Black women into the profession, we have that as a problem.

And then we have a serious, serious problem of retention, very, very serious. Even once those women get in, they leave for a number of reasons, and because they've left there aren't any in leadership roles. It's something that the industry has paid a lot of attention to over the past six months, and it's starting to take some action, but previously, there was talk, and it was just talk. It was usually talk related to some sort of organizational output, such as "we're going to have a diversity training program, oh, we had six of those, we did a good job." I think there is awareness, but there was awareness before, just no action. Hopefully, this time there is awareness and action.

Parrish: I just hope that with our discussions of feminism, class and society, ideology, all of that theory, that the difference between a Black woman and a Latina woman doesn't get lost. . . . Because it is a very different experience, and when things go down or when experiences happen of racism and classism and for minority women, that's not necessarily the same for White women. My peers haven't had to move around as much as I have at universities because they hadn't experienced racism on their jobs. My peers who are White women, and they're so great, and they've all reached out and been supportive, but at the same time there's that true distinction.

Parrish: I would like to . . . emphasize the real irony in the losses of Ahmaud Arbery, Breonna Taylor, and George Floyd. Last year, I made a decision to leave [a professional association], to actually leave all PR communications associations. . . . And I was also considering leaving academia in general just because of my experience as a Black professor while trying to research African American practitioners, HBCUs [historically Black colleges and universities], and the current status of race relations in public relations. I've had people come to me and tell me my White male colleagues have whispered around that they're concerned about my scholarship and that I might not get tenure.

It's crazy how what happened in the real world like with Black people losing their lives. Even though we've been mad the whole time, like I was mad last year, I was mad the year before, but now the madness has kind of reached a new bubble. What I have slightly braced myself for is for people's gaze to leave again, and for it not to be the popular opinion again that Black lives matter, and for us to still be experiencing issues in PR and other fields, too. But PR is what we're focused on, about African Americans coming in the field and deciding to leave because they're actually being pushed out of the field.

Hill: A group of women in the United States came together and had meetings [at my old job], and at one of those meetings were talking about the challenges of not being given opportunities and the challenges of not being considered leadership material, and what comes with the feeling of being discriminated against because of your gender. I actually remember speaking up about this and I said, yes, that is true. And there is also another issue here that has to do with gender and race. I said to the leader, the woman who had brought this group together, I said, you know the way that you feel that men in this company treat you, that's how you treat Black women in this company. It was just eye opening to her, because I put it in a context that she could relate to. After that she reached out to me to have lunch and to get to know me, and to hear me, although I had been at the company before. Yes, there is a huge gender issue . . . race is a separate issue, but for Black women, it is always, always, always both issues, you are never just a woman.

THE MODEL: IDEOLOGICAL LEVEL

Missing Pieces in Public Relations

Rakow: [The ideological level] seems a good place to bring in democracy and the economy and so forth as not just kind of these ideas that seeped through down to the individual, but you used the term *structuration* in a couple of places, that's a great term for thinking through how ideology—how institutions really—have the function of structuration holding together ideology and then our practices and processes.

Defining Public Relations

Hill: I think one thing we can also look at is the U.S. definition of public relations, and the standard definition, or one of the definitions that always centers around this two-way communication and being mutually beneficial. I think we need to look at the mutually beneficial aspect, and this goes not just to corporate. If we look at mutual—being mutually beneficial, and if we take, for example, the modern feminism movement in the United States and if we look at what followed the modern civil rights movement, and if we look at some of the work that was done in the feminist movement in the 1970s. And we look at how organizations responded to that or didn't respond, and then we look at the role of the organization now and what the organization—what organizations have done to promote feminism and to promote gender equality—let's take, for example, work-life balance, it is not good. So, when you look at gender and race, I think we also need to look at it within the context of what public relations supposedly is, this mutually beneficial aspect, and say, is it really mutually beneficial?

Sha: I think the primary ideological influence on both the research and the practice is the idea that public relations should be a management function. I think it's highly problematic, because, first, yeah, we all want to be managers because we don't want to be workers, that hierarchy thing and the privileging of the higher stratum. But, also, while having a seat at the management table is a place to influence change, blah, blah, I think in reality it has really become a place where public relations is co-opted into the existing power structures for the benefit of the organization. So, that begs the question of who public relations really serves, and the ideology is that we serve organizations and publics, but maybe our ideology needs to shift to where we're really serving society. And if we shift that ideology from serving organizations to really serving society, then maybe the public relations function being in a management role isn't where that service to society really happens, because we're too co-opted and we're too bought-in to the existing power structure.

Topic: There is this problem that PR is just a strategic management function. And then from my perspective that's everything that is wrong with the world, because management is associated with masculinity, and then women inherently are not seen as always as fit for managers except if they raise masculine characteristics. So, if we would see PR more as communication—you know, if we would define it differently than just management, maybe that would also improve the position of women.

THE MODEL: ORGANIZATIONAL LEVEL

Organizational Norms and Expectations Dictate Status

Sha: What exactly constitutes organizational? So, for some people that's their immediate supervisor, for other people it's the top organizational leadership, and I think that part of the problem with a lot of our scholarship has been we have treated the concept of organization as monolithic, and it's not. I can't even answer that question because I don't know what part of the organization you're talking about.

Topic: That's really interesting, actually. And there is a big thing with the language here in England, actually, because you have this so-called BBC accent and then you have the common accent, which would be the working classes and the poor, and this upper-class kind of BBC accent. And this often also conditions your opportunities to pass an interview or to get a job or to get into certain positions. It's definitely relevant how organizations talk and who is allowed to actually present the organization.

You also have that in other European countries. I know in Croatia you have it—so, I'm from the coast and we have this stretchy accent, similar to Texas in the United States. We would not be allowed to be on TV with that accent, you'd have to change to northern. I think it's across Europe, I've heard quite some countries talking about that.

Moreno: We have a couple of insights about organizations that I want to read to you. We asked in the last Communication Monitors about the reasons that are hindering women from reaching top positions in communication and public relations. We established three levels, the macro level, professional associations and bodies, the micro level for the practitioners and the meso level, the organizational. Practitioners clearly state that the main reasons for the glass ceiling perpetuation is at the organizational level. They also think that organizations have the responsibility for changing that. A clear majority of European practitioners believe that organizations have the greatest influence to change things, more than professional associations or more than the practitioners themselves.

Organizations Obstruct Change

Hill: What often happens within organizations is they are sort of perpetuating the structures and systems that already exist in society, and we see right now where organizations have responded to social, recent social injustice, and they are trying to take a stand in addressing that whereas previously they did not. I see organizations, for the most part, not working to try to dismantle the problems structurally in society with race and gender, but instead perpetuating those. And they will work to dismantle those if there were a societal force that requires them to do so. So, if we look at movements in—if we look at social movements that involve gender and race historically, those movements have usually not been started by organizations, organizations react to those, but they are not the leaders of those movements.

Rakow: That's where I'm at in terms of what role the organizations play in actually obstructing change. And I think we have to stop thinking of organizations as givens in society and think about them as problems, and ask why do we have them. How is it they have usurped the role of the rest of us to actually be participating members of society, because they have the voice, they have the power, they have the economy, all of that. Public relations has been absolutely complicit in enabling them to do that, that's who does it for organizations, is public relations. We have to hold public relations accountable and say stop it. You are exercising power in society in a way that is silencing the rest of us and disempowering the rest of us to actually function as the motivating energy behind making decisions. We can't do it, organizations are in the way.

And I'll draw on John Dewey, who public relations in the United States draws on all the time wrongly, he never said what everybody says he said. He says essentially public relations, news, publicity, propaganda, it is all the problem, because it is in the hands of corporate actors who stand in the way between us and our government. How are we going to get organizations out of the way? In public relations scholars need to stop acting like it doesn't matter or that it's—they're givens. They're not—where did they come from? Why do we have them? Why don't we do it in different ways?

So, yeah, I can get really worked up about the fact that we have to reconfigure power, and it starts with organizations. And I think it's helpful to think of them—think of institutions and organizations and separate those apart and think about political institutions, think about economic institutions, legal, which go beyond a particular organization, who are functioning by—how do I say this—they're given the ability to do this by our legal frameworks, so we can't leave that out. . . . What kind of society do we have? What kind of a political system do we have? What kind of an economic system do we have? What about democracy? Why don't we ever talk about democracy in the field of public relations? Oh, because the power lies with the organizations that we're helping exercise power, you know, it's a catch-22.

Place: I totally agree with what you said. . . . I've got a piece coming out soon about African American women, activists, that I've been working with. And there was this myth that, hey, if we go online, on social media, our voice will be heard and we will do things to really save the community, but the current status of corporate America and social media is you've got to pay to play. And, so if you are a group of low-income African American women and you can't pay to boost your posts or pay to get seen, you're going to fall flat.

We did a lot of work of just really dealing with this myth of this all-empowering notion of advertising and PR, you have to have money, so bringing in that socioeconomic status, there's class, there's so much that intersects to really help us understand why some groups of individuals remain completely oppressed or disempowered. And going to the political institutions, too, some of the women that I interviewed said things like this, and I hadn't really lived this, but just how [the local legislative bodies] would hold their meetings at eleven o'clock at night. These White men who were in charge of the money, in charge of the decisions, they would hold them late at night so that low-income women would be home taking care of their children, and it would silence them and keep them from participating in those democratic discourses.

Lack of Organizational Accountability

Parrish: I appreciate everything all of you said on this point, and I think one additional thing that we can look at is the cosmetic and pseudo efforts of organizations and how we fail to hold them accountable. One chapter that I've published this year, we mentioned the term *cosmetic diversity*, and for whatever reason they'll hire a woman. Everyone is talking about feminism, they'll hire a woman and then we'll all look away, right, like "yay, they got a woman in there," and then we'll look away. But then they'll be having their meetings at 11:00 p.m. and they know she has kids, and they know that she can't like participate. But when our gaze is not there and when our efforts are not there to hold these organizations we build up, that's when those pseudo efforts and cosmetic efforts, they happen over and over again, we see it all the time.

I just submitted a paper today for publication about diversity-related crisis in the fashion industry, and literally seven things happened back-to-back. There was no corporate crisis learning at all, and it was all of them that said, oh, hey, we're going to hire a new diversity person, and it's been a year and we don't know exactly what they have done. That's because when they hired someone we looked away, we turned our backs and we didn't hold them accountable for the actions that we said we would.

Place: It seems like the same old kind of masculine norms, discourses, are still there. They bring individuals of color, bring women. Instead, what we have to do is just change the standards, change the system, change discourse. And I don't know, it makes me think of the research method that I love so much. We, as qualitative scholars, we co-create meaning, so why can't we all just come together and co-create new meanings and new practices for PR right now? Come on, guys, let's revamp the whole everything.

THE MODEL: PROFESSIONAL LEVEL

Professional Associations Not Reflecting Diverse Reality

Fitch: [A professional association in Australia] released its first ever diversity and inclusion report, . . . and I was so disappointed on so many levels with it. They hadn't made any engagement with academics who've written about issues of race, gender, diversity in the field, it was just paying lip service, I think, to the idea of diversity. I think it was well intentioned, but their main concern echoed precisely the dialogues that were happening in the '50s and '60s and '70s and '80s about the field threatened by a woman, particularly the feminization of PR. Actually, threatened by it being a feminized industry. I mean, this is not new, and the number-one priority was to get more men into PR, and this was the end of 2016. So, it was like who wrote this, and why didn't they speak to any of us who are actually researching this stuff and might have been able to contribute.

I think, in some ways, our professional associations [are] strong . . . struggling financially, not representative of the industry probably in Australia. . . . And they're often—so, they're underresourced. . . . I know in the last month or two they've [used] over their social media feed to promote LGBTQ issues within PR. And I thought, this is great, they're actually trying to engage in these dialogues. Like the initiatives I've seen in the UK and in the United States around race and changing the recruitment in the field, we don't see that tackling of the classed and raced nature of the industry in Australia. A lot of the research is based on the very small membership base of the industries, which, I don't think is representative of people working in communication roles in Australia at all. Some of that research was done with practitioners, who said, "Oh, no, race isn't a problem." And I would always challenge that. It's so obviously a problem, if you look at the professional association newsroom images . . . listing pictures of themselves, it's clearly a very, very White industry in Australia. So, the sort of strategizing that might go on for practitioners who are othered in some way to try and fit in, I think was something that probably should have been tackled in the academic work that was done, but there hasn't been a lot of research in the Australian context around that.

Greater Advocacy Needed by Professional Associations

Vardeman: My student did her thesis on disability, practitioners with disabilities. And one of her findings was that she looked at [a professional association] and the diversity statements—it includes gender, people of all genders and races and ethnicities and sexual identities and orientations, but not disabilities. So, that's problematic.

Rakow: It seems to me, there's this opportunity that professional associations could take. What I've seen is that they are very much concerned about an individual level of practice and their ethics are more about the individual level. . . . There is an inherent conflict of interest that you're practicing public relations from an institution that is paying you and you have no greater professional commitment beyond that.

Now, we could say, well, it's the legal model, it's the attorney model, you know, you have a client. Well, fine, but who is representing the public—nobody, which is why they don't have any power. We have the clients who have the money to afford legal representation, PR representation, and their case wins over and over and over. So, we really need the associations to step up and take on the bigger question of discourse. . . . We need PR to talk about who's not telling the truth, who's withholding. We need full publicity, meaning full access to what organizations are doing, because they ought to be subservient to the rest of us, but they're not, we're subservient to them. I wish we could get our professional associations to step up to the plate.

RECOMMENDED REVISIONS
TO THE SOCIO-ECOLOGICAL MODEL

Sha: I'm wondering if the rendering in the model is individual, professional, organizational, and societal, if that—because for me, it's seems more logical to have it be individual, organizational, professional, and then societal. Because if you take the perspective of any individual practitioner, their most immediate layer surrounding them is their employing organization, whereas the professional association is something that is a choice and also sometimes the organizations are the members in a professional association as opposed to the individuals being members. It seems, somehow, counterintuitive to me, that professional is closer to the individual before organizational.

Parrish: When I look at the model and I think of all of the things that impact us on different levels, it seems like there's a place within each level for those aspects to be considered. One thing that doesn't necessarily need to go in the model but maybe can be explored is the reasons why people lean to one area or the other, especially in dealing with intersectionality or even in dealing with the model. I know for myself, feminism takes a backseat to race just because that's—I live in America, I'm an American, and that's America's biggest problem with me, is my race. And then comes my gender, so that's kind of the tug-of-war that I experience, for someone else it might be different, it might be, I don't know, it could be their religion makes them focus on something first and then the—so, I think it might be worth mentioning, especially when you think about intersectionality, why someone—why a woman might lean more towards one area or be more active in another area versus another just based upon pertinence in life.

Moreno: I was thinking about when I reviewed the model if in the first level, the ideological level, there are other intersections such as race that are real in the practitioner level, identity and our question of identity. But they are also in the societal level. So, I was wondering if first that identity will be also in the—maybe a societal level. And my second question was if we should—should we talk about cultural level that includes ideological, core media, societal.

Rakow: I just so much appreciate how much you're trying to grapple with all of this, it's unbelievably difficult. One thing that I felt was needed is the political and the economic, to talk about democracy for other political systems and also capitalism and other economic systems. And I know you do have capitalism in a couple of places, I saw that, but I really didn't see democracy at all, and that gets back to how to push the field toward thinking about what is it that PR does, how is this going to function, why isn't it functioning.

What I see is a lot of functionalism and systems theory behind your model, when you talk about the pieces all kind of fit together and work together. . . . I'm not sure I'd agree that that's really functionalism. So, really pushing us to all think about our social theories about politics and economics and then what role organizations play, should or shouldn't play in it, I think would be a helpful addition to what a mammoth task you're already doing.

Fitch: If we were going to talk about ideology, I would have talked about neoliberalism and these ideas about individual agency and getting ahead. When I looked at the model, I was kind of musing about women and work and precarious employment indeed, that the trends in PR for women to go into consultancy work and to freelance did kind of affect corporate sectors as well. I've been thinking a lot around women and precarious employment. I guess my query was about the model, how would that kind of freelance/agency/consultancy work fit into it? I was just kind of musing when I was looking at the model about women's employment patterns generally.

Hill: One question I had about the model has to do with the individual level, and I wasn't clear if that was individual, like how somebody perceives themselves as a human being or individual in terms of being a practitioner. Because sometimes, if it's the latter, what happens is sometimes your individual perception of yourself as a practitioner gets absorbed by the organization that you work for. So, my perception of myself as a practitioner when I worked at X company was different than when I worked at a different company or at a different agency.

Vardeman: I think that we're still not studying and theorizing enough about the context within which gender and race in public relations play out. If there were some way to incorporate in the model the different context that might vary between the different levels, like what does gender during a crisis mean for an individual versus ideological ways we look at gender roles, for instance, during a particular crisis and how do media communicate different things to genders based on who's preparing. I think about like different contexts that are very important right now, like crisis, social media, disinformation, the histories of our theories, and then what I said earlier about the identities of scholars as politics in our research institutions. And I wanted to mention one thing here, and this might be a little sensitive, but I was brought up in the strategic management and excellence theory tradition, and more and more I question it every single time I teach it. I feel like it's—I think it's losing relevance even though it holds a huge piece of real estate in my mind, but I definitely don't know that it's where our field is. I have this question of, are we looking at what has been or are we suggesting what should be, like, as the way that we kind of look at the paradigms for public relations?

12

Putting the Socio-Ecological
Model to Use

OUTLINE OF CHAPTER CONTENT

- Themes across the public relations literature
- Neglected areas of study
- Strengths of the model
- Limitations of the book and model
- Responses to the dialogue and future recommendations
  o A revised model: Repositioning the levels
  o Continuing the struggle for feminism in public relations
  o Redefining the organizational level
  o Experimenting with methodology
  o Creating and promoting new narratives
  o Changing scholarly discourse by advancing feminist criticism
- Conclusion

This book proposed a socio-ecological model and attempted to achieve three goals with it. The first goal of the book was to offer a comprehensive review of the literature in public relations that has addressed feminism, gender, race, LGBTQ practitioners, and related underrepresentations and marginalizations in the field. We synthesized the scholarly territory of the 2000s on, added some historical snapshots, and used the new model to categorize the literature and view it from a feminist lens. Most of the literature included in this book derived from the United States and other Western countries and addressed women in public relations. There is a growth in work addressing gender and race, but LGBTQ issues were virtually ignored with a few exceptions. Some of the literature offered critiques on class, power, voice, and identity, and a few essays suggested intersectionality as a theoretical lens. All this literature, however, can fit into a socio-ecological model as it is a prescriptive model that helped delineate and clarify existing research and its level of influence. It displayed where influences co-construct our understanding of public relations and how it substantiates and reifies marginalization, power, and disparity.

The second goal of the book was to analyze and critique the multiple factors that have constituted meaning about women, people of color, and LGBTQ practitioners using the new model. There are ideological, societal, mediated, and organizational factors constructing norms and expectations for gender and race in public relations. These factors play out in the practice of public relations and in the research of the field. The socio-ecological model of influence was used successfully as an analytical tool to reflect on how public relations is constituted as a body of meaning that is raced, gendered, and economically bound. It explained why certain voices remain unheard and how disparities and discrimination continue. Through social, professional, and institutional norms and expectations, practitioners face oppression and marginalization and in fact reify hegemonic assumptions about identity—both personal and professional identity—that is contested.

Finally, the new model was used to facilitate a dialogue with public relations scholars and practitioners who helped evaluate and refine our thoughts about feminism for the field. To that end, this chapter summarizes some dominant themes from the literature, gaps that need to be addressed, and recommended future work. We respond here to the recommendations from our dialogue participants by introducing a revised socio-ecological model based on their feedback.

THEMES ACROSS THE PUBLIC RELATIONS LITERATURE

We noted several patterns after sifting through the public relations literature and analyzing it via the multiple socio-ecological levels. We quickly list here the most prominent themes, which summarize the details that are provided in the book:

- Most of the research published on feminism, gender, and race is at the individual practitioner level.

- *Gender* is the term used in the literature, though it is actually biological sex that is being measured and in binary category. Cis women are the primary focus of most feminist and gender research.
- Sexism is discussed as being only a women's problem. Even though we were able to find a couple of studies that asked men about their perceptions, most of the literature does not consider men gendered.
- Race and racism are discussed as being only for people of color. Parrish and Gassam (2020) argued that the White majority believes diversity is "only for minorities" (p. 178) and will lead to their loss of power and status within society. This may be a reason for the lack of discourse in the feminist literature that includes analysis of White privilege in public relations. By the same token, literature on multiculturalism and diversity does not unpack gender or class.
- The literature remains very much a social scientific paradigm where empirical studies reign.
- Public relations is viewed as an organizational activity that works to maintain organizational success and status. While a political economy of public relations bounds its practice, the scholarly discourse does not start from this vantage point.

NEGLECTED AREAS OF STUDY

From the themes, we decipher the gaps in the literature and the concepts and arguments that have essentially remained invisible and ignored. These gaps are quickly summarized below, and again, greater detail can be found in the chapters of the book:

- There are few studies about racism and the ideological and organizational complicity in sustaining racist practices. There is even less work interacting gender and race to showcase the influences on the lived experiences of women of color in public relations.
- Research on LGBTQ populations and practitioners is rare. We can identify the same few authors over and over again who publish about this. There is a lack of accountability for this invisibility as well.
- The core function of public relations is to sustain capitalism and a class system justified by organizations. This ideological constraint is missing from most public relations literature.
- Public relations scholarship is lacking discourse that moves beyond the binary examination of sex differences and that intertwines gender with race and other identities.
- Socio-ecological levels that are severely lacking in analysis and affect studies include ideological, professional, and organizational. Scholarship needs to examine and critique their influences on public relations and identity.

STRENGTHS OF THE MODEL

Our socio-ecological model is multilayered and relational. It not only shows each level that influences public relations but also exhibits the relationships between layers and signifies the amount of impact each level has. It is not one theory, nor does it reduce influence to one cause, which much of the public relations research has done. It instead complicates understandings of public relations and layers on influences that rarely get discussed in the extant literature. However, it does so through a rather simplistic visual that presents some borderlines and clarity for purposes of usefulness. Therefore, our model is at one time comprehensive and ideological but also heuristic and applicable.

The model advances a feminist perspective about feminism and does not attempt to oversimplify how feminism exists, in the field or in our framework. While we described the history of feminism with three philosophical categories—liberal, socialism/Marxist, and radical—we interconnected these stances in this book and present an eclectic version of feminism that works for us. It permits a deeper and broader look at the barriers in public relations. We struggled with the title of this book for a long time because we were creating a feminist model to address the influences on public relations and its practitioners, and we wanted to create a public relations model for feminism and feminist work in public relations. We eventually became comfortable with the esoteric awareness that, as feminists, we were doing both.

The model helps expose the location for subdisciplines, how they overlap and encroach on public relations work. Strategic communication, for example, brings together various knowledge sets and skills in communication in order to benefit organizations. With the model, we see how the extant research in strategic communication has been restricted to the organizational level and has been neglectful in its examination of ideological, cultural, and professional impacts that have marginalized practitioners. Strategic communication was created as a "more professional"—in other words, more legitimate—work space in a bid to help retain men within the practice and assist male practitioners in aspiring to elite status in the profession.

The new model highlighted influences that have rarely been exposed in public relations and have remained virtually invisible to the field, though they have been significant and powerful. For example, we highlighted organizational barriers that are driven by classism and racism. These barriers include equitable pay and advancement; inconsistent work-life integration; unfair social media labor practices; mixed mentoring practices; diminished leadership roles for women; and a dearth of transparent, scholarly dialogue about current sexual harassment and microaggressions in the workplace. Summarizing what we know about public relations scholarship with an organizational-level view revealed the dominance of functional presuppositions.

Our analysis of the professional level revealed how little scholarship has had to say about the legitimacy of a sexist, racist, classist profession. For the most part, the work in professional aspirations has remained silent about these critical oppressions that have existed, thereby defaulting to masculine, Euro-centric, and heteronormative traits that pose as valuable, such as expertise, autonomy, codes of ethics that go unaccounted for, and organization-centered roles. Fitch (2016) argued that efforts at professionalization were to stave off the increasing numbers of women entering public relations. However, our analysis of the professional level's influence on public relations and gender found that the meaning of public relations as a profession is so diffused that it has little positive or negative impact on gender issues. What our analysis of public relations as a profession identified were issues of encroachment, discrimination, problems in public relations education, and postfeminist beliefs. Some promising feminist research on the profession of public relations came from Rakow (1989), L. A. Grunig et al. (2000), and Fitch and Third (2014), who argued for the worthiness of feminist values.

Without question, the most studied level is the individual practitioner. We venture to estimate that 90 percent of all literature about gender, race, and feminism lie within this base level. The body of literature has supplied a wealth of understanding on the lived experiences of individual public relations practitioners. Several studies offered evidence of pay inequities, role disparities, the evolving meaning of "public relations manager," and leadership. Yet the real value of this knowledge is that it offered an accurate depiction of the prototypical White female practitioner; it sorely lacks an exposé of the levels of influence on the practitioner. The practitioner is affected by hegemony, capitalism, ideological norms that support racism, sexism and homophobia, gendered and raced professional constraints around legitimacy and value, and oppressive policies and practices by organizations, to name just a few of the factors that create meaning for the self about public relations and their place in it. We collected studies that gave voice to the experiences of American women and men, gay men, and multicultural entry-level and midcareer-level practitioners. These are important voices; however, they reside within the barriers of societal ideologies and the organizations that employ them.

Students, scholars, and other authors can use the new model to locate themselves and their work, establishing for themselves an awareness of their unit of analysis and focal, referent point. As Shoemaker and Reese (2014) suggested with their hierarchy of influences model, our model can be used as a guide "on how questions are posted and relationships defined for investigation" (p. 2). It also has the advantage of considering a topic from multiple angles and intersecting perspectives (p. 15). For example, these are some future research questions: How do entry-level public relations practitioners who enter professional associations learn best practices that are gendered? How do White public relations practitioners reify racist norms and expectations as they advocate communication strategies for their employers? How are organizational choices influenced by professional associations and vice versa? How do practitioners perceive microaggressions and sexual harassment to be part of their organization's culture?

LIMITATIONS OF THE BOOK AND MODEL

We believe that the act of proposing a socio-ecological model has more benefits for public relations than weaknesses, but at the same time, we acknowledge that it does have its limitations. First, we could not feasibly address all the linkages and relationships between levels that exist and that offer areas of potential and critique. We also recognize that each of the issues or topics we addressed here under one level could certainly be addressed in different ways across levels. For example, we purposely addressed mentorship narrowly as an organizational structure that could hinder or facilitate women's advancement in their field. Mentorship can and should be considered informally as well and outside boundaries of organizations. It is experienced at the individual level, and frankly, most of the research is done at the individual unit of analysis, but we wanted to bring attention to its larger influence when done within organizational settings. There are several examples of this where we had to make decisions about where to put an issue. Another example is with sexual harassment and microaggressions. We discussed at length whether they should be at the organizational level or individual level. They actually play out in both arenas. But in order to limit the book length to fewer than thousands of pages, we made some difficult choices. Here we wish to acknowledge that the overlaps and repetition of issues across levels could and should be fodder for future research. For example, we believe that it is important to have a professional layer because one's membership in a professional organization should result in taking on specific principles of practice that are presented and shared through membership activities. But one's identity as a "professional" could be very individually formed; that is, it is one's avowed identity that encourages an individual practitioner to join a professional organization. Another way of looking at the overlap is that hundreds of people working in public relations have little need for an ascribed professional identity obtained through professional associations. They might claim a personal identity of "professionalism" that is quite different from the characteristics learned in professional associations. This is an appropriate area of study and begs several research questions around these contestations.

Another limitation of the book and model is the lack of direction regarding methodology. We have not directed researchers to types of methodologies that might capture the intertwining influences on gender inequities in public relations practice. We will need researchers to advance new methods yet to have entered the mainstream of academic acceptance as acknowledged in peer review and successful grants gained. Some methods may be ethnographic, examinations of gendered discourses, or collaborations with global feminists who challenge Western perspectives. We agree with Thornton Dill and Zambrana (2009) that we need multidomain and multidisciplinary approaches to get at the roots of hegemony, power, and intransigent power structures.

An important limitation that we acknowledge is the ultimate functional approach we take with the premise of the book. Any model, including ours, is essentially yet another structure with assumptions about process and a system of inputs and outputs. We have bought in to a functional approach, as hard as we tried to be critical feminist scholars who break down systems and structures. We categorized public relations phenomena as distinct and discrete. This was a criticism brought out during the dialogue, and it is essential to expose here as a limitation to any organizing system for scholarship. To offset this criticism, we believe that this layering approach gives us the possibility of synergy and fluidity of theories. Synergies and layers should not hide divisive outcomes, biases, or faulty assumptions. The term *ecological* should embrace one-way, asymmetrical as well as synergistic relationships.

Finally, does any written work avoid the assumptions about ideology and the economic and political systems that are hegemonic to its creators? We can only be aware of what we are aware of, what we learned in this process, and what the dialogue helped to make visible for us. However, we are still limited in our ability to understand and explain, due to our worldview, background, race, and culture. We encourage feedback and criticism that will open up greater avenues to scholarship and to improving the field of public relations.

RESPONSES TO THE
DIALOGUE AND FUTURE RECOMMENDATIONS

The dialogue we engaged in with other scholars and practitioners helped form not only a revised perspective on the new model we developed but also a list of future recommendations for scholarly discourse in public relations. The dialogue moved us from our original interpretations of the field to a co-constructed meaning about what is important for the field and how to address what is important. Below we first describe the changes to the model based on the dialogue, and then we end the chapter, and the book, with recommendations for future research.

A Revised Model: Repositioning the Levels

We propose revising our socio-ecological model by repositioning the professional level and the organizational level. Our colleagues helped us see how this new depiction is more logical because individual public relations practitioners are more likely influenced by their employers, whereby they may or may not choose to join a professional association. This relocation reflects a less influential role of the profession directly on to the professional aspirations of practitioners. Our summary of the public relations scholarship on "the profession" of public relations supports this recommendation. Realistically, we found that few practitioners, according to U.S. Census data, joined professional associations. Having individual choice as to whether to join a professional association works against achieving a cohesive identity that would influence public relations standards. The seven associations that we analyzed gave varied meanings to the terms *gender* and *diversity*, sometimes including women (only), heterosexuality, or LGBTQ references. While we found some glimmers of association advocacy, they were unnoticed by our dialogue participants. Associations have not "stepped up to the plate" to question the bigger issues of the industry's discourse or how organizations play into oppressive societal relations of power. Little in our analysis of public relations associations suggests a prioritization on the public interest unless it fits the association's interests.

We had initially chosen to follow Shoemaker and Reese's hierarchy of influences model by mimicking the position of professional influence. However, we have now reassessed this and realize that this is one place where journalism is different from public relations. Journalists look first to the ethical standards of their professional association, the Society of Professional Journalists, for example, rather than to their employing media organization. The journalism field has one professional association that may have only partial membership of practicing journalists, but its ethical standards are fixed and hegemonic, whereas we do not see this in the practitioners of public relations. Moreover, today's digital mediascape allows user-generated journalism and independent journalism in ways that disconnect the individual journalist from their organization even more so than in public relations today.

Thus, our revised, final model is illustrated in Figure 12.1. The revised model shows the new positionality of the professional level being below media and the organizational level connecting more closely to practitioners. This, of course, adds a new concern, of putting more emphasis on the organizational influence directly onto the practitioner. This visual depiction of the role of organizations butts up against a desire to decouple the organizational, hegemonic assumptions about where public

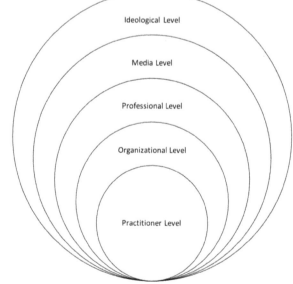

Figure 12.1. Final Socio-Ecological Model for Public Relations

relations is practiced and how it is bounded. We recognize this danger in the new model, and yet we wish to make clear here that we are not normalizing this organizational context for all public relations nor recommending it. Until today's public relations structure and scholarship radically changes, the new model depicts a reality about where most public relations is in fact enacted.

Continuing the Struggle for Feminism in Public Relations

Academic resistance to antiracist and feminist scholarship as told to us by our dialogue participants is disheartening. Their stories propel us to call it out for what it is: racist, xenophobic, and misogynistic—beliefs that have no place in scholarly spaces. These beliefs reify traditions we faced ourselves as graduate students, and to hear that they continue to exist oppresses the new scholars of the field. The field's systems of oppression insist on depicting public relations theory and practice as genderless and raceless, while White, Western, masculine norms guide the actual worldviews of what is acceptable and what is excluded. Scholarly hegemony has forced us to find small clusters of feminist colleagues who encourage us to publish wherever we can to circumvent the mainstream barriers.

Feminism and feminist theories are not your 1980s versions. Brooks's (2020) opinion is that feminism has failed all women, regardless of race, class, and politics, as evidenced by the ferociousness by which "decades' worth of progress are likely to be undone toward gender equity in America, having been hidden until the year of Covid-19; . . . the unworkableness of the status quo" in which women relied on childcare outside the home so as to return immediately to employment lest they be penalized for lapses in employment or frowned on as lacking professional dedication (p. 4). Brooks called for a new feminism for all women that embraces "more sustainable, inclusive models of women's empowerment buttressed by truly progressive policies like health care for all, paid leave for anyone caring for a baby and a universal basic income for anyone raising children in the home" (p. 4). Feminism exerts direction to revealing gendering and gender inequities in the practice of public relations. Feminism seeks diversity and inclusion goals to overcome White privilege. It champions social justice for the many whose identities have been oppressed for the benefit of one identity—the modeled patriarchal White heterosexual male. Our feminism addresses racism, sexism, classism, and ethnocentrism in a continuing struggle to make known the realities of public relations practice and the insidiousness of patriarchy that blinds it from professional aspirations and societal contributions.

Redefining the Organizational Level

We originally imagined the concept of the organization as a bounded reality for groups of people who agree to common goals. Our thinking on the organization level was sharpened from the dialogue. Our peers challenged us to consider what exactly constitutes the organizational. In our discussion, we left the impression of a monolithic concept and embraced the notion of organizations as variant. Organizations have different languages, caste systems, power discourses, and levels of sensitivity toward issues such as racism and homophobia. Public relations plays a complicit role in resisting organizational power and contesting its capitalistic assumptions that are destructive to democratic ideals. We agree that organizations should be defined by their resistance to advance social movements. If we look merely at our public relations body of knowledge, though, our viewpoint defaults to traditional. When working from the organizational-level view, we must remain skeptical of organizational lip service to social justice for the oppressed and disempowered.

Experimenting with Methodology

Give up on the oversimplifications in the name of quantitative parsimony. Deference to quantitative binaries in research should come with clear limitations about overgeneralizing to all genders based on binary comparisons. Quantitative methodologies will not fade away; they can be contextualized much more with notations of "snapshots in time," the limits of homogenizing data even if separated by gender, race, class, geography, and so forth. Always, quantitative results are better explained with accompanying qualitative study either at the front end or the back end of quantitative survey research. Future studies of "big data" will need further explanation and qualifiers in place when interpreting findings. Finally, we urge experiential ethnographies, biographies, and autobiographical methodologies—recognizing the postmodern and historical moments in which we study feminism and public relations practice.

Creating and Promoting New Narratives

Despite our efforts to counter the dominant management paradigm with which we introduced the organizational level, our peers helped call into question the functionalism our model sustains. The strategic management and excellence theory traditions overshadowed the different contexts we examined, such as in crisis communication and social media disinformation. We are mindful of the shadow cast by the management paradigm in our public relations scholarship and how our work has been tied to a liberal feminist perspective.

We are in need of new narratives. Fledgling narratives have come from Ciszek's work on activism, queer theory's contesting of sexuality, and Place's call to "revamp everything." We heard new narratives in our dialogue, especially around communication rather than management, community rather than organization, and democracy rather than oppression. These are not only in need of creation, though; we need to promote them as well. Academic and professional leaders need not be afraid of reputation problems but instead need to become vocal advocates for the new narratives that help dismantle the very power those leaders hold.

Changing Scholarly Discourse by Advancing Feminist Criticism

One way to create and promote new narratives is to challenge and change scholarly discourse. Feminist criticism can take on an intersectional approach to countering racism and sexism found in research. Our model exposed how and in what ways a female White majority in management does not equate with power and influence yet marginalizes many voices nonetheless. The stories of a few White female practitioners are too often framed with an optimism of overcoming barriers. Their stories continue to be told within the lens of masculine values and narratives, and we have not looked at the reinforcing discourses between male and female practitioners that reify gendered stereotypes.

However, we should no longer accept the invisibility of gender and race in published literature. The gendered and raced experiences of all public relations practitioners should be explored as their experiences influence how they practice public relations and are influenced by practice. We should start with capitalism, race, ethnicity, and sexual orientation as standpoints alongside gender. We have oversimplified and stereotyped gender theory to one prototype, the majority White female public relations practitioner, leaving out the masculine experience and the intertwining of masculine, feminism, raced, classed, and sexual, the marginalized, and the subaltern that are enacted in the public relations workplace. We call on researchers to ascribe race, gender, sexuality, and other markers of identity to their participants. We ask journal editors and reviewers to expose the cloaks that keep invisible dominance, hierarchy, inequity, and power. These terms might help get us past the liberal ideas that we have clung to that keep us at individualistic levels of acceptance of the hegemonic norms in public relations.

CONCLUSION

This project encourages further professional and scholarly discourse that deepens an understanding of the problems of racism, sexism, and homophobia in public relations. The model here is new and has not been used before, but we hope it will become a helpful tool for future research.

References

Aldoory, L. (2001a). Making health messages meaningful for women: Factors that influence involvement. *Journal of Public Relations Research, 13*, 163–185.

Aldoory, L. (2001b). The standard white woman in public relations. In E. L. Toth & L. Aldoory (Eds.), *The gender challenge to media: Diverse voices from the field* (pp. 105–149). Hampton Press.

Aldoory, L. (2005). A (re)conceived feminist paradigm for public relations: A case for substantial improvement. *Journal of Communication, 55*, 668–684.

Aldoory, L., & Toth, E. L. (2002). Gendered discrepancies in a gendered profession: A developing theory for public relations. *Journal of Public Relations Research, 14*, 103–126.

Aldoory, L., & Toth, E. L. (2004). Leadership and gender in public relations: Perceived effectiveness of transformational and transactional leadership styles. *Journal of Public Relations Research, 16*, 157–183.

Aldoory, L., Jiang, H., Toth, E. L., & Sha, B.-L. (2008). Is it still just a women's issue? A study of work-life balance among men and women in public relations. *Public Relations Journal, 2*(4), 1–20.

Aldoory, L., Reber, B. H., Berger, B. K., & Toth, E. L. (2009). Provocations in public relations: A study of gendered ideologies of power-influence in practice. *Journalism and Mass Communication Quarterly, 85*, 735–750.

Altheide, D. L. (1976). *Creating reality: How TV news distorts events.* Sage.

Alvesson, M., & Billing, Y. D. (2009). *Understanding gender and organizations* (2nd ed.). Sage.

Alvesson, M., & Willmott, H. (2002). Identity regulation as organizational control: Producing the appropriate individual. *Journal of Management Studies, 39*, 619–644.

American Press Institute. (2015). *Facing change: The needs, attitudes and experiences of people in media.* Accessed: https://www.americanpressinstitute.org/publications/reports/survey-research/api-journalists-survey/

Applebaum, L., Walton, E,. & Southerland, E. (2015). *An examination of factors affecting the success of underrepresented groups in the public relations profession.* Public Relations Society of American Foundation (pp. 1–55). http://static1.squarespace.com/

static/55c03b22e4b0f9e68b052dab/t/563392f5e4b0bdd8b857e59c/1446220795551/CC NY+Diversity+Study+Report+FINAL.pdf

Arenstein, S. (2019, January 16). PR News' top women in PR speak: Onus on us and industry to close leadership gap. *PR News.* https://www.prnewsonline.com/women -Top+Women+in+PR-leadership

Arthur W. Page Society. (2020a). *About Page.* https://page.org/about

Arthur W. Page Society. (2020b, May 29). *Diversity and the future of work.* https://page.org/blog/hot-topics-diversity-the-future-of-work

Arthur W. Page Society. (2020c). *Page principles.* https://page.org/site/the-page-principles

Arthur W. Page Society. (2020d). *Professional development.* https://page.org/professional -development

Ashcraft, K. L. (2006). Back to work: Sights/sites of difference in gender and organizational communication studies. In B. J. Dow & J. T. Wood (Eds.), *The Sage handbook of gender and communication* (pp. 97–122). Sage.

Association for Women in Communications. (2020). Home page. https://www.womcom.org/content.aspx?page_id=22&club_id=903060&module_id=193266

Banks, S. (1995). *Multicultural public relations.* Sage.

Banks, S. P., & Riley, P. (1993). Structuration theory as ontology for communication research. *Annals of the International Communication Association, 16,* 167–196.

Barnes, S. (2020). *COVID-19's impact on Black communications professionals.* Report by Media Frenzy Global and Black Public Relations Society of Atlanta. file:///Users/laldoory/Desktop/MFG-COVID-Black-Professionals-Report.pdf

Basar, U. (2019). Critical public relations and cultural public relations: Two theoretical exits before the bridge for the lopsided, practice-focused public relations field. *Global Media Journal: Turkish Edition, 9*(18), 1–23.

Baumgardner, J. (2011). *F'em: Goo goo, gaga, and some thoughts on balls.* Seal Press.

Berger, B., Meng, J., & Hayman (2017). Gender differences deepen, leader-employee gap remains and grades slide. *Plank Center Report Card 2017 on PR Leaders.* http://plankcenter.ua.edu/resources/research/research-library/report-card/

Bond, M. A., & Pyle, J. L. (1998). The ecology of diversity in organizational settings: Lessons from a case study. *Human Relations, 51,* 3–38.

Botan, C. H., & Taylor, M. (2004). Public relations: State of the field. *Journal of Communication, 54,* 645–661.

Boulton, C. (2016). Black identities inside advertising: Race, inequality, code switching, and stereotype threat. *Howard Journal of Communication, 27,* 130–144.

Bourne, C. (2019). The public relations profession as discursive boundary work. *Public Relations Review, 45,* 1–8.

Brenner, J. (2014). Socialist-feminism in the 21st century. *Against the Current, 39,* 20–23.

Bridgen, L. (2011). Emotional labour and the pursuit of the personal brand: Public relations practitioners' use of social media. *Journal of Media Practice, 12,* 61–76.

Broadfoot, K. J., & Munshi, D. (2007). Diverse voices and alternative rationalities. *Management Communication Quarterly, 21,* 249–267.

Broadfoot, K. J., & Munshi, D. (2015). Agency as a process of translation. *Management Communication Quarterly, 29,* 469–474.

Bronfenbrenner, U. (1979). *The ecology of human development: Experiments by nature and by design.* Harvard University Press.

Bronstein, C., & Fitzpatrick, K. (2015). Preparing tomorrow's leaders: Integrating leadership development in journalism and mass communication education. *Journalism and Mass Communication Educator, 70,* 75–88.

Brooks, K. (2020, December 23). Feminism has failed women. *New York Times.* https://www.nytimes.com/2020/12/23/opinion/coronavirus-women-feminism.html

Broom, G. M., & Dozer, D. M. (1982). A comparison of sex roles in public relations. *Public Relations Review, 8,* 17–22.

Broom, G. M. (1986). Advancement for public relations role models. *Public Relations Review, 12,* 37–56.

Broom, G. M. (2009). *Cutlip and Center's effective public relations* (10th ed.). Prentice Hall.

Broom, G. M., & Smith, G. D. (1978, August). *Toward an understanding of public relations roles: An empirical test of five role models' impact on clients.* Paper presented at Public Relations Division, Association for Education in Journalism and Mass Communication, Memphis, TN.

Broom, G. M., & Smith, G. D. (1979). Testing the practitioner's impact on clients. *Public Relations Review, 5,* 47–49.

Brown, C. F. (2020, May). An advocate for diverse professionals. *PRSA Strategies and Tactics, 3*(5), 4.

Bruning, S. D., & Ledingham, J. A. (1999). Relationships between organizations and publics: Development of a multi-dimensional organization-public relationship scale. *Public Relations Review, 25,* 157–170.

Burrell, G., & Morgan, G. (1979). *Sociological paradigms and organisational analysis.* Burlington, VT: Ashgate.

Butler, J. (1990). *Gender trouble: Feminism and the subversion of identity.* Routledge.

Byerly, C. (2006). Questioning media access: Analysis of FCC women and minority ownership data. *Does Bigger Media Equal Better Media?* Social Science Research Council and Benton Foundation. https://www.howardmediagroup.org/sites/default/files/Does_Bigger_Media_Equal_Better_Media.pdf

Byerly, C. (2011). Behind the scenes of women's broadcast ownership. *Howard Journal of Communications, 29,* 24–42.

Byerly, C. (2013). Factors affecting the status of women journalists: A structural analysis. In C. Byerly (Ed.), *Palgrave international handbook on women and journalism* (pp. 11–23). Palgrave Macmillan.

Byerly, C. (2018). Feminism, theory, and communication: Progress, debates, and challenges ahead. In D. Harp, J. Loke, & I. Bachmann (Eds.), *Feminist approaches to media theory and research* (pp. 19–35). Palgrave Macmillan.

Byerly, C., & Ross, K. (2006). *Women and media: A critical introduction.* Blackwell.

Caldera, A. (2020). Challenging capitalistic exploitation: A Black feminist/womanist commentary on work and self-care. *Feminist Studies, 46,* 707–716.

Carragee, K. M., & Roefs, W. (2004). The neglect of power in recent framing research. *Journal of Communication, 54,* 214–233.

Center for the Study of Social Policy. (2019, September). *Key equity terms and concepts: A glossary for shared understanding.* https://cssp.org/wp-content/uploads/2019/09/Key-Equity-Terms-and-Concepts-vol1.pdf

Centers for Disease Control and Prevention. (2014). *The social ecological model: A framework for prevention.* https://www.cdc.gov/violenceprevention/publichealthissue/social-ecologicalmodel.html?CDC_AA_refVal=https%3A%2F%2Fwww.cdc.gov%2Fviolenceprevention%2Foverview%2Fsocial-ecologicalmodel.html

Champlin, S., & Li, M. (2020). Communicating support in Pride collection advertising: The impact of gender expression and contribution amount. *International Journal of Strategic Communication, 14*, 160–178.

Chen, X., Hung-Baesecke, C-J. F., & Chen, Y-R. R. (2020). Constructing positive public relations in China: Integrating public relations dimensions, dialogic theory of public relations and the Chinese philosophical thinking of Yin and Yang. *Public Relations Review, 46*, np.

Chen, Y-N. K. (2011). Social capital, human capital, and career success in public relations in Taiwan. *Chinese Journal of Communication, 4* (4), 430–439.

Choi, J. (2012). A content analysis of BP's press releases dealing with crisis. *Public Relations Review, 38*, 422–429.

Ciszek, E. L. (2015). Bridging the gap: Mapping the relationship between activism and public relations. *Public Relations Review, 41*, 447–455.

Ciszek, E. L. (2017a). Activist strategic communication for social change: A transnational case study of lesbian, gay, bisexual, and transgender activism. *Journal of Communication, 67*, 702–718.

Ciszek, E. L. (2017b). Advocacy communication and social identity: An exploration of social media outreach. *Journal of Homosexuality, 64*, 1993–2010.

Ciszek, E. (2018). Queering PR: Directions in theory and research for public relation scholarship. *Journal of Public Relations Research, 30*, 134–145.

Ciszek, E. (2020). "We are people, not transactions": Trust is a precursor to dialogue with LGBTQ publics. *Public Relations Review, 46*, 1–7.

Ciszek, E. L., & Pounders, K. (2020). "The bones are the same": An exploratory analysis of authentic communication with LGBTQ publics. *Journal of Communication Management, 24*, 103–117.

Cline, C. G., Toth, E. L., Turk, J. V., Walters, L. M., Johnson, N., & Smith, H. (1986). *The velvet ghetto: The impact of the increasing percentage of women in public relations and business communication.* IABC Foundation.

College Board. (2016). *Total group profile report: 2016 college-bound seniors.* https://reports. collegeboard.org/pdf/total-group-2016.pdf

Collins, P. H. (2000). *Black feminist thought.* Routledge.

Constantine, M. G., & Sue, D. W. (2007). Perceptions of racial microaggressions among black supervisees in cross-racial dyads. *Journal of Counseling Psychology, 54*, 142–153.

Coombs, W. T. (2001). Interpersonal communication and public relations. In R. L. Heath (Ed.), *The handbook of public relations* (pp. 105–114). Sage.

Coombs, W. T., & Holladay, S. J. (2012). Fringe public relations: How activism moves critical PR toward the mainstream. *Public Relations Review, 38*, 880–887.

Coombs, W. T., Holladay, S. J., Hasenauer, G., & Signitzer, B. (1994). A comparative analysis of international public relations: Identification and interpretation of similarities and differences between professionalization in Austria, Norway and the United States. *Journal of Public Relations Research, 6*, 23–29.

Cottle, S. (1998). Making ethnic programmes include the BBC: Professional pragmatic and cultural containment. *Media, Culture and Society, 20*, 295–317.

Commission on Public Relations Education. (2017). *Fast forward: Foundations + Future State. Educators + Practitioners.* www.CommissionPRed.org

Commission on Public Relations Education. (2020). *About the commission.* http://www.com missionpred.org/about-the-commission/

Creedon, P. J. (1993). Acknowledging the infrastructure: A critical feminist analysis of systems theory. *Public Relations Review, 19*, 157–166.

Creedon, P. J., & Cramer, J. (2007). *Women in mass communication* (3rd ed.). Sage.

Crenshaw, K. (1989). Demarginalizing the intersection of race and sex: A black feminist critique of antidiscrimination doctrine, feminist theory and antiracist politics. *University of Chicago Legal Forum, 1989* (1, Article 8). https://chicagounbound.uchicago.edu/uclf/vol1989/iss1/8/

Crenshaw, K. (1991). Mapping the margins: Intersectionality, identity politics, and violence against women of color. *Stanford Law Review, 43*, 1241–1299.

Cross, W. E., Jr. (1987). A two-factor theory of Black identity: Implications for the study of identity development in minority children. In J. S. Phinney & M. J. Rotheram (Eds.), *Children's ethnic socialization* (pp. 117–133). Newbury Park, CA: Sage.

Crossley, A. D. (2017). *Finding feminism: Millennial activists and the unfinished gender revolution.* New York University Press.

Cutlip, S., & Center, A. (1958). *Effective public relations.* Prentice Hall.

Cutlip, S., Center, A., & Broom, G. (1985). *Effective public relations.* Prentice Hall.

Dalton, H. L. (1995). *Racial healing: Confronting the fear between blacks and whites.* Doubleday.

Daniels, C. (2017). A tale of two narratives: *The PRWeek US 2017 Salary Survey.* https://www.prweek.com/article/1425769/tale-two-narratives-prweek-us-2017-salary-survey

Davies, C., & Hobbs, M. (2020). Irresistible possibilities: Examining the use and consequences of social media influencers for contemporary public relations. *Public Relations Review, 46*, np.

Davis, C. (1996). The sociology of the professions and the profession of gender. *Sociology, 30*, 661–678.

Davis, S. M. (2019). When sistahs support sistahs: A process of supportive communication about racial microaggressions among Black women. *Communication Monographs, 86*, 133–157.

Daymon, C., & Demetrious, K. (Eds.). (2016). *Gender and public relations: Critical perspectives on voice, image and identity.* Routledge.

Delgado, R., & Stefancic, J. (2001). *Critical race theory: An introduction.* New York University Press.

Demirhan, K., & Cakir-Demirhan, D. (2015). Gender and politics: Patriarchal discourse on social media. *Public Relations Review, 41*, 308–310.

Deuze, M. (2006). Participation, remediation, bricolage: Considering principal components of a digital culture. *The Information Society, 22*, 63–75.

Deuze, M. (2011). Media life. *Media, Culture and Society, 33*, 137–148.

Di Gennaro, K., & Brewer, M. (2019). Microaggressions as speech acts: Using pragmatics to define and develop a research agenda for microaggressions. *Applied Linguistics Review, 10*, 725–744.

Dill, B. T., & Kohlman, M. H. (2012). Intersectionality: A transformative paradigm in feminist theory and social justice. In S. Hesse-Biber (Ed.), *Handbook of feminist research: Theory and praxis* (2nd ed., pp. 154–174). Sage.

Dodd, M. D. (2016). Intangible resource management: Social capital theory development for public relations. *Journal of Communication Management, 20*, 289–311.

Dozier, D. M. (1988). Breaking public relations' glass ceiling. *Public Relations Review, 14*(3), 6–14.

Dozier, D. M., & Broom, G. M. (2006). The centrality of practitioner roles to public relations theory. In C. H. Botan & V. Hazelton (Eds.), *Public relations theory II* (pp. 137–170). Lawrence Erlbaum Associates.

Dozier, D. M., Place, K., Vardeman, J., Sisco, H. F., & Sha, B-L. (Winter, 2019). A longitu-dinal analysis of the gender income gap in public relations in the U.S. 1979–2014. *Media Report to Women, 47*(1), 12–19.

Dozier, D. M., Sha, B-L., & Shen, H. (2013). Why women earn less than men: The cost of gender discrimination in U.S. public relations. *Public Relations Journal, 7*, 1–15.

Dubrowski, M., McCorkindale, T., & Rickert, R. (2019). *Mind the gap: Women's leadership in public relations.* https://instituteforpr.org/mind-the-gap-womens-leadership-in-public-relations/

Dyer, R. (1997). The matter of whiteness. Reprinted in P. S. Rothenberg (Ed.), *White privilege* (2nd ed.; pp. 9–14). Worth Publishers.

Edwards, L. (2008). PR practitioners' cultural capital: An initial study and implications for research and practice. *Public Relations Review, 34*, 367–372.

Edwards, L. (2009). Symbolic power and public relations practice: Locating individual practi-tioners in their social context. *Journal of Public Relations Research, 21*, 251–272.

Edwards, L. (2010). "Race" in public relations. In R. L. Heath (Ed.), *The Sage handbook of public relations* (2nd ed.; pp. 205–221). Sage.

Edwards, L. (2013). Institutional racism in culture production: The case of public relations. *Popular Communication, 11*, 242–256.

Edwards, L. (2014). Discourse, credentialism and occupational closure in the communication industries: The case of public relations in the UK. *European Journal of Communication, 29*, 319–334.

Edwards, L. (2018a). Public relations, voice and recognition: A case study. *Media, Culture and Society, 40*, 317–332.

Edwards, L. (2018b). *Understanding public relations: Theory, culture and society.* Sage.

Edwards, L., & Hodges, C. E. M. (2011). *Public relations, society and culture: Theoretical and empirical explorations.* Routledge.

Ehling, W. P. (1992). Estimating the value of public relations and communication to an orga-nization. In J. E. Grunig (Ed.), *Excellence in public relations and communication management* (pp. 617–638). Routledge.

Elliott, P. (1972). *The sociology of the professions.* Herder & Herder.

Entman, R. M. (1993). Framing: Toward clarification of a fractured paradigm. *Journal of Communication, 43*, 51–58.

Evetts, J. (2011). A new professionalism? Challenges and opportunities. *Current Sociology, 59*, 406–422.

Ferguson, M. A. (1984, August). *Building theory in public relations: Interorganizational rela-tionships.* Presented at the Association for Education in Journalism and Mass Communica-tion, Gainesville, FL.

Ferguson, M. A. (1990). Images of power and the feminist fallacy. *Critical Studies in Mass Communication, 7*, 215–230.

Figueroa, M. E. (2017). A theory-based sociological model of communication and behavior for the containment of the Ebola epidemic in Liberia. *Journal of Health Communication, 22*, 5–9.

Fitch, K. (2015). Promoting the Vampire Rights Amendment: Public relations, post feminism and True Blood. *Public Relations Review, 41*, 607–614.

Fitch, K. (2016). Feminism and public relations. In J. L'Etang, D. McKie, N. Snow, & J. Xifra (Eds.), *The Routledge handbook of critical public relations* (pp. 54–63). Routledge.

Fitch, K. (2020). The PR body: Aesthetic labor in public relations work. *Media Report to Women, 48*, 5–22.

Fitch, K., & Third, A. (2010). Working girls: Revisiting the gendering of public relations. *PRism*, *7*(4), 1–13.

Fitch, K., & Third, A. (2014). Ex-journos and promo girls: Feminization and professionalization in the Australian public relations industry. In C. Daymon & K. Demetrious (Eds.), *Gender and public relations: Critical perspectives on voice, image and identity* (pp. 247–268). London.

Fitch, K., James, M., & Motion, J. (2016). Talking back: Reflecting on feminism, public relations and research. *Public Relations Review*, *42*, 279–287.

Ford, R., & Brown, C. (2015). State of the PR industry: Defining and delivering on the promise of diversity. White paper of the National Black Public Relations Society, Inc. https://instituteforpr.org/wp-content/uploads/NBPRS-State-of-the-PR-Industry-White-Paper.pdf

Frohlich, R., & Peters, S. B. (2007). PR bunnies caught in the agency ghetto? Gender stereotypes, organizational factors and women's careers in PR agencies. *Journal of Public Relations Research*, *19*, 229–254.

Future Directions of Strategic Communication. (2017, May 25). Pre-conference program at International Communication Association, San Diego, CA.

Gaille, B. (2017, May 20). 23 statistics on sexual harassment in the workplace. https://brandon gaille.com/23-statistics-on-sexual-harassment-the-workplace/

Gallicano, T. D. (2013). Internal conflict management and decision making: A qualitative study of a multitiered grassroots advocacy organization. *Journal of Public Relations Research*, *25*, 368–388.

Gallicano, T. D., Curtin, P., & Matthews, K. (2012). I love what I do, but . . . A relationship management survey of millennial generation public relations agency employees. *Journal of Public Relations Research*, *24*, 222–242.

Gamson, J. (2003). Reflections on queer theory and communication. *Journal of Homosexuality*, *45*, 385–389.

Gandy, O. (1980). Information in health: Subsidised news. *Media, Culture and Society*, *2*, 103–115.

Gandy, O. H. (1982). *Beyond agenda setting: Information subsidies and public policy*. Ablex.

Gans, H. J. (1979). *Deciding what's news: A study of CBS Evening News, NBC Nightly News, Newsweek, and Time*. Northwestern University Press.

Gatta, M. (2009). Developing policy to address the lived experiences of working mothers. In B. Thornton Dill & R. E. Zambrana (Eds.), *Emerging intersections: Race, class, and gender in theory, policy, and practice* (pp. 101–122). Routledge.

Gesualdi, M. (2019). Revisiting the relationship between public relations and marketing: Encroachment and social media. *Public Relations Review*, *45*, 372–382.

Giddens, A. (1984). *The constitution of society: Outline of the theory of structuration*. Cambridge, UK: Polity Press.

Gilkerson, N., Anderson, B., & Swenson, R. (2018). Work-life balance 2.0? An examination of social media management practice and agency employee coping strategies in a 24/7 social world. *Public Relations Journal*, *12*(2). https://epublications.marquette.edu/cgi/viewcontent.cgi?article=1526&context=comm_fac

Gitlin, T. (1980). *The whole world is watching: Mass media in the making and unmaking of the new left*. University of California Press.

GLAAD. (2016, October). *GLAAD media reference guide* (10th ed.). https://www.glaad.org/sites/default/files/GLAAD-Media-Reference-Guide-Tenth-Edition.pdf

Global Alliance. (2020). Home page. https://www.globalalliancepr.org/who-we-are

Goffman, E. (1974). *Frame analysis: An essay on the organization of experience.* Northeastern University Press.

Golombisky, K. (2015). Renewing the commitments of feminist public relations theory from Velvet Ghetto to social justice. *Journal of Public Relations Research, 27,* 389–415.

Gordon, C. (2002, August–September). Communicators: Forty-six years of shaping the corporate world. *Communication World,* 31–33.

Gramsci, A. (1971). *Prison notebooks, Volume 1.* Columbia University Press.

Gregory, A., & Halff, G. (2013). Divided we stand: Defying hegemony in global public relations theory and practice? *Public Relations Review, 39,* 417–425.

Grimes, D. S. (2002). Challenging the status quo? Whiteness in the diversity management literature. *Management Communication Quarterly, 15,* 381–409.

Grunig, J. E. (1984). Organizations, environments and models of public relations. *Public Relations Research and Education, 1,* 6–29.

Grunig, J. E. (1992). An overview of the book. In J. E. Grunig (Ed.), *Excellence in public relations and communication management* (pp. 1–28). Lawrence Erlbaum Associates.

Grunig, J. E. (2006). Furnishing the edifice: Ongoing research on public relations as a strategic management function. *Journal of Public Relations Research, 18,* 151–176.

Grunig, J. E., & Grunig, L. A. (2000). Public relations in strategic management and strategic management of public relations: Theory and evidence from the IABC Excellence project. *Journalism Studies, 1,* 303–321.

Grunig, J. E., & Hunt, T. (1984). *Managing public relations.* Holt, Rinehart & Winston.

Grunig, L. A. (1991). Court-order relief from sex discrimination in the foreign service implications for women working in development communication. *Public Relations Research Annual, 3*(1-4), 85–113.

Grunig, L. A. (2005). *Communicating for diversity.* Proceedings of the Second World Public Relations Festival. Global Alliance for Public Relations and Communication Management and Federazione Reiazoni Pubbliche Italiana (FERPI). Trieste, Italy.

Grunig, L. A., Grunig, J. E., & Dozier, D. M. (2002). *Excellent public relations and effective organizations: A study of communication management in three countries.* Lawrence Erlbaum Associates.

Grunig, L. A., Toth, E. L., & Hon, L. (2000). Feminist values in public relations. *Journal of Public Relations Research, 12,* 49–68.

Grunig, L. A., Toth, E. L., & Hon, L. (2001). *Women in public relations: How gender influences practice.* Guilford Press.

Hallahan, K. (1999). Seven models of framing: Implications for public relations. *Journal of Public Relations Research, 11,* 205–242.

Hallahan, K., Holtzhausen, D. R., van Ruler, B., Vercic, D., & Sriramesh, K. (2007). Defining strategic communication. *International Journal of Strategic Communication, 1,* 3–35.

Halperin, D. M. (2003). The normalization of queer theory. *Journal of Homosexuality, 45,* 339–343.

Hardin, M., & Whiteside, E. (2010). Framing through a feminist lens. In P. D'Angelo & J. A. Kuypers (Eds.), *Doing news framing analysis: Empirical and theoretical perspectives* (pp. 312–330). Routledge.

Harris, T. M., & Moffitt, K. (2019). Centering communication in our understanding of microaggressions, race, and otherness in academe and beyond. *Southern Communication Journal, 84,* 67–71.

Harris, T. M., Janovec, A., Murray, S., Gubbala, S., & Robinson, A. (2019). Communicating racism: A study of racial microaggressions in a southern university and the local community. *Southern Communication Journal, 84*, 72–84.

Harter, L. M., Kirby, E. L., & Gerbensky-Kerber, A. (2010). Enacting and disrupting the single-sex mandate of the YWCA: A post-structural feminist analysis of separatism as an organizing strategy. *Women & Language, 33*, 9–28.

Hayden, S. (2010). Lessons from the Baby Boon: "Family-friendly" policies and the ethics of justice and care. *Women's Studies in Communication, 33*, 119–137.

Heath, R. L. (1992). The wrangle in the marketplace: A rhetorical perspective of public relations. In E. L. Toth & R. L. Heath (Eds.), *Rhetorical and critical approaches to public relations* (pp. 17–36). Hillsdale, NJ: Lawrence Erlbaum Associates.

Heath, R. L. (Ed.). (2001). *The handbook of public relations*. Sage.

Heath, R. L. (2006). Onward into more fog: Thoughts on public relations research directions. *Journal of Public Relations Research, 18*, 93–114.

Heath, R. L. (2009). The rhetorical tradition. In R. L. Heath, E. L. Toth, & D. Waymer (Eds.), *Rhetorical and critical approaches to public relations II* (pp. 17–47). Routledge.

Heath, R. L., McKie, D., Munshi, D., & Xifra, J. (2019). Public relations critical intersections special section introduction. *Public Relations Review, 45*, np.

Heath, R. L., Toth, E. L., & Waymer, D. (Eds.). (2009). *Rhetorical and critical approaches to public relations II*. Routledge.

Heath, R. L., Waymer, D., & Palenchar, M. J. (2013). Is the universe of democracy, rhetoric, and public relations whole cloth or three separate galaxies? *Public Relations Review, 39*, 271–279.

Herz, M., & Johansson, T. (2015). The normativity of the concept of heteronormativity. *Journal of Homosexuality, 62*, 1009–1020.

Hesmondhalgh, D., & Baker, S. (2015). Sex, gender and work segregation in the cultural industries. *The Sociological Review, 63(S1)*, 23–36.

Hispanic Public Relations Association. (2020). *About us*. https://hpra-usa.org/about-us/

Hobbs, M. J. (2020). Conflict ecology: Examining the strategies and rationales of lobbyists in the mining and energy industries of Australia. *Public Relations Review, 46*.

Hoffman, J., & Hamidati, A. (2016). Beyond professional snail races: Contextualizing corporate communication in Indonesia. *Journal of Public Relations Research, 28*, 51–66.

Hoffman, J., Rottger, U., & Jarren, O. (2007). Structural segregation and openness: Balanced professionalism for public relations. *Studies in Communication Sciences, 7*, 125–146.

Hofstede, G. (2001). *Culture's consequences: Comparing values, behaviors, institutions, and organizations across nations* (2nd ed.). Sage.

Holder, A. M. B., Jackson, M. A., & Ponterotto, J. G. (2015). Racial microaggression experiences and coping strategies of Black women in corporate leadership. *Qualitative Psychology, 2*, 164–180.

Holtzhausen, D. R. (2002). Towards a postmodern research agenda for public relations. *Public Relations Review, 28*, 251–264.

Holtzhausen, D. R. (2015). The unethical consequences of professional communication codes of ethics: A postmodern analysis of ethical decision-making in communication practice. *Public Relations Review, 41*, 769–776.

Holtzhausen, D. R. (2016). Datafication: Threat or opportunity for communication in the public sphere? *Journal of Communication Management, 20*, 21–36.

Holtzhausen, D. R., & Voto, R. (2002). Resistance from the margins: The postmodern public relations practitioner as organizational activist. *Journal of Public Relations Research, 14*, 57–84.

Holtzhausen, D. R., & Zerfass, A. (2013). Strategic communication—pillars and perspectives on an alternative paradigm. In A. Zerfass, L. Rademacher, & S. Wehmeir (Eds.), *Organisationscommunikation und public relations, Forschungsparadigmen und neue perspektivenI* (pp. 73–94). Springer VS. Reprinted in Sriramesh, K., Zerfass, A., & Kim, J-N. (Eds.), *Current trends and emerging topics in public relations and communication management*. Routledge.

Holtzhausen, D. R., & Zerfass, A. (2015). *The Routledge handbook of strategic communication*. Routledge.

Hon, L. C. (1995). Toward a feminist theory of public relations. *Journal of Public Relations Research, 7*, 27–88.

Hon, L. C., & Grunig, J. E. (1999). *Guidelines for measuring relationships in public relations*. Institute for Public Relations. https://www.instituteforpr.org/wp-content/uploads/Guidelines_Measuring_Relationships.pdf

Hon, L. C., Grunig, L. A., & Dozier, D. M. (1992). Women in public relations: Problems and opportunities. In J. E. Grunig (Ed.), *Excellence in public relations and communication management* (pp. 419–438). Routledge.

Hou, J. Z. (2019). Understanding public relations: Theory, culture and society, by Lee Edwards. *Journalism and Mass Communication Quarterly, 97*, 553–555.

Howson, R., & Smith, K. (2008). Hegemony and the operation of consensus and coercion. In R. Howson & K. Smith (Eds.), *Hegemony: Studies in consensus and coercion* (pp. 1–15). Routledge.

Huang, Y.-H. (2001). OPRA: A cross-sectional, multiple-item scale for measuring organizational-public relationships. *Journal of Public Relations Research, 13*, 61–90.

Huang, Y.-H., & Zhang, Y. (2013). Revisiting organization-public relations research over the past decade: Theoretical concepts, measures, methodologies and challenges. *Public Relations Review, 39*, 85–87.

Hughes, C., & Southern, A. (2019). The world of work and the crisis of capitalism: Marx and the Fourth Industrial Revolution. *Journal of Classical Sociology, 19*, 59–71.

Human Rights Campaign. (2020). *Glossary of terms*. https://www.hrc.org/resources/glossary-of-terms?utm_source=GS&utm_medium=AD&utm_campaign=BPI-HRC-Grant&utm_content=454854043833&utm_term=lgbt%20community&gclid=CjwKCAiAudD_BRBXEiwAudakX9jtW1DgYHUVy3W7eK-FhsqnbHv173lwm6zSSsF-l4CN46-xrbXNqRoCyvEQAvD_BwE

Hung, C. F. (2005). Exploring types of organization-public relationships and their implications for relationship management in public relations. *Journal of Public Relations Research, 17*, 393–426.

Ihlen, O., van Ruler, B., & Fredriksson, M. (2009). *Public relations and social theory: Key figures and concepts*. Routledge.

International Association of Business Communicators. (2020a). *About us*. https://www.iabc.com/about-us/

International Association of Business Communicators. (2020b). *Diversity and inclusion statement*. https://www.iabc.com/about-us/purpose/iabc-diversity-and-inclusion-statement/

International Association of Business Communicators. (2020c). Home page. https://www.iabc.com/

Jenkins, H. (2004). The cultural logic of media convergence. *International Journal of Cultural Studies, 7*, 33–43.

Jiang, H. (2012). A model of work-life conflict and quality of employee-organization relationships (EORs). Transformational leadership, procedural justice, and family-supportive workplace initiatives. *Public Relations Review*, *38*, 241–245.

Jiang, H., & Shen, H. (2018). Supportive organizational environment, work-life enrichment, trust and turnover intention: A national survey of PRSA membership. *Public Relations Review*, *44*, 681-689.

Jiang, H., Ford, R., & Long, P. A. C. (2016). Diversity and inclusion: A case study of the current status and practices of Arthur W. Page Society members. Special report of the PRSA Foundation. https://princolor.files.wordpress.com/2016/02/arthur-w-page-topline-diversity-study-findings.pdf

Jiang, H., Luo, Y., & Kulemeka, O. (2016). Social media engagement as an evaluation barometer: Insights from communication executives. *Public Relations Review*, *42*, 679–691.

Jiang, H., Luo, Y., & Kulemeka, O. (2017). Strategic social media use in public relations: Professionals' perceived social media impact, leadership behaviors, and work-life conflict. *International Journal of Strategic Communication, 11*, 18–41.

Jiang, H., Luo, Y., & Kulemeka, O. (2017). Strategic social media use in public relations: Professionals' perceived social media impact, leadership behaviors, and work-life conflict. *International Journal of Strategic Communication, 11*, 18–41.

Jin, Y., Sha, B.-L., Shen, H., & Jiang, H. (2014). Tuning in to the rhythm: The role of coping in strategic management of work-life conflicts in the public relations profession. *Public Relations Review, 40*, 69–78.

Johansen, P. (2001). Professionalisation, building respectability and the birth of the Canadian public relations society. *Journalism Studies, 2* (1), 55–71.

Katz, D., & Kahn, R. L. (1966). *The social psychology of organizations*. Wiley.

Katz, D., & Kahn, R. L. (1978). *The social psychology of organizations* (rev. ed.). Wiley.

Keating, M. (2016). Changing the subject: Putting labour into public relations research. *Media International Australia, 160*, 20–31.

Kennedy, A. K., & Sommerfeldt, E. J. (2015). A postmodern turn for social media research: Theory and research directions for public relations scholarship. *Atlantic Journal of Communication, 23*, 31–45.

Kent, M. L., & Li, C. (2020). Toward a normative social media theory for public relations. *Public Relations Review, 46.*

Kent, M. L., & Taylor, M. (1998). Building dialogic relationships through the world wide web. *Public Relations Review, 24*, 321–334.

Kern-Foxworth, M. (1989). Status and roles of minority PR practitioners. *Public Relations Review, 15*, 89–98.

Ki, E.-J., & Hon, L. C. (2007). Testing the linkages among the organization-public relations and attitude and behavioral intentions. *Journal of Public Relations Research, 19*, 1–23.

Ki, E.-J., Kim, J.-N., & Ledingham, J. A. (2015). *Public relations as relationship management: A relational approach to the study and practice of public relations* (2nd ed.). Routledge.

Kim, J.-N., & Ni, L. (Eds.). (2010). *The Sage handbook of public relations*. Sage.

Kim, S-Y., & Reber, B. H. (2009). How public relations professionalism influences corporate social responsibility: A survey of practitioners. *Journalism and Mass Communication Quarterly, 86*, 157–174.

Kleinnijenhuis, J., Schultz, F., & Utz, S. (2013). The mediating role of the news in the BP oil spill crisis 2010. *Communication Research, 42*, 408–428.

Kuypers, J. A. (2010). Framing analysis from a rhetorical perspective In P. D'Angelo & J. A. Kuypers (Eds.), *Doing news framing analysis: Empirical and theoretical perspectives* (pp. 286–311). Routledge.

Lattimore, D., Baskin, O., Heiman, S., & Toth, E. L. (2012). *Public relations: The profession and the practice* (2nd ed.). McGraw-Hill.

Lawniczak, R. (2009). Re-examining the economic roots of public relations. *Public Relations Review, 35,* 346–352.

Ledingham, J. A. (2003). Explicating relationship management as a general theory of public relations. *Journal of Public Relations Research, 15,* 181–198.

Ledingham, J. A., & Bruning, S. D. (Eds.). (2000). *Public relations as relationship management: A relational approach to the study and practice of public relations.* Lawrence Erlbaum Associates.

Lee, H., Place, K. R., & Smith, B. G. (2018). Revisiting gendered assumptions of practitioner power: An exploratory study examining the role of social media expertise. *Public Relations Review, 44,* 191–200.

Lee, S. T., & Lin, J. (2017). An integrated approach to public diplomacy and public relations: A five-year analysis of the information subsidies of the United States, China, and Singapore. *International Journal of Strategic Communication, 11,* 1–17.

Lee, T. L., & Basnyat, I. (2013). From press release to news: Mapping the framing of the 2009 H1N1 A influenza pandemic. *Journal of Health Communication, 28,* 119–132.

L'Etang, J. (1999). Public relations education in Britain: An historical review in the context of professionalism. *Public Relations Review, 25,* 261–289.

L'Etang, J. (2003). The myth of the "ethical guardian": An examination of its origins, potency and illusions. *Journal of Communication Management, 8,* 53–67.

L'Etang, J. (2005). Critical public relations: Some reflections. *Public Relations Review, 31,* 521–526.

L'Etang, J. (2008). *Public relations: Concepts, practice and critique.* Sage.

L'Etang, J. (2014). Public relations and historical sociology: Historiography as reflexive critique. *Public Relations Review, 40,* 654–660.

L'Etang, J. (2015). "It's always been a sexless trade"; "It's clean work"; "There's very little velvet curtain." *Journal of Communication Management, 19,* 354–370.

L'Etang, J., McKie, D., Snow, N., & Xifra, J. (Eds.). (2015). *The Routledge handbook of critical public relations.* Routledge.

Let's Get Acquainted. (1941, March). *NBC Transmitter,* p. 5.

Lind, R. A., & Salo, C. (2002). The framing of feminist sand feminism in news and public affairs programs in U.S. electronic media. *Journal of Communication, 52,* 211–228.

Lininger, M. R., Wayment, H. A., Craig, D. I., Huffman, A. H., & Lane, T. S. (2019). Improving concussion-reporting behavior in national collegiate athletic association division 1 football players: Evidence for the applicability of the socioecological model for athletic trainers. *Journal of Athletic Training, 54,* 21–29.

Lock, I., Wonneberger, A., Verhoeven, P., & Hellsten, I. (2020). Back to the roots? The applications of communication science theories in strategic communication research. *International Journal of Strategic Communication, 1,* 1–24.

Logan, N. (2011). The white leader prototype: A critical analysis of race in public relations. *Journal of Public Relations Research, 23,* 442–457.

Lukitsch, C. (2016). Shattering the glass ceiling: Fixing the wage gap in PR. *PR News Online.* https://www.prnewsonline.com/wage-gap-in-pr

Lumpkins, C. Y., Bae, J., & Cameron, G. T. (2010). Generating conflict for greater good: Utilizing contingency theory to assess Black and mainstream newspapers as public relations vehicles to promote better health among African Americans. *Public Relations Review, 36,* 73–77.

Martin, C. (2019). In their own little corner: The gendered sidelining of NBC's information department. *Journal of Radio and Audio Media, 26,* 88–103.

Mason, C. (2019, September). The "gender say gap": 5 ways to identify the gap and champion change. *PRSA Strategist.* https://www.prsa.org/article/the-'gender-say-gap'-5-ways-to-identify-the-gap-and-champion-change

Matheson, B., & Petersen, E. J. (2020). Tactics for professional legitimacy: An apparent feminist analysis of Indian women's experiences in technical communication. *Technical Communication Quarterly, 29,* 376–391.

McChesney, R. (1999). *Rich media, poor democracy: Communication politics in dubious times.* University of Illinois Press.

McChesney, R. (2014). Be realistic, demand the impossible: Three radically democratic internet policies. *Critical Studies in Media Communication, 31,* 92–99.

McCorkindale, T., & Rickert, R. (2020, August 3). *Mind the gap: Women's leadership in public relations presentation of survey findings.* Unpublished data from Institute for Public Relations presentation.

McDonald, J. (2015). Organizational communication meets queer theory: Theorizing relations of "difference" differently. *Communication Theory, 25,* 310–329.

McKie, D., & Munshi, D. (2009). Theoretical black holes. In R. L. Heath, E. L. Toth, & D. Waymer (Eds.), *Rhetorical and critical approaches to public relations II* (pp. 61–75). Routledge.

McQuail, D. (1972). *Sociology of mass communications.* Penguin Books.

McRobbie, A. (2009). *The aftermath of feminism: Gender, culture and social change.* Sage.

Meisenbach, R. J., & Feldner, S. B. (2009). Dialogue, discourse ethics, and Disney. In R. L. Heath, E. L. Toth, & D. Waymer (Eds.), *Rhetorical and critical approaches to public relations* (pp. 253–271). Routledge.

Mellado, C., & Barria, S. (2012). Development of professional roles in the practice of public relations in Chile. *Public Relations Review, 38,* 446–453.

Meng, J., & Berger, B. (2013). An integrated model of excellent leadership in public relations: Dimensions, measurement, and validation. *Journal of Public Relations Research, 25,* 141–167.

Meng, J., & Neil, M. S. (2020). *PR women with influence.* Peter Lang.

Meng, J., Berger, B., Heyman, W., & Reber, B. H. (2019). *Public relations leaders earn a "C+" in the Plank Center's report card 2019.* http://plankcenter.ua.edu/wp-content/uploads/2019/09/Report-Card-Full-Report.pdf

Meyer, A. L., & Leonard, A. (2014). Are we there yet? En route to professionalism. *Public Relations Review, 40,* 375–386.

Michell, D., Szabo, C., Falkner, K., & Szorenyi, A. (2018). Towards a socio-ecological framework to address gender inequity in computer science. *Computers and Education, 126,* 324–333.

Molleda, J. C., Moreno, A., & Navarro, C. (2017). Professionalization of public relations in Latin America: A longitudinal comparative study. *Public Relations Review, 43,* 1084–1093.

Montiel, A. V. (2012). Intersections between feminism and the political economy of communication: Women's access to and participation in Mexico's media industries. *Feminist Media Studies, 12,* 310–316.

Moreno, A. (2018). *Fact or fiction: Rewriting the text on gender inequities in communication management.* Institute for Public Relations. https://instituteforpr.org/fact-fiction-re-writing-text-gender-inequalities-communication-management/

Moss, D., Newman, A., & DeSanto, B. (2005). What do communication managers do? Defining and refining the core elements of management in a public relations/corporate communication content. *Journalism and Mass Communication Quarterly, 82,* 873–890.

Motion, J., & Leitch, S. (1996). A discursive perspective from New Zealand: Another world view. *Public Relations Review, 22,* 297–310.

Munshi, D., & Edwards, L. (2011). Understanding "race" in/and public relations: Where do we start and where should we go? *Journal of Public Relations Research, 23,* 349–367.

Munshi, D., & Priya, K. (2005). Imperializing spin cycles: A postcolonial look at public relations, greenwashing, and the separation of publics. *Public Relations Review, 31,* 513–520.

Munshi-Kurian, A., Munshi, D., & Kurian, P. (2019). Strategic interventions in sociology's resource mobilization theory: Reimagining the #MeToo movement as critical public relations. *Public Relations Review, 45,* np.

Myers, C. (2017). Publicists in US public relations history: An analysis of the representations of publicists, 1815–1918. *American Journalism, 34,* 71–90.

National Black Public Relations Society. (2020a). *About us.* https://nbprs.org/about-us/

National Black Public Relations Society. (2020b). Home page. https://nbprs.org/

Navarro, C., Moreno, A., Molleda, J. C., Khalil, N., & Verhoeven, P. (2020). The challenge of new gatekeepers for public relations. A comparative analysis of the role of social media influencers for European and Latin American professionals. *Public Relations Review, 46,* np.

Nicolini, K. M., & Hansen, S. S. (2018). Framing the Women's March on Washington: Media coverage and organizational messaging alignment. *Public Relations Review, 44,* 1–10.

O'Brien, T. (2020, May). PR pros adjust to working from home offices. *PRSA Strategies and Tactics, 3*(5), 7.

O'Dwyer's. (2020). *Public relations associations, clubs, societies.* https://www.odwyerpr.com/pr_services_database/associations.htm

O'Neil, J. (2003). An analysis of the relationships among structure, influence, and gender: Helping to build a feminist theory of public relations. *Journal of Public Relations Research, 15* (2), 151–179.

O'Sullivan, T. (1994). Profession. In T. O'Sullivan, J. Hartley, D. Saunders, M. Montgomery, & J. Fiske (Eds.), *Key concepts in communication and cultural studies.* Routledge.

Otusanya, A. D., & Bell, G. C. (2018). "I thought I'd have more trouble with white people!": Exploring racial microaggressions between West African immigrants and African Americans. *Qualitative Research Reports in Communication, 19,* 44–50.

Overton-de Klerk, N. O., & Verwey, S. (2013). Towards an emerging paradigm of strategic communication: Core driving forces. *Communication, 39,* 362–382.

Park, S., Bier, L. M., & Palenchar, M. J. (2016). Framing a mystery: Information subsidies and media coverage of Malaysia airlines flight 370. *Public Relations Review, 42,* 654–664.

Parkin, F. (1979). *Marxism and class theory: A bourgeois critique.* Taylor and Francis.

Parrish, C. P., & Gassam, J. Z. (2020). African-American professionals in public relations and the greater impacts. In E. M. Thomas (Ed.), *Diversity resistance in organizations* (2nd ed.; pp. 178–194). Routledge.

Pasquarelli, A. (2018, November 19). The other "ism": Pockets of the industry are beginning to address its youth bias. *Advertising Age, 89*(23), 20.

Pavlik, J. (2001). *Journalism and news media.* Columbia University Press.

Penning, T. S., & Sweetser, K. D. (2015). Role enactment, employer type, and pursuit of APR. *Public Relations Review, 31,* 135–137.

Petrosillo, I., Zurlini, G., & Aretano, R. (2015). Socioecological systems. In S. A. Elias (Ed.), *Reference module in earthy systems and environmental sciences* (pp. 1–7). Elsevier.

Phillips, R., & Cree, V. E. (2014). What does the "Fourth Wave" mean for teaching feminism in twenty-first century social work? *Social Work Education, 33,* 930–943.

Pieczka, M. (2002). Public relations expertise deconstructed. *Media, Culture and Society, 24,* 301–324.

Pieczka, M. (2018). Critical perspectives of engagement. In K. A. Johnston & M. Taylor (Eds.), *The handbook of communication engagement* (pp. 549–568). Wiley-Blackwell.

Pieczka, M., & L'Etang, J. (2001). Public relations and the quest for professionalism. In R. L. Heath (Ed.), *Handbook of public relations* (pp. 223–235). Sage.

Pieczka, M., & L'Etang, J. (2006). Public relations and the quest for professionalism. In J. L'Etang & M. Pieczka (Eds.), *Public relations: Critical debates and contemporary practice* (pp. 265–278). Lawrence Erlbaum Associates.

Place, K., & Vardeman-Winter, J. (2015). *Status report: Public relations research 2005–2015.* Lillian Lodge Kopenhaver Center for the Advancement of Women in Communication, Florida International University.

Place, K. R., Smith, B. G., & Lee, H. (2016). Integrated influence? Exploring public relations power in integrated marketing communication. *Public Relations Journal, 10,* 1–36.

Plowman, K. D. (2008). Hot waste in Utah: Conflict in the public arena. *Journal of Public Relations Research, 20,* 403–420.

Plowman, K. D., & Wilson, C. (2018). Strategy and tactics in strategic communication: Examining their intersection with social media use. *International Journal of Strategic Communication, 12,* 125–144.

Poleshuck, E., Perez-Diaz, W., Wittink, M., ReQua, M., Harrington, A., Katz, J., Juskiewicz, I., Stone, J. T., & Bell, E. (2017). Resilience in the midst of chaos. *Journal of Community Psychology, 47,* 1000–1013.

Pompper, D. (2005a). "Difference" in public relations research: A case for introducing critical race theory. *Journal of Public Relations Research, 17,* 139–169.

Pompper, D. (2005b). Multiculturalism in the public relations curriculum: Female African American practitioners' perceptions of effects. *The Howard Journal of Communication, 16,* 295–316.

Pompper, D. (2007). The gender-ethnicity construct in public relations organizations: Using feminist standpoint theory to discover Latinas' realities. *The Howard Journal of Communication, 18,* 291–311.

Pompper, D. (2012). On social capital and diversity in a feminized industry: Further developing a theory of internal public relations. *Journal of Public Relations Research, 24,* 86–103.

Pompper, D. (2016). Interrogating inequalities perpetuated in a feminized field. In C. Daymon & K. Demetrious (Eds.), *Gender and public relations: Critical perspectives on voice, image and identity* (pp. 67–86). Routledge.

Pompper, D., & Adams, J. (2006). Under the microscope: Gender and mentor-protégé relationships. *Public Relations Review, 32,* 309–315.

Pompper, D., & Jung, T. (2013). Outnumbered yet still on top, but for how long? Theorizing about men working in the feminized field of public relations. *Public Relations Review, 39,* 497–506.

Pooley, J. (2014). Sociology and the socially mediated self. In S. Waisbord (Ed.), *Media sociology: A reappraisal* (pp. 224–246). Polity Press.

Public Relations Society of America. (2020a). *About public relations.* https://www.prsa.org/all-about-pr/

Public Relations Society of America. (2020b). *Diversity and inclusion plan.* https://www.prsa.org/docs/default-source/about/diversity/d-i-strategic-plan-20-22.pdf?sfvrsn=e259e47b_0&spMailingID=32201525&spUserID=MzM

Public Relations Society of America. (2020c). *Getting it right.* https://apps.prsa.org/Learning/Calendar/display/12203/Getting_It_Right_Diversity_and_Inclusion_in_LGBTQ#.XrMgQxNKiog

Public Relations Society of America. (2020d). Home page. https://www.prsa.org/home

Public Relations Society of America. (2020e). *Membership.* https://www.prsa.org/membership/

Public Relations Society of America. (2020f). *PRSA certification guidelines.* https://prssa.prsa.org/chapter-firm-resources/start-a-prssa-chapter/pr-program-certification/

Public Relations Student Society of America. (2020). *Listing of chapters.* http://collegeguide.prsa.org/listing/united-states-of-america-programs

Public Relations Council. (2020a). Home page. https://prcouncil.net/

Public Relations Council. (2020b). *PR Council's anti-discrimination and anti-harassment statement.* https://prcouncil.net/news/pr-council-member-firms-anti-harassment-non-discrimination-zero-tolerance-statement/

Public Relations Council. (2020c). *PR Council's code of ethics.* https://prcouncil.net/join/the-pr-council-code-of-ethics-and-principles/

Public Relations Council. (2020d). *PR Council's pay equity statement.* https://prcouncil.net/pr-council-pay-equity-statement/

Public Relations Council. (2020e). *SHEQUALITY.* https://prcouncil.net/shequality-podcast/

Rakow, L. F. (1989). From the feminization of public relations to the promise of feminism. In E. L. Toth & C. G. Cline (Eds.), *Beyond the velvet ghetto* (pp. 287–298). IABC Research Foundation.

Rakow, L. F. (2016). Foreword. In C. Daymon & K. Demetrious (Eds.), *Gender and public relations* (pp. xiii–xv). New York: Routledge.

Rakow, L. F., & Nastasia, D. I. (2018). On Dorothy E. Smith: Public relations and feminist theory at the crossroads. In O. Ihlen & M. Fredriksson (Eds.), *Public relations and social theory* (2nd ed.; pp. 252–277). Routledge.

Rakow, L. F., & Wackwitz, L. A. (Eds.). (2004). *Feminist communication theory: Selections in context.* Sage.

Ramaker, T., van der Stoep, J., & Deuze, M. (2015). Reflective practices for future journalism: The need, the resistance and the way forward. *Javnost-The Public, 22,* 345–361.

Reese, S. D., & Shoemaker, P. J. (2016). A media sociology for the networked public sphere: The hierarchy of influences model. *Mass Communication and Society, 19,* 389–410.

Reinharz, S. (1992). *Feminist methods in social research.* Oxford University Press.

Reinharz, S. (1993). Neglected voices and excessive demands in feminist research. *Qualitative Sociology, 16,* 69–76.

Reskin, B. F., & Roos, P. A. (1990). *Job queues, gender queues.* Temple University Press.

Revers, M., & Brienza, C. (2018). How not to establish a subfield: Media sociology in the United States. *American Sociologist, 49,* 352–368.

Richard, L., Gauvin, L., & Raine, K. (2011). Ecological models revisited: Their uses and evolution in health promotion over two decades. *Annual Review of Public Health, 32,* 307–326.

Riordan, E. (2002). Intersections and new directions: On feminism and political economy. In E. R. Meehan & E. Riordan (Eds.), *Sex and money: Feminism and political economy in the media* (pp. 3–15). University of Minnesota Press.

Risman, B. J. (2004). Gender as a social structure: Theory wrestling with activism. *Gender and Society, 18*, 429–450.

Risman, B. J. (2009). From doing to undoing: Gender as we know it. *Gender and Society, 23*, 81–84.

Risman, B. J., & Davis, G. (2013). From sex roles to gender structure. *Current Sociological Review, 61*, 733–755.

Robbins, S. P. (1990). *Organizational theory: Structure, design and applications* (3rd ed.). Englewood Cliffs, NJ: Prentice-Hall.

Robinson, K. (2018). *#METOO: Examining communication toward meaningful change.* Blogpost. https://instituteforpr.org/metoo-examining-employee-organization-relationships-organizational-culture-and-transparent-communication-toward-mea

Robinson, S. (2018). *Networked news, racial divides: How power and privilege shape public discourse in progressive communities.* Cambridge University Press.

Roos, P. A., & Stevens, L. M. (2018). Integrating occupations: Changing occupational sex segregation in the United States from 2000 to 2014. *Demographic Research, 38*, 127–154.

Roper, J. (2005). Symmetrical communication: Excellent public relations or a strategy for hegemony? *Journal of Public Relations Research, 17*, 69–86.

Rothenberg, P. S. (2005). *White privilege: Essential readings on the other side of racism* (2nd ed.). Worth Publishers.

Rottger, U., & Preusse, J. (2013). External consulting in strategic communication: Functions and roles within systems theory. *International Journal of Strategic Communication, 7*, 99–117.

Ruoho, I., & Torkkola, S. (2018). Journalism and gender: Toward a multidimensional approach. *Nordicom Review, 39*, 67–79.

Sacket, P. R., Kuncel, N. R., Beatty, A. S., Rigdon, J. L., Shen, W., & Kiger, T. B. (2012). The role of socioeconomic status in SAT-grade relationships and in college admissions decisions. *Psychological Science, 23*, 1000–1007.

Salihu, H. M., Wilson, R. E., King, L. M., Marty, P. J., & Whiteman, V. E. (2015). Socio-ecological model as a framework for overcoming barriers and challenges in randomized control trials in minority and underserved communities. *International Journal of MCH and AIDS, 3*, 85–95.

Sallot, L. M., & Johnson, E. A. (2006). To contact . . . or not? Investigating journalists' assessments of public relations subsidies and contact preferences. *Public Relations Review, 32*, 83–86.

Sallot, L. M., Steinfatt, T. M., & Salwen, M. B. (1998). Journalists' and public relations practitioners' news values: Perceptions and cross-perceptions. *Journalism and Mass Communication Quarterly, 75*, 366–377.

Sanchez, G. M., Nejadhashemi, A. P., Zhang, Z., Woznicki, S. A., Habron, G., Marquart-Pyatt, S., & Shortridge, A. (2014). Development of a socio-ecological environmental social justice model for watershed-based management. *Journal of Hydrology, 518*, 162–177.

Sawyer, K., & Thoroughgood, C. (2020). Diversity resistance and gender identity. In K. M. Thomas (Ed.), *Diversity resistance in organizations* (pp. 58–76). Routledge.

Scheufele, D. (1999). Framing as a theory of media effects. *Journal of Communication, 49*, 103–122.

Scheufele, D., & Tewksbury, D. (2007). Framing, agenda setting, and priming: The evolution of three media effects models. *Journal of Communication, 57*, 9–20.

Serini, S. A., Toth, E. L., Wright, D. K., & Emig, A. (1997). Watch for falling glass . . . Women, men, and job satisfaction in public relations: A preliminary analysis. *Journal of Public Relations Research, 9*, 99–118.

Serini, S. A., Toth, E. L., Wright, D. K., & Emig, A. (1998). Power, gender and public relations: Sexual harassment as a threat to the practice. *Journal of Public Relations Research, 10*, 177–192.

Sha, B-L. (2006). Cultural identity in the segmentation of publics: An emerging theory of intercultural public relations. *Journal of Public Relations Research, 18*, 45–65.

Sha, B-L. (2011). Does accreditation really matter in public relations practice? How age and experience compare to accreditation. *Public Relations Review, 37*, 1–11.

Sha, B-L. (2018). Editor's essay: Identity and/in/of public relations. *Journal of Public Relations Research, 30*, 129–133.

Sha, B-L., & Dozier, D. M. (2011, August). *Women as public relations managers: Show me the money.* Paper presented to the Association for Education in Journalism and Mass Communication, St. Louis, MO.

Sha, B-L., & Toth, E. L. (2005). Future professionals' perceptions of work, life and gender issues in public relations. *Public Relations Review, 31*, 93–99.

Shah, A. (2017, September 12). Why do PR firms pay women, people of color less? *The Holmes Report.* https://www.holmesreport.com/long-reads/article/why-do-pr-firms-pay -women-people-of-color-less

Shen, H., & Jiang, H. (2013). Drivers of public relations professionals' life-work conflict: A pilot study of PRSA members. *Public Relations Review, 39*, 226–228.

Shenoy-Packer, S. (2015). Immigrant professionals, microaggressions, and critical sensemaking in the U.S. workplace. *Management Communication Quarterly, 29*, 257–275.

Sherwood, M., Nicholson, M., & Marjoribanks, T. (2017). Access, agenda building and information subsidies: Media relations in professional sport. *International Review for the Sociology of Sport, 52*, 992–1007.

Shoemaker, P. J., & Cohen, A. (2006). *News around the world: Content, practitioners and the public.* Routledge.

Shoemaker, P. J., & Reese, S. D. (1996). *Mediating the message: Theories of influences on mass media content* (2nd ed.). Longman Trade/Caroline House.

Shoemaker, P. J., & Reese, S. D. (2014). *Mediating the message in the 21st century: A media sociology perspective* (3rd ed.). Routledge.

Simorangkir, D. (2011). The impact of the feminization of the public relations industry in Indonesia on communication practice. *International Journal of Strategic Communication, 5*, 36–48.

Sison, M. D. (2009). Whose cultural value? Exploring public relations' approaches to understanding audiences. *PRism, 6*(2). https://www.prismjournal.org/uploads/1/2/5/6/125661607/v6-no2-a4.pdf

Smith, B. G. (2013). The internal forces on communication integration: Co-created meaning, interaction, and postmodernism in strategic communication. *International Journal of Strategic Communication, 7*, 65–79.

Smith, B. G., & Place, K. R. (2013). Integrating power? Evaluating public relations influence in an integrated communication structure. *Journal of Public Relations Research, 25*, 168–187.

Smudde, P. (2015). *Managing public relations: Methods and tools.* New York: Oxford University Press.

Sommerfeldt, E. J., & Yang, A. (2018). Notes on a dialogue: Twenty years of digital dialogic communication research in public relations. *Journal of Public Relations Research, 30,* 59–64.

Spector, S., & Spector, B. (2018). *Diverse voices: Profiles in leadership.* PRMuseum Press.

Stokes, A. Q., & Holloway, R. L. (2009). Documentary as an activist medium: The Wal-Mart movie. In R. L. Heath, E. L. Toth, & D. Waymer (Eds.), *Rhetorical and critical approaches to public relations* (pp. 343–359). Routledge.

Strayer, J. F. (2015, December 15). *Sexual harassment: A workplace pandemic.* https://institute forpr.org/sexual-harassment-workplace-pandemic/

Strayer, J. F. (2016, August 8). *Five key communication strategies to combat sexual harassment in the workplace.* https://instituteforpr.org/five-key-communication-elements-combat-sexual -harassment-workplace/

Strong, F. (2018, March 6). *Breaking down the results from the 2018 PR salary survey: Are you earning what you are worth?* https://www.swordandthescript.com/2018/03/pr-salary -survey-2018/

Sue, D. W. (2010). *Microaggressions in everyday life.* Wiley & Sons.

Sweetser, K. D., & Brown, C. W. (2008). Information subsidies and agenda-building during the Israel-Lebanon crisis. *Public Relations Review, 34,* 359–366.

Swirsky, J. M., & Angelone, D. J. (2016). Equality, empowerment, and choice: What does feminism mean to contemporary women? *Journal of Gender Studies, 25,* 445–460.

Taft, H. P. (2003, February/March). Times have changed? IABC Research Foundation's the Velvet Ghetto Revised. *Communication World,* 10–11.

Tam, S. Y., Dozier, D. M., Lauzen, M. M., & Real, M. R. (1995). The impact of superior-subordinate gender on the career advancement of public relations practitioners. *Journal of Public Relations Research, 7,* 259–272.

Tench, R., Topic, M., & Moreno, A. (2017). Male and female communication, leadership styles and the position of women in public relations. *Interactions: Studies in Communication and Culture, 8,* 231–248.

Theofilou, A. (Ed.). (2021). *Women in PR history.* Routledge.

Thiefels, J. (2017, February 7). 5 company initiatives that improve office culture. *Engage: The Employee Engagement Blog.* https://www.achievers.com/blog/5-company-initiatives -improve-office-culture/

Thompson, P. (2020). Capitalism, technology and work: Interrogating the tipping point thesis. *The Political Quarterly, 91,* 299–309.

Thornton Dill, B., & Zambrana, R. E. (Eds.). (2009). *Emerging intersections: Race, class, and gender in theory, policy, and practice.* Rutgers University Press.

Thornton, M. (2010). "Post-feminism" in the legal academy. *Feminist Review, 95,* 92–98.

Tindall, N. T. J. (2009a). In search of career satisfaction: African-American public relations practitioners, pigeonholing, and the workplace. *Public Relations Review, 35,* 443–445.

Tindall, N. T. J. (2009b). The double bind of race and gender: Understanding the roles and perceptions of Black female public relations faculty. *Southwestern Mass Communication Journal, 25,* 1–16.

Tindall, N. T. J. (2013). Invisible in a visible profession: The social construction of workplace identity and roles among lesbian and bisexual public relations professionals. In N. T. J. Tindall & R. D. Waters (Eds.), *Coming out of the closet: Exploring LGBT issues in strategic communication with theory and research* (pp. 24–53). Peter Lang.

Tindall, N. T. J., & Waters, R. D. (2012). Coming out to tell our stories: Using queer theory to understand the career experiences of gay men in public relations. *Journal of Public Relations Research, 24,* 451–475.

Tindall, N. T. J., & Waters, R. D. (2013). (Eds.). *Coming out of the closet: Exploring LGBT issues in strategic communication with theory and research.* Peter Lang.

Topic, M., Cunha, J. M., Reigstad, A., Jelen-Sanchez, A., & Moreno, A. (2020). Women in public relations (1982–2019). *Journal of Communication Management, 24,* 391–407.

Toth, E. (2009). The case for pluralistic studies of public relations. In R. L. Heath, E. L. Toth, & D. Waymer (Eds.), *Rhetorical and critical approaches to public relations II* (pp. 48–60). Routledge.

Toth, E. L., & Cline, C. G. (1989). *Beyond the velvet ghetto.* IABC Research Foundation.

Toth, E. L., & Cline, C. G. (2007). Women in public relations. In P. J. Creedon & J. Cramer (Eds.), *Women in mass communication* (3rd ed.; pp. 85–106). Sage.

Toth, E. L., & Heath, R. L. (Eds.). (1992). *Rhetorical and critical approaches to public relations.* Lawrence Erlbaum Associates.

Trujillo, N., & Toth, E. L. (1987). Organizational perspectives for public relations research and practice. *Management Communication Quarterly, 1,* 199–231.

Tsetsura, K. (2011). Is public relations a real job? How female practitioners construct the profession. *Journal of Public Relations Research, 23,* 1–23.

Tuchman, G. (1978). *Making news: A study in the construction of reality.* Free Press.

Ursino, N. (2019). Dynamic models of socio-ecological systems predict catastrophic shifts following unsustainable development. *The Science of the Total Environment, 654,* 890–894.

U.S. Bureau of Labor Statistics. (2019). *Occupational employment and wages, May 2019.* https://www.bls.gov/cps/cpsaat11.htm

U.S. Bureau of Labor Statistics. (2020). *Occupational outlook handbook.* https://www.bls.gov/ooh/

Valdivia, A. (1995). *Feminism, multiculturalism, and the media.* Sage.

Valentini, C. (2015). Is using social media "good" for the public relations profession? A critical reflection. *Public Relations Review, 41,* 170–177.

van Dijck, J. (2013). *The culture of connectivity: A critical history of social media.* Oxford.

Van Ruler, B. (2005). Commentary: Professionals are from Venus, scholars are from Mars. *Public Relations Review, 31,* 159–173.

Van Zoonen, L. (1994). *Feminist media studies.* Sage.

Vanc, A., & White, C. (2011). Cultural perceptions of public relations gender roles in Romania. *Public Relations Review, 37,* 103–105.

Vardeman, J. (2013). Feminization theory. In R. L. Heath (Ed.), *Encyclopedia of public relations* (2nd ed.; pp. 338–341). Sage.

Vardeman, J., & Sebesta, A. (2020). The problem of intersectionality as an approach to digital activism: The Women's March on Washington's attempt to unite all women. *Journal of Public Relations Research, 32,* 7–29.

Vardeman-Winter, J. (2011). Confronting whiteness in public relations campaigns and research with women. *Journal of Public Relations Research, 23,* 412–441.

Vardeman-Winter, J., & Place, K. R. (2017). Still a lily-white field of women: The state of workforce diversity in public relations practice and research. *Public Relations Review, 43,* 326–336.

Vardeman-Winter, J., Jiang, H., & Tindall, N. T. J. (2013). Information-seeking outcomes of representational, structural, and political intersectionality among health media consumers. *Journal of Applied Communication Research, 41,* 389–411.

Vieira, E. T., & Grantham, S. (2014). Defining public relations roles in the U.S.A. using cluster analysis. *Public Relations Review, 40*, 60–68.

Vogt, E. (2020, January 1). How motherhood made me a better PR pro. *PR Strategist.* https://www.prsa.org/article/how-motherhood-made-me-a-better-pr-pro

Wagemans, A., Witschge, T., & Deuze, M. (2016). Ideology as resource in entrepreneurial journalism: The French online news startup Mediapart. *Journalism Practice, 10*, 160–177.

Waisbord, S. (Ed.). (2014). *Media sociology: A reappraisal.* Polity.

Warner, M. (1991). Introduction: Fear of a queer planet. *Social Text, 9*(4), 3–17.

Waymer, D., Brown, K. A., Baker, K., & Fears, L. (2016). Socialization and pre-career development of public relations professionals via the undergraduate curriculum. *Communication Teacher, 32*, 117–130.

Weaver, C. K. (2016). A Marxist primer for critical public relations scholarship. *Media International Australia, 160*(1), 43–52.

Werder, K. P., & Holtzhausen, D. (2011). Organizational structures and their relationship with communication management practices: A public relations perspective from the United States. *International Journal of Strategic Communication, 5*, 118–142.

Werder, K. P., Nothhaft, H., Vercic, D., & Zerfass, A. (2018). Strategic communication as an emerging interdisciplinary paradigm. *International Journal of Strategic Communication, 12*, 333–351.

West, C., & Fenstermaker, S. (1995). Doing difference. *Gender and Society, 9*, 8–37.

White, C. L., & Boatwright, B. (2020). Social media ethics in the data economy: Issues of social responsibility for using Facebook for public relations. *Public Relations Review, 46*, np.

Wildman, S. M., & Davis, A. D. (1996). Making systems of privilege visible. In S. M. Wildman (Ed.), *Privilege revealed: How invisible preference undermines America* (pp. 7–24). New York University Press.

Wilensky, H. (1964). The professionalization of everyone? *American Journal of Sociology, 70*, 137–158.

Wills, C. M. (2020). Diversity in public relations: The implications of a broad definition for PR practice. *Public Relations Journal, 13*(3) https://prjournal.instituteforpr.org/wp-content/uploads/Wills_final_formatted_June2020.pdf

Wilson, L. J., Ogden, J. D., & Wilson, C. E. (2019). *Strategic communications for PR, social media and marketing* (7th ed.). Kendal Hunt.

Witmer, D. F. (2006). Overcoming system and culture boundaries: Public relations from a structuration perspective. In C. H. Botan & V. Hazleton (Eds.), *Public relations theory II* (pp. 361–374). New York: Routledge.

Wittig, M. (1997). One is not born a woman. In L. Nicholson (Ed.), *The second wave* (pp. 265–271). Routledge.

Wright, D. K., Grunig, L. A., Springston, J. K., & Toth, E. L. (1991). *Under the glass ceiling: An analysis of gender issues in American public relations.* PRSA Foundation Monographs Series, Vol. 1, No. 2. PRSA Foundation.

Wrigley, B. J. (2002). Glass ceiling? What glass ceiling? A qualitative study of how women view the glass ceiling in public relations and communication management. *Journal of Public Relations Research, 14*, 27–55.

Xifra, J. (2017). Recognition, symbolic capital and reputation in the seventeenth century: Thomas Hobbes and the origins of critical public relations historiography. *Public Relations Review, 43*, 579–586.

Xifra, J., & Collell, M.-R. (2014). Medieval propaganda, longue duree and new history: Towards a nonlinear approach to the history of public relations. *Public Relations Review*, 40, 715–722.

Xifra, J., & Heath, R. L. (2015). Reputation, propaganda, and hegemony in Assyriology studies: A Gramscian view of public relations historiography. *Journal of Public Relations Research*, 27, 196–211.

Yeomans, L. (2016). Gendered performance and identity work in PR consulting relationships: A UK perspective. In C. Daymon & K. Demetrious (Eds.), *Gender and public relations: Critical perspectives on voice, image and identity* (pp. 87–107). Routledge.

Yep, G. A. (2016). Toward thick(er) intersectionalities: Theorizing, research, and activating the complexities of communication and identities. In K. Sorrells & S. Sekimoto (Eds.), *Globalizing intercultural communication: A reader* (pp. 86–94). Sage.

Yep, G. A., & Lescure, R. (2019). A thick intersectional approach to microaggressions. *Southern Communication Journal*, 84, 113–126.

Yep, G. A., Lovass, K. E., & Elia, J. P. (2003). Introduction: Queering communication: Starting the conversation. In G. A. Yet, K. E. Lovaas, & J. P. Elia (Eds.), *Queer theory and communication: From disciplining queers to queering the discipline(s)* (pp. 1–10). Routledge.

Zerfass, A., Vercic, D., Northhaft, H., & Werder, K. P. (2018). Strategic communication: Defining the field and its contribution to research and practice. *International Journal of Strategic Communication*, 12, 487–505.

Zerfass, A., Vercic, D., & Wiesenberg, M. (2016). The dawn of a new golden age for media relations? How PR professionals interact with the mass media and use new collaboration practices. *Public Relations Review*, 42, 499–508.

Zhang, L. (2018). The contradictions of "women's work" in digital capitalism: A "non-Western"/Chinese perspective. *Feminist Media Studies*, 18, 147–151.

Zoller, H. M. (2004). Manufacturing health: Employee perspectives on problematic outcomes in a workplace health promotion initiative. *Western Journal of Communication*, 68, 278–301.

Index

White, C. L., 58, 92
White leader prototype, 46–47
Whiteness, 46–48; in CRT, 42–45; gender
    and, 4; in public relations published
    research gaps, 4–5
White privilege, 45, 193
Whiteside, E., 60
White women, 78–79, 158, 164, 195; in
    glass ceiling, 73–74
Wilson, L. J., 25
Witmer, 84, 92
Wittig, M., 49
Women in Public Relations (Grunig, L. A.), 7
women of color, distinct experiences of,
    176–77
Women's March on Washington (2017),
    29, 61
women's work, 100–101, 109, 160

work-life policies and practices:
    discrimination in, 71–72; race in,
    72; stigma in, 72; transformational
    leadership style in, 73; workplace
    initiatives in, 72–73
workplace diversity, 14
workplace sexual harassment, 144–45, 190

Yeomans, L., 157
Yep, G. A., 163
young women, 27–28
YWCA, 88–89

Zambrana, R. E., 14, 32
Zerfass, A., 26
Zhang, L., 42
Zoonen, L. van, 27

Lightning Source UK Ltd.
Milton Keynes UK
UKHW021322251022
411069UK00005B/216